DIGITAL MARKETING

**Everything you
need to know**

Eddie O' Mahony

My Motivation

When I recently participated in an online course on digital marketing I discovered that many of the participants had either limited or no knowledge of the role of the subject matter. This motivated me to write an easy-read book for people who would like to know more about digital marketing, often referred to as online marketing or Internet marketing. The book takes us through the fascinating and ever changing world of digital marketing: where it originated, where it is now and where it is likely to be in the future.

In simple terms, digital marketing is about the promotion of brands via one or more forms of electronic media. It differs from traditional marketing activity in that it involves the use of channels and methods that allow a company to analyse its marketing campaigns and establish what is working and what isn't, usually in real time. Digital marketing can work in tandem with traditional marketing activities.

Among the comments from my fellow participants were:

"I want to be at the cutting edge of Digital Marketing."

OL, Russia

"I want to explore contemporary marketing methods."

GL,South Africa

"I have very limited experience of Digital Marketing."

BB, England

"I hope to learn all about Digital Marketing."

AJ, Thailand

"I want to get a better understanding of Digital Marketing."

LMcM, Ireland

"I would like to be Digital Marketing savvy."

GM, USA

"Digital Marketing is a new discovery for me."

HR,South Korea

"I want to know what Digital Marketing is all about."

EM,Czech Rep.

"I'd like to know more about Social Media and Internet Marketing."

FS, Greece

"I'd like to learn new things about Digital Marketing."

DM, Nigeria

"I hope to learn new things in the marketing field."

F D, Italy

"I want to understand the Digital Marketing jigsaw."

RS, Wales

'Digital Marketing fascinates me."

QW, China

"A landscape that's in constant change."

GO, Ireland

"I'm looking forward to upskilling in Direct Marketing."

RT,New Zealand

"I want to see how the old and new ways to market are blending."

HT, France

Contents

Chapter 1: Reflecting on the Internet

The Internet and the World Wide Web

The Internet and the World Wide Web (WWW) are not the same thing, yet some individuals are unaware of this. The Internet is made up of a vast number of different networks. Millions of computers are connected together throughout the world, making up a network in which a person can communicate with others so long as they are all connected to the Internet. Information moves around the Internet in a number of languages referred to as protocols, which are a set of rules controlling the exchange of data between devices.

The Web is a method of getting information over the Internet and is constructed on top of the Internet. The Web involves hypertext transfer protocol (HTTP), which is just one of the languages used over the Internet, to dispatch data. The Web also uses browsers like Internet Explorer, Firefox and Safari to access documents referred to as web pages that are connected to each other via hyperlinks which the reader can directly follow by clicking or by hovering over the link to open it. Web documents can include visual graphics, copy content, videos and audios. The Web causes information to be spread throughout the Internet. The Internet facilitates e-mail, which relies on simple mail transfer protocol (SMTP), Usenet bulletin board newsgroups, instant messaging and transfer protocol (FTP) for transferring files between a number of computers. The Web is part of the Internet, but a large part. As previously stated, the two terms mean different things and should not be confused as the same thing.

Where it all began
It is not my intention to provide a detailed history of the Internet, which has been covered extensively in many other publications during the past twenty-five-odd years since its introduction. Instead, I will cover some key milestones that I hope will be of interest about this incredible technological invention. Speaking at the One Young World Summit 2014, Sir Bob Geldof[1] said that the Internet was probably the most important innovation ever in our history.

However, there was a lot of bemusement and misunderstanding about the Internet at the start, including what it was going to be used for, and more importantly how to use it.

What some individuals said about the Internet
Entrepreneur Bill Gates[2] referred to the new phenomenon on May 26, 1995 when he sent a communication entitled "The Internet tidal wave" to all the Microsoft executive staff. He believed it changed the rules, offering an incredible opportunity and challenge to people and businesses. He later said that the Internet was turning into the town square for the worldwide town of tomorrow. Gate's contribution to the Economist Group's 'The World in 2001'[3] recognised the growing potential of the Internet and predicted that the biggest advances in digital technology were still to come. Today, he continues to work with Microsoft in a part-time strategic role

alongside its CEO. Gates thankfully became a philanthropist and has since devoted his considerable skills and financial fortune to help reduce the inequity in the world.

Not everybody was enthusiastic about the Internet. Some people did not support the predictions prevalent at the time that the Internet would replace newspapers as a source for news and analysis and books for leisure reading. To paraphrase Don Tapscott,[4] a leading authority on innovation and media, the Internet is similar to the disclosure of the printing press, just it's altogether different. The Internet helps us to learn things, as well as acquire knowledge contained in individuals' crania and gives access to the insight of individuals on a worldwide scale.

Significant milestones

The World Wide Web (WWW) was twenty-five years old in 2014. This most important part of the network of computer networks that make up the Internet gave rise to transforming the Internet from a system used by specialists into a technology used by hundreds of millions of people around the world today. There were a number of crucial innovations before the arrival of the Internet. In 1969, computers connected with each other for the first time at two US Universities, UCLA and Stanford. 1971 witnessed the introduction of the first email, which was not as refined as it is today. It was the brainchild of Ray Tomlinson,[5] who also introduced the @ symbol to separate the user name from the name of the computer being used, which later became the domain name. 1977 was a significant year for the development of the Internet when the first PC modem was introduced. A year later we had the first unsought commercial email message, now known as spam, sent to 600 California Arpanet users. By 1987, there were some 30,000 hosts on the Internet, made possible with the introduction of the TCP/IP standard, an important communication language and set of rules used to connect hosts on the Internet. In 1989, America Online (AOL) was launched and made the Internet popular amongst the general population. At its peak, it had over 30 million members as part of an enclosed subscription-based community. In that role it was key in shaping the Internet and gave people a preview of what would become the high-speed broadband we have today.

How the Internet evolved
Unlike inventions such as Thomas Edison's light bulb and Graham Bell's telephone, the Internet has no one individual inventor at a particular point in time. Instead, it has evolved over a number of years. As we have seen, the Internet is basically a network connecting many other smaller networks into a single global network. In the beginning, the Internet connected and facilitated university networks and research organisations within the United States. The Internet evolved from a military concern for the safety of the United States more than fifty years ago. Government was concerned about the consequences of a Soviet attack on the United States' telephone system. A single missile, they claimed, would be a disaster and had the potential to destroy the whole

network of lines and wires that made efficient long-distance communication possible. Throughout the 1980s, university scientists and researchers used the system to dispatch files and data between computers.

In 1989 the Internet changed again. A computer programmer in Switzerland called Tim Berners-Lee had spent over ten years working on a design originally developed in 1973 and published in 1974. The result of this extensive work was the World Wide Web (WWW). It was not just about sending files from one place to another but was itself a "web" of information that anyone on the Internet could access. Berners-Lee, who wrote a code for the Web,[6] is really the person who created the Internet that we are familiar with today. Since then there have been many changes and upgrades to the Internet. In 1992, a sophisticated browser called Mosaic was introduced and offered a non-threatening way to use the Web, allowing users to view text and visuals on the same screen and to surf using scrollbars and clickable links. Mosaic brought Internet into the public domain. Its dominance, however, was brief. Netscape Navigator arrived the following year and it soon became the market leader. Netscape exited in 2008 when Microsoft focused on the Web, bringing us Internet Explorer, still available today along with Firefox and Safari and others.

The commercialisation of the Internet.
US Congress announced that the Web could be adapted for commercial purposes. As a result, many types of businesses set up websites. They began to use the Internet to sell products and services directly to

customers. The web was commercialised in 1995. Encryption, probably the most efficient way to offer data security, was created by Netscape, which made it more secure to conduct financial transactions on the Web, including the use of credit cards online. From there the Internet grew enormously over a brief period of time. In 1994 and 1995 the powerful e-commerce concern Amazon.com and online eBay forever changed the way consumers would eventually shop for anything from electronics to clothing. In 1996, more than twenty-five million computers had been connected to the Internet across one hundred and eighty different countries. In 1998, Google was launched, completely changing the way people found information online. Wikipedia was founded in 2001, which some argue was the start of social media. Facebook overtook MySpace, once the most popular social media network. In 2004, we had the emergence of social networking companies. YouTube began streaming videos in 2005. The Internet was a way for people of all ages to stay connected. In 2006, Saddam Hussein's hanging went viral from a cell phone and was seen by millions worldwide. On April 16, 2007 a cell phone video of the Virginia Polytechnic Institute and State University shooting, which resulted in 32 people killed and 17 wounded, was uploaded to CNN's news report and went global. 2008 saw first reports of the China earthquake appear on Twitter.

People began sharing personal information over the Internet with the arrival of MySpace and LinkedIn in 2003. In 2007, the iPhone gave a huge impetus to mobile web applications and design. In 2008 national politicians availed of the Internet to communicate their policies and their capabilities in the US Presidential Election. Hillary Clinton promoted herself using videos on YouTube. It was the first time that election candidates used the Internet to promote themselves and their policies in the US presidential election. In 2010, the Internet as the primary news source overtook newspapers for Americans. One of the great things about the Internet was its facility to allow people to communicate successfully and on a global scale. 2010 saw the arrival of a group of social movements in the Middle East that became known as the Arab Spring. This resulted mainly in young people getting others to revolt in large numbers against governments who enforced strict and unpopular laws restricting personal freedom.

Global Internet User Survey 2012[7]
This survey reveals that over eighty per cent of the sample felt that access to the Internet was a basic human right, allowing freedom of expression about everything to everybody. Over 60 per cent of respondents agreed that Internet access had contributed significantly to civil action and political awareness in their country. 98 per cent agreed the Internet was essential for their access to knowledge and education. Over 80 per cent agreed that the Internet played a positive role in their individual lives as well as society at large; 96 per cent of those accessed the Internet at least once a day. More than 90 per cent used social media and 60 per cent used it every day.

Internet of Things

So what does the future hold for the Internet and what's this phenomenon called the Internet of Things all about? We are already beginning to be part of the Internet of Things, a concept that encapsulates a future where commonly used physical objects will be connected to the Internet and in turn will connect with other devices. Although the idea wasn't articulated until 1999, the Internet of Things has been discussed for decades. An example often quoted is about a Coke machine installed at Carnegie Melon University in the early 1980s, where computer programmers connected to the machine over the Internet and were able to ascertain whether or not there would be a cold drink available from the machine. We inhabit a society where devices are connected to devices as well as to our bodies, including heart monitors that can be connected to weighing scales for added convenience, or smartphones that can be connected to electric lights in our homes. We could soon have a situation where billions of devices will be connected to each other, everything from devices we will wear to domestic appliances. This creates a set of challenges and opportunities for businesses and consumers alike. Dr John Barrett, Cork Institute of Technology (CIT)[8] spoke about the Internet of Things in a talk entitled 'Creating our future together'. He predicts things connected to the Internet will include vehicles, animals, soil as well as people. Through 'tagging', smartphones will be able to read all they need to know from such physical objects or people. Individuals will be able to check with Google to establish where they are supposed to be at a given time, where their office keys are. It will check fridge contents and give details of traffic flow on a given city or country route. The national grid will control washing machines and tumble driers.

Overall, it is hoped that the Internet of Things will create a better and more efficient way to manage things. On a grand scale, it could have many benefits for society in general, for example better traffic control, resulting in fewer deaths on our roads, better ways to manage energy, better climate control. The Internet of Things will improve and keep an eye on individuals in a more comprehensive way, leading to a better public and private health care service for all the population. From a business perspective it could improve marketing tactics, allowing advertising messages to be aimed at consumers through their mobile devices. People might argue that such activity could intrude on people's privacy. It could increase incidences of computer hacking, with implications for security. On the other hand, more efficient technology could mean better security software being available. Dr Barrett predicts that by 2032, each person will be surrounded by 3000 to 5000 connected everyday things. Over the next few years, we will hear a lot more about the Internet of Things, which is only in its infancy at this stage of its development.

The Pew Research Center, Washington D.C.[9] confirms many of Dr Barrett's predictions, stating that the extending system of everything and everybody, the development of Internet of Things in addition to implanted and wearable gadgets would have far-reaching and useful impacts by 2025. The majority of the gadgets will be inserted into our bodies. The majority of gadgets will be conveying information for our benefit.

Remote control apps will allow phones to monitor and adjust household activities from heating the oven to running a bath. They may even prevent fires in the home while people are away. All of this could be at the price of privacy. Positive and negative aspects will continue to be part f the Internet; it will be balanced by the desires of those who use it. There is one certainty: the Internet has changed our lives.

Tim Berners-Lee,[10] at a recent seminar, said that he wants an Internet that would be a good basis for the majority rules system and that will be available to the people who do not have it at present. He urges individuals to create a Magna Carta that will allow him to speak to people he wants to engage with.

Early entrepreneurs

A number of entrepreneurs emerged during the early years of the Internet. Computer programmers are more associated with having coding capabilities than having business acumen; Pierre Omidyahad[11] both qualities and created eBay, the online auction site that made him a billionaire. He wrote web codes that let him put a laser pointer up for auction online. EBay is now virtually synonymous with online auctions and around 100 million registered users access the site where consumers can find almost anything online in a matter of minutes. Just as Bill

Gates does, Omidyar spends a great deal of his time with his philanthropy organisation, which donates hundreds of millions of dollars for social and economic change.

Two graduate students set up Google in the late 1990s. Once the company hit the big time they realised they needed more experience at the helm of their search engine invention. They invited a technological visionary, Eric Schmidt,[12] to improve Google's capabilities. Schmidt became CEO of Google in 2001, charged with the mission of steering Google into the future. Schmidt was well known throughout Silicon Valley for his leadership experience. He was noted for his strengths in Internet business strategies and for his fearlessness in backing new and unproven technologies. In 2004, Schmidt orchestrated Google's public stock offering and the company flourished.

In the mid 1990s, many business people were looking at ways of using the Internet to make themselves a fortune. Jeff Bezos[13] emerged with a vision for a new idea in shopping, which resulted in the introduction of extra large shopping malls. The attraction of the Internet encouraged him to set up a business selling books online. With Amazon.com, Bezos went on to successfully get customers by the millions with hugely discounted products from detergent to power tools and included free shipping. In just a few years, millions of people who said they would never abandon shopping malls moved over to online shopping with Amazon.com.

In 2014, The Internet Society (ISOC) published A Global Internet Report, titled 'Open and Sustainable Access for All'.

The report is the first in a series to celebrate the progress of the Internet, covering trends and depicting the business principles that will continue to increase its growth. It deals with the positive aspects the Internet brings, and how to deal with the negatives that can inhibit consumers going online. Given the unbelievable pace of change, the report says it is important to crystallise and spread the benefits of the open Internet, rather than assuming they will happen. It tells us that the Internet has transformed the world. Unlimited access to the Internet has revolutionised the way people communicate and collaborate, how business people and large corporations carry out business, and how governments and citizens communicate with each other. The development of the Internet relied critically on establishing an open process. The open Internet has created a medium unlike anything else, one that merges the most notable characteristics of traditional media with the new digital channels.

The Internet allows traditional forms of communication, but is more interactive than old-style broadcast and the conventional telephone conversation. As a result, Internet users are both creators of information as well as consumers of brands. Websites, blogs, videos, and tweets can all be broadcast and accessed in the largest mass medium of our time. Audio and video conference calls can be arranged by groups to avoid unnecessary travel. Companies can develop new markets for their brands and raise money online to finance their business projects online. The ISOC[14] concluded that as we near close to three billion Internet clients it is appropriate to venture back and wonder about the velocity of changes that have occurred to date. It is clear that the open Internet model, which served to fuel the development and explore all the obstructions, continues to be the ideal approach to guarantee that the Internet stays supportable and keeps on growing. In the meantime, we can address the advanced gap that divides areas and individuals, and ensure that once on the Web, everybody has the same client experience. With open and widespread online access, anything is possible.

Areas of concern

Today's revolution in digital communications involves a fundamental rethink about how people perceive their environment and express what they understand. The constant presence of images, concepts and ideas, and their almost instant transmission from around the globe, have profound consequences, both positive and negative, for the psychological, ethical, moral and social development of individuals as private and business people. An important point is the gap between consumer demographics and regions, a form of discrimination dividing the rich from the poor. It underlines the fact that everybody should have access to the new technology created primarily by the Internet in order to share in the promised benefits of globalisation and development. Ways need to be found to make the Internet accessible to groups in unfavourable circumstances, either directly or at least by tying it in with lower-cost traditional media. The benefits of the new worldwide movement towards communications integration created by the Internet need to be available to everybody around the world. The causes and consequences of the divide are not only economic but also technical, social, and cultural. The question of freedom of expression on the Internet is complex and gives rise to other concerns. Freedom of expression and the free exchange of ideas should be available to everybody. Freedom to seek and know the truth is a fundamental human right. Freedom of expression is a cornerstone of democracy. Governments should not be able to deprive people of access to information on the Internet or any other media because they find it doesn't suit them. Authoritarian regimes are usually the greatest culprits but the problem also exists in democracies where mass communication of political views often depends on wealth. Governments and their advisors can manipulate and misrepresent truthfulness and fairness by the use of clever sound bites. The Internet is a highly effective medium for bringing instant news and information rapidly to people. Therefore we must ensure that Internet journalism does not contribute to sensationalism and misinformation. Honest journalism is essential to the common good of all nations and the international community.

The Internet brings with it other areas of great concern, including cyber bullying and exposure to sexual predators. The online world opens the door for trusting young people to interact with virtual strangers and people they'd normally avoid in real life. Children and teenagers have been sexually solicited online, while sexual predators target children in chat rooms and wherever young people go online; predators are now scouring social networking sites where very often children's profiles including photos, hobbies and blogs are freely available. Predators may take on fake identities and feign interest in children's activities to exploit unsuspecting and vulnerable young people. On the Internet, cyber bullying exploits children who are ignorant of its dark side. Cyber bullies don't witness their victims' reactions. Some cyber bullies pose as their victims and send out harassing messages to others. Cyber bullies have also begun posting humiliating videos of people they dislike. The Internet can result in unsavoury photographs being published online. Camera phones, digital cameras and web cams are everywhere these days, and children can be victims of their own inexperience with these new devices. They can post pictures, videos or text online that they later regret. A child's online reputation is a growing concern with the rise of online activity.

Is the Internet, like other communication vehicles, a force for both good and evil? We will come back to this in Chapter 30.

Chapter 2: Have the basics of fundamental marketing changed in the digital age?

Diverse views on traditional marketing

Consulting groups and marketing academics and practitioners hold different views on the relevance of traditional marketing. At one extreme some believe that the fundamentals of traditional marketing haven't changed very much in today's business environment. Business guru and academic Dr Philip Kotler is noted for his strategic approach to marketing. He is an advocate of the marketing mix, or the 4P's, framework, representing product, price, place and promotion. It encourages marketers to decide what customers to attract and set about meeting their requirements. Kotler says his framework is a plan that marketers can use to influence customers' responses. The 4P's help companies to develop a basic selling promise as well as developing desired brand imagery. With the growing popularity of the Internet and its new communication channels, some argue that the 4P's concept is outdated. Kotler disagrees and staunchly defends the concept as being still very relevant today, despite the new marketing landscape and arrival of digital media. Kotler[15] said that marketing has a better reputation today than in earlier times. Marketing used to be perceived as an advertising or communications function. Eventually marketing taught companies to put the consumer at the centre of things and give marketers greater insights into the buying and selling process. Today, Chief Marketing Officers have a greater say in company affairs that includes identifying new markets. On the other hand, there are still some companies who take a narrower view of the marketing function. Kotler goes on to argue that the ideal marketing team is one promoting a traditional and digital-age approach to marketing strategy and implementation. Traditional advertising, which embraces TV and radio commercials, is still needed to communicate the company's brand proposition and promise. He concludes social media should be used to deliver brand communications with individually focused messages to different customers and prospects in real time. Social media messages should reflect the core brand message.

J. Wesley Hutchinson on marketing

J. Wesley Hutchinson, Professor of Marketing at the University of Pennsylvania,[16] said that there are endless truths in advertising that still hold and haven't changed in decades. Regardless of how you achieve your client you have to think about dividing and figuring client lifetime esteem. He went on to argue that change is inevitable and will continue to be part of every business, particularly in a management discipline that deals with brand promotion amongst consumers, namely marketing. The needs and requirements of the consumer will still require current brands to be repackaged and reinvented and new products brought to the marketplace.

David Edelman on marketing

To paraphrase David Edelman of McKinsey's,[17] he said that shoppers today interface with brands in a broad sense in new ways, which implies customary promoting procedures must be overhauled to accord with how brand relationships have changed.

Peter Drucker on marketing[18]

To paraphrase Peter Drucker, who said some years ago, and it is still very relevant today, promoting is basic to the point that it can't be viewed in a different capacity. It is the entire business seen from the perspective of its last result, that is, from the client's perspective.

Harvard Business Review on marketing

At the other extreme, some believe that traditional marketing is a dying breed, giving way to the new kid on the block, 'inbound' marketing. More about that anon. Harvard Business Review,[19] published an article recently titled 'Rethinking Marketing', said that in light of the fact that organisations can now associate straightforwardly with clients, they should profoundly revamp to put developing connections in front of building brands. It advocates that marketers should always move from being brand management driven, where companies concentrate on driving communications in one direction towards the customer as opposed to engaging in a two-way communications dialogue. In my view, traditional marketing practice continues to put the consumer at the centre of everything but recognises that consumers today engage with brands in a host of new ways and have different relationships with brands than before. Today's consumers have a very different array of options and will want to continue to engage with the company and its brands long after they have considered and made their purchase. Marketing departments will need to accommodate this shift in consumer activity in their strategic marketing planning and implementation programmes. Consumers will still require an attractive brand offering that they can value and appreciate. What has changed is the need to be able to discern what contact points are most open to influence and how marketers can engage with them in these areas. This is what marketers have to be aware of promoting brands in the digital age of new and diverse communication channels. Customer orientation is not just a marketing function but requires total company effort. I believe marketing will need to synergise its brand imagery, brand proposition and brand positioning through the traditional media with the diverse range of digital media channels that are changing by the day. Companies with a strong marketing ethos will continue to develop and achieve incisive market segmentation, competitor market analysis, consumer insights, and brand positioning and brand proposition in a more focused way with the help of digital marketing concepts. Weighing up the arguments for and against the role of traditional marketing today, it is true that while the Internet is fast becoming the centrepiece of marketing there is still a need for marketers to consider both online and offline approaches to reach its target market with timely consumer messages. Traditional marketing can work quite well with online marketing and need not be viewed as a separate discipline. The objective of traditional marketing is to communicate with prospects offline and if necessary connect with them online. Both traditional and digital marketing can assist marketers achieve their business goals. Each of them has their own skills, with advantages and disadvantages.

Marketing needs to be reassessed

The marketing concept needs to be reassessed. Traditional marketing methods need to be revised but not abandoned and marketers need to be well versed in the traditional way of marketing before they adopt new ways of developing a marketing strategy and implementing a marketing programme. More than ever, the traditional marketing concept needs to reflect what is happening in the marketplace. The important elements of the marketing concept include customer satisfaction and total company input, with profit as the ultimate goal. Nowadays, customer satisfaction in itself is not enough. Companies must strive to secure customer emotional attachment to their brands. To compete, companies need to change from trying to force their brands on the consumer to building long-lasting customer relationships through well-thought-out online communication programmes.

The Internet may have changed the way consumers engage with brands and each other but the process for companies getting prospects into their sights hasn't changed. It would appear that many companies would still need traditional strategic marketing planning and implementation before they consider the implications of the new digital media channels in their overall marketing plan.

Market segmentation

Arriving at pre-agreed subsets of consumers is called market segmentation. It is the opposite of selling the same brand to everyone. It is generally held that it is better to retain and sell to existing customers than trying to find new customers. The purpose of market segmentation is to concentrate marketing energy on certain consumer groups so that competitive advantage can be achieved. Digital marketing will help companies interact with and form relationships with their current customers and give them what they want. The objective will be to do as much business as possible with their best customers. The marketing plan will start with the target market and will have a comprehensive and detailed account of its make up. The main types of buyer characteristic used to segment consumer markets are behavioural, demographic, geographic and psychographic. The easy bit will be agreeing the demographics, the geographic location, age group and gender of the prospects for their brand offering. The more difficult task will be building up a lifestyle profile of their target customers including their aspirations and values, with nuances. The profile will include factors that affect the target market. What are they influenced by? What type of music do they like? What TV and Internet programmes do they like? What is their educational background? What are their family relationships like? Do they feel secure? Do they rate it important to be connected with other people? Do they live at home? Are they in a partnership/relationship? What do they do for relaxation and leisure? Are they ambitious? Do they want to succeed in life? What are their aspirations? Are they wary of change? Do they have traditional values that emphasise the importance of family life? Do they have a relatively ethnocentric outlook, with low levels of trust and tolerance? Are they into environmental protection? Into gender equality and a desire to get involved in local political life?

A market worth targeting has a number of characteristics. It's sizeable enough to be profitable, it's a growth market, it's not overcrowded with competitors, it's easily accessible, the company has the money to compete in it, and the target market fits in with the company's ethos and mission statement. Having built up a comprehensive customer profile will make it easier for marketing to carry out a competitor market analysis.

Competitor market analysis

Apart from understanding its customers, a company needs to pay close attention to its competition. Marketers needs to constantly review their brand characteristics, including pricing, selling channels, customer service, sales force strategy, R&D, advertising and promotion programmes, against their close competitors so that they can identify areas of competitive advantage and disadvantage. Once a company has identified its competitors it needs to assess and evaluate their objectives, strategies, strengths and weaknesses as well as likely competitor reactions.

SWOT analysis is a useful tool used by companies. It analyses the company's internal strengths and weaknesses, its external opportunities and threats, as well as those of its competitors so that corrective action can be taken to deal with any problems that surface during the analysis phase. SWOT analysis could pick up issues such as a lack of marketing focus in the company, a brand that's too expensive, an increase in competition, a change in consumer taste and lifestyles choices, or a high threat of substitutes. It can also offer an opportunity to expand a brand's range and offerings. Marketers can also use Porter's Five Forces to establish a) threat of new entrants, substitutes; b) bargaining power of buyers, suppliers; c) intensity of competitive rivalry; and d) company's core competence.

Consumer insights
Marketers develop consumer insights when they gather both quantitative and qualitative information about their customers. Consumer insights can result from the interpretation of investigations into the consumer mindset, aspirations and motivations that can trigger the customer's interpretation and attach them to a company brand. This information will help marketers to acquire, develop and build a relationship with current and new customers. It's a revelation about target consumers that links consumers and brands that fuels overall business strategy. It helps concept development. It keeps the consumer at the centre of the decision making process. It is something a marketer knows that their competitors do not. It's getting to the heart of why consumers do what they do.

Brand positioning

Brand positioning is all about discussing and agreeing what core benefits the brand has to offer the consumer in preference to others. It is at the heart of marketing strategy. Brand positioning, often referred to as the brand statement, is the place the marketer wants the brand to be in the mind of the consumer relative to competing brands. Positioning involves tailoring a brand so that it stands out from its competitors to encourage consumers to purchase it. Marketers will sometimes reposition a brand to move it to a different place in the consumer's mindset. Brands need to be perceived as different from competitors by consumers.

Brand proposition

A brand proposition should clearly state the benefits that a consumer will experience from using a brand. A well-thought-out brand proposition will include the brand's unique selling proposition (USP), which should ideally include benefits that no other brand can offer. It is not always necessary to have a rational point of difference as long as there is an opportunity to have an emotionally unique brand attribute. A brand proposition should be easy to understand and be relevant to the target audience. It should appeal to the target's current needs and assimilations. A good brand proposition should be persuasive and connect with its target at all levels.

Implementation of the strategic marketing plan

Having completed the strategic planning stage the remaining marketing process covers the implementation phase. This involves determining how the strategic plan can be put into operation to achieve the goals set out in the marketing plan. The next stage of the marketing process can involve all the staff, particularly in a small company, who should take ownership of the marketing plan. This includes detailing specific tasks to individuals and departments to successfully execute a detailed plan of action.

If you can't measure it you can't improve it

The final stage of the traditional marketing process is carrying out a return on investment (ROI) analysis. To do this effectively, the company will have had to establish a system for tracking and monitoring the key elements of the overall marketing plan. Managers will be tasked with monitoring performance on a regular basis. Web analytics software can be used to measure consumer activity in relation to the company's website; It should identify the promotions that result in the greatest sales and identify those that do not work and contribute to the company's ROI. This helps managers to achieve the company's and brand's business objectives. They can set goals to be achieved laid out in the marketing plan.

Chapter 3: If the fundamentals of marketing haven't changed, what is digital marketing all about, and what's different today?

What is digital marketing?

- The use of electronic media to promote brands amongst consumers and to assess the success of marketing campaigns.
- The advertising and promotion of brands using digital marketing including social media channels to target consumers effectively in real time.
- Digital marketing is the fastest growing way of launching and promoting new brands and repositioning existing ones by using digital media channels in a two-way dialogue that will help deliver a company's branding and communications programmes.

Put simply, digital marketing is about promoting brands over the Internet using various digital devices. It can also be called Internet marketing, online marketing, or web marketing. Digital marketing focuses specifically on making company brands visible on the web. This way, potential customers can easily gather information about them. This visibility can be achieved on a company's own website, in a host of social media channels, paid media marketing like Google AdWords, and non paid media including search engine optimisation, which generates a natural placement on search engine listings. One way a company can increase good organic search results is through a company blog. This can be a series of informal articles which the company posts on its website for the public to read and eventually develop a relationship with the company. Another great way to get started is to achieve visibility with social media by having a Facebook fan page, a Twitter account or running a video on YouTube, starting a group on LinkedIn and so on.

Once a company gets visibility online, it needs to maintain consistent interaction that will extend its reach to potential buyers and direct them to its website or the platform where they can access the company's brands. The objective of digital marketing is to help a company increase sales and revenue. It is therefore important to generate leads, and to be able to do that it will need to engage its customers. The best thing about digital marketing is that it is not only cost effective, but it's also easy to measure and track. Tracking a brand's online marketing is important as it allows a company to find out what is performing well and, more importantly, what is not performing well. It can focus on what is working and target that aspect to maximise its profits accordingly. If it finds that a certain channel is not performing well, it can transfer that budget to a better-performing platform so as to increase its returns with a similar budget. It is very important for a company to have a customer base that returns to its brands over and over again. It can do this through digital marketing tools including email marketing and so on.

How does digital marketing differ from traditional marketing?

Digital marketing is in some ways very different from traditional marketing, although the core business principles remain the same. The Internet has affected long-term brand relationships now that customers can quickly check out online specific brand propositions as well as competitive brands. Although consumers have a lot of resources to evaluate brands at their disposal, companies can use similar resources to enhance the value of their brands. Traditionally, branding has been about repetition of messages and imagery. Today a company can get consumers to interact with brands in a host of new ways with innovative and creative thinking. Traditional marketing needs to adjust to and be in tune with how brand relationships have changed.

Consumers are now meeting, interacting and socialising through social networks. They are now empowered by information on their mobile phones. They are able to check out data about the brand, not just the price of things but what people are saying about brands and what other online options are available to them. They are demanding more and more from the companies they choose to form relationships with. Digital marketing enables companies to glean a great deal of information about a prospect from the web search term that they use and in turn have a brand offering to suit the prospect at a given point in time. Most consumers are connected 24/7/365 via mobile devices. The digital space is now an ever-growing source of entertainment, news, and shopping and social interaction. It no longer means simply having a website, but includes customer interaction through mobile apps, digital television, interactive billboards, video and so on.

Digital marketing may not always be an easy option for a company's brand. While many brands do have a successful online presence, companies need to realise that it takes a lot of perspiration and hard work and failed attempts to find success through digital marketing. When it comes to digital marketing there are several strategies and media channels a brand can follow. Often it's a matter of trial and error to find what works best for a particular brand. Knowing your customers very well, their motivations, their interests, needs and requirements, combined with some trial and error can give a company an idea of how it should proceed. Digital marketing is an ever-evolving discipline where new ideas and concepts emerge frequently. Being adaptable and open to new ideas is paramount. A company needs to develop its strategy and its campaigns accordingly, give them time to work, testing and measuring and tweaking along the way. Then it needs to evaluate them with its data as its guide. The good news is that digital marketing is really in its infancy and companies have the opportunity to get up to speed quickly.

Why do companies use digital marketing?
Companies use digital marketing to increase traffic to their website, improve brand recognition, generate sales leads, increase business from existing customers, and improve a company's communications internally and externally. It is hard to believe that ten years ago digital

marketing was a relatively new form of marketing activity. Today the Internet is the first port of call for consumers to get information about a business and its brands. With digital marketing we now have a whole range of armoury and new digital communication channels to choose from. The trick is to work out which ones and how to use them. Digital marketing is revolutionising the way companies interact with consumers, giving them the power to share knowledge and brands in real time, anywhere. Companies can publish ideas, presentations, videos, promotions, and catalogues across a broad range of digital spaces. Companies can reach their targets at the right time with the right communication and real-time measurement techniques allowing them to identify consumer segments and target the right messages at consumers in these spaces. Companies can implement a wide range of digital channels so as to engage customers in a more personalised way. Digital marketing trends that organisations are rapidly embracing include mobile and social media. The opportunity for companies is to be able to communicate with customers and prospects where and when and how they are most receptive to the company's messages. Companies will need to have a consolidated view of their customers' preferences and expectations across all media channels both offline and online. They can use this information to create customer experiences and interactions that will build trust and encourage purchase and subsequent recommendation through word of mouth. The point here is that instead of focusing on how and where to allocate spending across a range of media companies should target stages in the customer's decision journey.

Key benefits of digital marketing

- Digital marketing is less expensive than offline marketing. Marketing a company's brands on the Internet is cheaper than selling them through retail stores. Companies only concern is how efficient it is, with no more expensive inventory costs and sales calls throughout the country.
- Digital marketing allows a company to sell 24/7/365. By a simple click customers and prospects can access and browse in the privacy of their homes or in their offices brands to suit their schedules day or night, Digital marketing allows companies to give a personalised service to their customers. By building a customer database a company can tailor its special offers to suit the profile and requirements of its customer base and encourage new prospects.
- Digital marketing allows a company to build relationships with its customer base. It can have a dialogue with its customers on social media. It can also link its offline advertising and promotion campaigns to its social network campaigns.
- Digital marketing allows companies to sell to more people anywhere. Once a prospect is online they can access a company's brand offering and place an order, assuming the company is equipped to dispatch the product by post or courier. Companies

are able to build in delivery costs into their pricing structures.

- Instant access to a wide reaches of Internet users both locally and internationally in a single click.
- A well-planned and targeted digital marketing campaign can help a company's business reach its target audience at a lower cost compared to traditional marketing tactics. Marketing brands through a physical retail outlet is much more expensive than marketing them on the Internet.
- A company's website is available to a company's target audience 24/7/365.
- Increases customer retention and loyalty by engaging with customers in a more personalised way when it advertises its products and services.
- Creates community building and reputation with social media to increase customer loyalty and create strong online reputations.
- Provides the possibility for an immediate response and feedback from today's connected consumer.
- It's measurable. A company can track its online campaign's success in real time.

Companies who ignore digital marketing will do so at their peril.
It should be clear to everyone that consumers or companies cannot avoid the new phenomenon, the digital landscape. For nearly 900 million people Facebook is an integral part of their daily lives. As digitalisation advances at an extraordinary rate, it impacts on people's personal lives and businesses' commercial futures. Digital media is

having a major effect on the relationship between companies and their customers and prospects. Consumers can play a major role in influencing the success of brands by sharing their personal experiences through social networks. Word-of-mouth recommendations are becoming a powerful driver of purchase decisions. Consumers' trust in their friends' experiences and recommendations may one day be more powerful and influential than advertising imagery and messages. Digitalisation is having a strong effect on the world's future development.

The relationship between a company and its customers has to be redefined.
The digital phenomenon is beginning to pose new challenges to a company's branding philosophy in the digital arena. Will the company be able to adapt its traditional brand and value propositions to the new selling environment? How will it manage digital media channels in a new media environment? What will its customers' expectations be in the new digital shopping environment?
One thing is certain, digitalisation should not be treated as an issue exclusive to the marketing function but as a critical and fundamental development for the company's business as a whole. The Internet has changed the way people give and receive information. Digital marketing allows companies to market their brands in exciting and innovative ways. Traditional media, nowadays referred to as 'push' marketing, is still used to promote brand imagery and includes above the line media like television,

radio, magazines and newspapers. Top-flight companies will continue to integrate traditional media with a digital marketing programme, using 'pull' channels like networks, blogs and search engine marketing. Digital marketing will continue to use Internet-connected devices like smartphones, laptops and tablets to engage with consumers online via the web and email channels, including display advertising and search engine optimization (SEO). A company wishing to get the edge over its competitors will continue using digital marketing strategies to create an even closer dialogue with its prospects and customers.

Creating the environment for the company and its customers and prospects to engage with each other.
If companies are serious about embracing digital marketing, one of the most important things to do is to create an environment amongst its entire frontline and back room staff that embraces engagement with its customers and prospects. This is easier said than done. It will mean delegating responsibilities for new management functions including social media, web design and management, and data-driven customer insights. Once a company decides how it will engage with its customers it needs to ensure that it has the organisational capabilities to create a successful, two-way meaningful engagement through the website and other customer touch points, i.e. the brand's point of customer contact from start to finish. The company's objective will be to create benefits that the customer or prospect will talk about with their

friends. This may influence them to buy from the company and is an effective marketing tool.

Building touch points is becoming an increasingly important aspect of digital marketing. As marketing becomes more pervasive in the digital environment the entire company will need to be more involved to agree a review of customer touch points and review if necessary. These touch points will have major benefits for the customer experience by using the important information generated by customers' feedback. Companies will need to listen constantly to their customers across all touch points so they can study their behaviour and gather relevant consumer insights. This will tell them when they need to respond more quickly to signs of changing needs.

Companies must be able to create, coordinate, measure, and develop campaigns for different channels.
In the digital world, traditional marketing techniques may play a supporting role instead of leading the marketing effort. To get consumers to engage with a company's brand, the company must develop high-impact digital marketing campaigns that cut through all the clutter. Because of the explosion of new marketing channels, digital campaigns are more labour intensive and complex than traditional advertising campaigns. Digital marketing is not only about delivering content to consumers, it's about stimulating conversations that create engagement, reflection and action.

Stories can be captivating.

In the digital arena consumer interest in credible stories means there are many ways to reach and engage people. If a company is considering using stories in its digital marketing plan it should consider a number of issues. What are its customers' goals? What are the challenges they face? How do they want to have their life changed? What is hindering it? What does the company wish to communicate? And, finally, how can the company engage its customers with a story that gets to the essence of the change they would like to see in their lives? The well-known comedian and singer Max Bygraves used to shout out to his audience, "I want to tell you a story." They say that people tend to remember good stories. Stories that are both informative and persuasive can leave a great impression on the person at the receiving end. People like to hear each other's stories; it's a fundamental human aspect of communication. Companies are using stories more and more, because they engage people, and they engage them on an emotional as well as a rational level. Storytelling can show people what a brand stands for. That's why proponents of digital marketing make use of real stories written by real people. These stories, often written by people working in the company, can convey the values of the company or its brands. They can also be stories about customers so that prospects can see how the brand is being used and how it can benefit them. People love to tell stories. It's the most natural thing in the world for many. Stories are a very powerful way of trying to influence each other. Stories are appealing to companies because sometimes rational explanations and a whole lot of statistics don't really engage people. Many of consumers' decisions are to do with wanting to feel better about something. Interesting stories can often connect people with those kinds of feelings, and engage them much more emotionally than facts and figures can. The best stories should emanate from within the company. A member of staff who has the interest of the company at heart and is familiar with the brands attributes should be designated to create stories that will capture the imagination of customers and prospects. All that is needed is a little creativity laced with lots of enthusiasm to connect with people. The stories should deal with the needs and values of the company and its customers and how they connect with each other. Once the company has established its narrative it's important to get it out there into the marketplace. In the business-to-business world, companies get most of their work through personal interaction frequently face-to-face communication. But it needs something else to back this up. This means either written/printed material or online activity. In today's world, prospects are looking for social proof that a company knows what it's about, delivers what it says it will, is likeable and is easy to deal with. They find it by searching for the company online. They may even check the company out on their mobile phone or tablet, so the company needs to have something good for them to find that delivers the social proof they are looking for. It's quite possible to waste a vast amount of time online, so companies need to be highly efficient and effective in the way they use the digital marketing tools at their disposal. The aim is to create an online presence that makes the company easy to find and which looks and sounds credible. Astute companies will share their stories offline when and where appropriate as well as online.

Chapter 4: Inbound marketing and content marketing: What's the relationship?

There is a lot of confusion amongst digital marketers on what the difference is between content and inbound marketing. Some believe that it's the same marketing discipline with two different names. Others see them as two distinct marketing tools. Both terms became popular around 2011 and both tools have increased in popularity ever since. Content marketing is the more popular of the two and probably the one more people have heard of.

What is inbound marketing?
According to Hubspot,[20] rather than the old outbound promoting systems for purchasing advertisements, purchasing email records, and petitioning God for leads, inbound showcasing concentrates on making quality content that pulls individuals towards the company and its brand, where they regularly need to be. By aligning content with customers' interests, a company will attract visitors that they can convert into contented customers. In recent times there have been a good deal of online explanations of inbound marketing techniques. Inbound marketing is the strategy that utilises both content and social media to accomplish its goals. Not that long ago, in the heyday of traditional marketing, below the line tactics such as tradeshows telemarketing, exhibitions and direct mail were effective ways to communicate with prospective customers. In today's era of information overflow disgruntled prospects have found ways to opt out of unwanted marketing communications. As a result, traditional marketing tactics on their own have been

declining in efficiency for a long time. Companies require other methods to increase brand awareness, improve relationships and increase leads, methods that seek to connect with customers and prospects when they are most open and amenable in real time. This activity is known under different names, and depends on whatever marketing guru or academic leader is presenting the idea. It can be inbound marketing, content marketing, social media marketing, etc. Each term has its own emphasis but they all describe a marketing activity that companies who are serious about promoting their brands cannot afford to ignore. Inbound marketing is basically about attracting the right visitors to a website. The expressions inbound marketing came into being when marketers began to seek alternatives to outbound 'interruption' marketing (like TV advertisements, billboards and direct mail). Marketers were beginning to fear that consumers were getting tired of being bombarded with advertising, so the idea behind inbound marketing is that instead of pushing marketing messages out to consumers, marketers use tactics to engage people and pull them in, including SEO, special events, PR and social media activity. Instead of interrupting consumers, marketers get their attention organically and provide value to consumers by using inbound strategies. How they did this would be different from company to company but it would have included the provision of content that would have caused confusion with the role of content marketing. There's a lot of crossover between content marketing and inbound marketing,

How then does inbound marketing work and what does it deliver?

In the world of inbound marketing, the company's objective is not to find leads, it is to help leads find the company. With inbound marketing, companies build up their own audience to attract prospects and customers with relevant content. Naturally buyers must find a company before they can purchase from it. Advocates of 'inbound marketing' say its fundamental role is about getting found online through search engines and social media pages. In this scenario 'content marketing' is the next strategic phase, which deals with ways of securing an engagement with company prospects. It goes without saying that if a company only focused on inbound marketing it wouldn't get very far achieving sales. With inbound marketing, companies can build awareness organically. The opposite of inbound marketing is outbound marketing, which includes cold-calling, direct paper mail, television and radio commercials and newspaper advertisements. These approaches are all forms of one-way communication, which attempt to reach out to consumers to promote a brand.

What is content marketing?

The Content Marketing Institute's[21] definition of content marketing is

"A marketing technique of creating and distributing valuable, relevant and consistent content to attract and acquire a clearly defined audience, with the objective of driving profitable customer action"

Content marketing is about developing content that will appeal to, engage and retain a predetermined audience of customers and prospects. Content marketers produce useful or entertaining content that's appreciated by the target market. It might be an email or a blog, infographics, videos, and newsletters and so on.

Content marketing is part of inbound marketing; the objective behind content marketing is to pull people in, as opposed to sending messages out to them. Visitors to websites will find the content themselves via social media or search engines, rather than it being forced upon them. If the content is interesting and useful, other people are likely to distribute it on a marketer's behalf. This helps increase the number of people who discover a company and its brands and can also improve its search engine rankings at the same time.

Both inbound marketing and content marketing are growing in popularity. Creating content that continually attracts potential customers has been proven to be more effective and less expensive than the interruption techniques of traditional marketing. It really doesn't matter what it is called: investing in high quality, valuable content will be beneficial to businesses. It will help improve search rankings, give something interesting to say on social media that will enhance brand recognition and encourage consumers to find a company's brands organically.

Where does content marketing fit in?

There is no inbound marketing without content. There are also important marketing inbound projects like search engine optimisation and interactive tools that exist outside the scope of content marketing. Companies not taking advantage of the full choices of inbound marketing practices are limiting the potential impact of their marketing activities. As the terms 'content marketing' and 'inbound marketing' become more known it's important to know when they are the same as and different from previous types of marketing and how they relate to each other. Smart companies believe that every one of their employees is in the customer service business and they help market the company's brands through their daily engagement with fellow staff, customers and prospects. The objective of marketing has not changed. Companies are still in the business of connecting the right people with the right brand at the right time at the right price.

Inbound marketing and content marketing, is one a subset of the other? Even though people may never agree on the difference between inbound marketing and content marketing it is feasible to define aspects of each of them before coming to a conclusion.

Content Marketing:

- Is specifically aimed to attract customers.
- Is the tactical promotion of onsite and offsite assets that can be inbound or outbound?

- It can embrace all aspects of marketing but people are usually referring to digital media being provided through earned media channels.
- It's about engaging editorial content for the purpose of building attention to brands and lead sources.
- Generally, content is about blogs posts, articles, email newsletters, eBooks, images, infographics, animations and videos.

Inbound Marketing

- Inbound marketing is a lead-generation tactic where companies track a lead's activity, whether on its website pages, blog, social networking sites and so on. Using appropriate software allows companies to be aware of the prospects' interests so they can be contacted at exactly the right time in real time. It also helps companies to build content that prospects and search engines are interested in.
- Inbound marketing on its own is never enough. An effective inbound marketing approach would involve a powerful combination of social media, marketing automation for repetitive tasks and content marketing,
- Inbound marketing involves a number of activities, with five supporting pillars. These support pieces are SEO, content to appeal to prospects, social media to deliver that content to customers and prospects, landing pages to bring them to a company site to capture and convert them, and then email to nurture them, because the company

has earned the right to speak with them. These five components or pillars are all-important and the wrapper around all of them is inbound marketing. It can be argued that content marketing is a subset of inbound, and that content is a critical aspect of inbound marketing.

Conclusion

Many companies don't care about what it's called, inbound or content marketing. They care whether or not they can expand their customer base, continue their relationship with existing customers and encourage them to discuss their brands with their family and friends. It should be done creatively and as cheaply as possible. Whatever it's called is really irrelevant as long as the task is achieved efficiently.

Basically, inbound marketing is the overall philosophy, strategy and implementation of providing consumers with something that's interesting and of value. Content marketing is the combination of tactics, techniques and marketing tools, that make this task a reality. Therefore, inbound marketing and content marketing is not the same thing but they aren't miles apart, rather two marketing systems that combine to achieve a common goal. Both have similar objectives, but their essential qualities are dissimilar.

I feel that there is a difference between inbound marketing and content marketing. However, the difference is not so great that they should be considered as completely separate entities. In reality, they are two marketing concepts that can work together and operate in synergy to deliver a successful outcome.

Content marketing has the ability to attract and keep customers, create a brand identity, increase brand exposure and improve a company's reputation. However it needs the strategic thinking and philosophical stature of inbound marketing to be effective and successful.

Chapter 5: How does content marketing fit with digital and traditional marketing?

Some definitions and explanations

There are many definitions and explanations of content marketing available online. The Content Marketing Institute states,

> "Content marketing refers to the creation and distribution of relevant and valuable content to attract, acquire, and engage a clearly defined and understood target audience with the objective of driving profitable customer action. A content marketing strategy can leverage all story channels (print, online, in-person, mobile, social, etc.), be employed at any and all stages of the buying process, from attention-oriented strategies to retention and loyalty strategies, and include multiple buying groups."[22]

The Institute's less formal definition reads:

> "Content marketing is comparable to what media companies do as their core business, except that in place of paid content or sponsorship as a measure of success, brands define success by ultimately selling more products or services. Content marketing is a process to attract customers by consistently creating content in order to change or enhance a consumer behaviour."[23]

Another quote, which is interesting and novel, is that 'Traditional marketing and advertising is telling the world you're a rock star.' A recent *Guardian* newspaper article[24] said that a definitive objective of content marketing is to develop business by sharing insightful and helpful information with the target market, which in turn will reward the company by purchasing its brands.

Content marketing concentrates on the customer or prospect's needs first. The real benefit of content marketing is in the engagement between a company and its customers and prospects. Traditional advertising tends to dictate to the target, whereas content marketing has a dialogue with them. Essentially, it is about the creation of and participation in interesting and meaningful conversations that will develop into a two-way relationship. Content marketing can benefit a company by increasing sales leads through increasing the number of visitors to its website. Content marketing can have tremendous value in different ways. The content a company creates and places on the web has a much longer shelf life at lower cost then traditional campaigns. A bigger collection attracts more interest. By embracing content marketing, companies can give customers and prospects the information they require in line with their interests. Content marketing works very efficiently with established traditional marketing tools. It offers a more personal approach to business and helps build trust. Content marketing can take many forms including blog posts, infographics, videos, podcasts, eBooks, and newsletters. Summing up, content marketing is about putting the emphasis on the customer or prospect, not the company. It attracts their attention with relevant content that is of interest to them. It is two-way dialogue instead of a monologue. It is more dynamic and easier to change. It costs less, involves less risk, has a longer shelf life and maximizes word-of-mouth referrals. It continues after a sale and it's easier to measure.

Creating a framework for a content marketing strategy
Content marketing needs a strategic approach of its own to fit into a company's overall integrated marketing strategy. The content marketing strategy is much more than creating content to engage audiences, generate leads and improve branding. The strategy needs to be integrated just like strategies regarding specific marketing techniques, including, for example, email, video, or social media. A content marketing strategy involves an analysis of the different ways content marketing can be used across the customer's touch points along the buying journey. A content marketing strategy deals in more detail than the company's overall marketing strategy with the type of information customers need during their buying journey and their preferred communication channels. It will look at ways the content marketing strategy can improve the overall marketing strategy of the company. The following is one of many structures for developing a content marketing strategic plan:

- Decide on the project team to manage the content marketing function within the company.
- Hold regular brainstorming sessions to generate a steady flow of ideas for content.

- Assemble the content to suit various channels and distribute it across the web.
- Generate customer and prospect traffic to read and view your content.
- Persuade and convert visitors to sales leads and entice them with opportunities to improve their situation.
- Analyse and improve performance. Before a company starts a content marketing plan it needs to be clear why exactly it is creating content in the first place and the entire marketing department should take ownership of it and in the case of small concerns the entire company.

Start with the different audiences.
A detailed evaluation of the company's different targets should take place on an ongoing basis, both internally and externally. One of the principles of content marketing is that the company needs to understand and write specifically for its audience. To do this it's essential to develop personas, a written representation of the company's intended users. The purpose of personas is to create reliable and realistic representations of a company's key audience segments. These representations should be based on insights from qualitative and quantitative internal and external research. Personas help to focus decisions surrounding website components. They also offer a quick and inexpensive way to test and prioritise those features throughout the development process. They can help management evaluate new website feature ideas. Designers can create the overall

look and feel of the website. Copywriters ensure the website content appeals to the different audiences. Personas development can discover coverage gaps and highlight new opportunities. A company may develop many personas for its website. Personas should concentrate on the major needs of the key user groups. Management should seek answers to the following key questions: Who are the users and why are they using the system? What behaviours, assumptions and expectations influence their view of the system? Elements should be organised into persona groups that represent the target users. Each group should be named or classified and refined into primary and secondary categories. Appropriate descriptions of each persona's background, motivations and expectations should be agreed and noted. Personas should include the following key pieces of information: job titles and major responsibilities, demographics such as age, education, ethnicity and family status, the goals and tasks they are trying to complete using the site, their physical, social and technological environment, a quote that sums up what matters most to the persona as it relates to the website. Persona information needs to be organised in an easy-to-read, logical format. In tandem with this management should clearly define and agree the purpose and vision for the website.

Build stories to appeal to social media.
Companies need to have different stories for different media channels. They should have a bank of material to fall back on when the need arises. When a company has

agreed its stories, it needs a strategic channel strategy in place. There is a maxim that content strategy defines channel strategy. A company needs to have a solid content strategy in place before it decides on a channel plan.

Getting it all together

Once a company has finalised its content, identified its audience and agreed its channel plan, it is ready to put its plan into action. To do this effectively it needs to have the right team in place to make the content the basis for a conversation. A response from the audience is now required. When the company receives comments it needs to have resources in place to respond and start a dialogue with the prospect. Knowledge of search engine optimisation will be helpful as well as being familiar with the different styles of the various social media channels.

How will a company know if the content is working?

Marketing guru Seth Godin,[25] academic and writer, once said that one should try not to quantify anything unless the information helps you settle on a superior choice or change your activities.

A company won't always get its content right. It is a continuous learning process, which can be helped by having an effective measurement process in place to assist it to change tack when necessary. Traditional advertising and marketing does not have effective ways of measuring its success, or otherwise. The only barometer is when the year-end ROI is known. A company needs to identify from the outset the metrics it intends to use to monitor performance and progress. Every standard of measurement, including video views, emails acknowledged, brand sales, can be assessed to find out what is working and what is not. Marketing is organic and it takes time to get it right. The thing to remember is that traditional advertising and marketing can be difficult to measure, while it is possible to measure content marketing. The crucial thing is to ensure the correct data is available for analysis. Reliable measurement is essential for the success of content marketing activity. Key performances indicators need to be agreed in advance to encourage management to focus on revenue performance.

Chapter 6: What exactly do we mean by social media and what is its role in digital marketing?

What is social media?
An important aspect of digital marketing concerns companies developing ongoing conversations with it their customers and prospects. Social media are is the online platforms and locations that enable people to participate in such conversations with others For companies, social media is a way to find out what interests its their customers and prospects, from which they can acquire key customer insights that will help them create more relevant and effective marketing strategies for their brands, which can be tweaked when necessary.

There are different kinds of social media
- Social networks like Google+ , Facebook, MySpace, Bebo, LinkedIn, Reddit, Pinterest, Tumblr, Vine, Snapchat, Instagram
- Blogs / Online journals including micro blogging such as Twitter
- Podcasts, including Apple iTunes
- Online community forums
- Wikis, including Wikipedia
- Content communities, including YouTube

Customers can use social media to let companies know what they think of their services and brands, what their customer service issues are and how they feel they are being treated. In turn, companies can respond and deal with any issues that may arise. Companies can also use social networking sites to run promotions and generate ideas for brand extensions. Companies need to be careful how they collect information about customers and prospects and how they manage that information so as not to alienate them if they feel they are being commercially exploited.

The ability to build up trust is key here. There is no denying the power of social media, online presence and digital advertising to spread a company's brand message. Even if it doesn't instantly translate into direct sales, it's still important as a tool for encouraging customer recruitment and keeping the brand prominent and top-of-mind for future prospects. The amount of consumer engagement online doesn't lessen the importance of the offline brand experience; they are probably of equal value. Consumers need to have a seamless shopping experience across all touch points.

Developing a marketing strategy using social media
Setting up a marketing strategy using social media is no different to planning any other marketing exercise. The company needs to be fully versed in the ins and outs of social media and be aware of the aspirations and needs of their target audience. The company will need to have set out in advance clear objectives against which all future actions can be assessed.

Start with the website.
Companies should have a website to act as an electronic brochure, catalogue and place for customer service. A website should represent what the company is all about and what it has to offer the consumer. It should be readily accessible and provide information on how consumers can contact the company. The purpose of the website is to encourage customers and prospects to engage with other visitors to the site as well as with the company about topics of mutual interest. The site should be search engine friendly and be accessible to customers and prospects using a desktop computer, laptop, tablet or mobile device. A company should ensure that its website has a unique domain name, preferably brief and easy to remember. The domain name should describe the nature of the business, with a hosting service that is fast and secure and can facilitate video content to maximise customers and prospect engagement. The website landing page needs to be compelling to convert visitors into sales or leads. It should be focused solely on capturing prospects' email addresses.

A company has the option of paying a developer to create its website. Content management system companies such as WordPress can be used to allow the company to create, publish, design and style its own templates and manage its own content online. It is important that the website has a clear and easy to understand navigation system and search function to support the company's brands Companies need to realise that search engines, like customers, thrive on interesting content and downloads that are fast and problem free. Blogs should be included to keep customers and prospects engaged in dialogue and to assist SEO pages. Email subscriptions should be encouraged on websites by adding an opt-in email subscription box. A popular way to extend the reach of websites is to add a Facebook or Twitter link to the home page.

A company's social media objectives need to be measured.
Before deciding on social media tactics the company needs to decide what its goals are so it knows what to measure to ensure it is doing the right things. If the company's goal is to increase traffic its standard of measurement should focus on visitors from social websites where the company has mounted social media campaigns. If the company's goal is to encourage a following of visitors its standard of measurement should be centred on subscribers. If a company's goal is to generate dialogue its standard of measurement should monitor quality of comments made. If revenue is key the value of each lead needs to be monitored.

Suggested social media tactics
- Devote a dedicated person to be responsible for social media marketing.
- Always have something worthwhile and meaningful to say.
- Keep it short and simple.
- Insightful understanding of target audience is important.
- Avoid spamming.

- Be proactive with content that focuses on users' interests.
- Gauge real-time market mood.
- Explore social data with a focused plan in mind.
- Be authentic, no waffle, draw on the company's own experiences.
- Be humorous where appropriate.
- Zero in on the customers' interests and needs.
- Remember conversation is a two-way street.
- Don't be too pushy, let relationships develop, Create trust.
- Use photographs and videos where possible.
- Use a conversational tone to engage readers.
- Be patient and encourage feedback.
- Outsource content development as needed, it may not be possible for it all to be done in house.
- Measure response, reaction and change frequently if necessary.
- Be polite at all times; never be aggressive with a point of view.
- Use blogging and make it mobile friendly.
- Make sure the company is talking to the right people.

Best ways to engage an audience
Marketing is about identifying consumer needs and satisfying those needs. Social media provides a real-time platform to do just that by creating dialogue.

- Create or source content that will resonate with potential prospects. It is assumed that the more a visitor likes a company's posts the more likely they are to engage with the company.
- Content is ideally suited for mobile devices. It is fast becoming the most popular way for people to view and engage.
- A company needs to ensure content is appropriate for mobile devices.
- Photos increase engagement. A company should consider posting backroom photos of its business activities, recent functions and media receptions, and share photos of its customers interacting with its brands. A company should also encourage its audience to share photos.
- Ask insightful questions about a variety of relevant topics to encourage discussion that may give more information about the target audience.
- Post infographics that will help the target audience understand and appreciate complicated issues that need to be communicated.
- Incorporate some humour into posts.
- A company should know how and when to use hash tags.
- Understand the importance of listening before speaking on topics raised.
- A company should have the resources to constantly update itself about social media matters and about the latest trends in an ever-changing social landscape.

- It is important to integrate traditional with social strategies.

Choosing effective social media management tools

A company needs to make sure that it has the appropriate social media management tools to be able to have regular dialogues with its customers and prospects. Companies who are serious about this will want a lasting presence with relevant content in media channels where they can create lasting relationships. Prior to adopting social media management tools a company should consider a number of things:

- It is important to establish why it needs a social media management tool in the first place and what it plans to get out of it, bearing in mind that it can be time consuming and costly. Relevant questions are: What is it trying to achieve? Is it to create a better workflow? Is it to monitor its use of keywords or to improve its management of content?
- What exactly does it feel it needs to measure? Is it for a one-off social media campaign or a series? Does it want to evaluate campaigns in relation to successful engagement or sales achievement? Does it want to see how it is doing against its competitors?
- Does the company care about its competitors' activity in this area? Is it using its competitors to decide what it should do? Does it wish to establish where prospects are interacting with competitors?

Does it wish to know the keywords its competitors are ranking for?

- What is the company's budget? This is often difficult to agree as companies may be unsure what value social media delivers to their bottom line and ROI. The company will need to have clear objectives before considering its options so it can decide on a tool that is most aligned to their objectives.

Just some of the companies that assist with improving online presence

Crowdbooster[26] is a social analytics tool that works with Twitter and Facebook and organises reports with real-time standards of measurements. Reports cover likes, shares, comments, replies, potential impressions, reach, followers and so on.

Raven Internet Marketing Tools[27] provides SEO, social media, content marketing, and PPC metrics and reporting and campaign tools.

How to find a target audience on social media.

Social media is in a state of constant change. New platforms are being introduced regularly with added features to help companies engage with ever increasing audiences. Companies new to this area need to start with basics like defining their target markets, the type of people they are, their likes and dislikes in order to start the process of creating meaningful engagement with their customers and prospects. As it moves on in the process the company needs to consider the target's psychographics so that it can develop relevant and innovative web content based on its targets' values and tastes.

Companies using social media

Companies have to consider which media channels are most appropriate for them to use to connect with their customers' and prospects' interests. They need to bear in mind that if they attract visitors, word of mouth will play a part in expanding their database. A detailed analysis of the various media channels' profiles will be required before companies decide which channels they need to have a presence on.

All social media platforms have their own individual identities.

These identities are created by the networks' user profiles. The Business Intelligence (BI) Journal[28] recently reported where it felt the biggest opportunities lay on the major networks. To paraphrase its findings,

- Facebook's users skew more youthful, and that means companies that promote the more luxurious brands are more likely to use print media than social media. Fast- moving consumer goods are more likely to be successful using channels like Facebook, which show more engagement with consumers. Facebook accounts for over half of all clicks on the Web.

- People have a tendency to utilise Twitter for news. In 2012, 83% of clients reported seeing news on Twitter. For brands, the best time to post on

Twitter is mid-day, between Monday and Thursday. The most noticeably negative time is after 3 p.m. on Fridays

- LinkedIn has the upside of being the spot for salaried experts, significantly, its populace is highly attractive to marketers since it is a high-salary and very educated client base. The best time to post on LinkedIn is Tuesday through Thursday, when experts are either starting or completing their workday.

- Pinterest is riding the wave of portable. It's truly the breakout tablet-first informal organisation. Pinterest clients as of now account for 48.2% of all social networking on iPads. Most of its followers are female who share information on items such as food and beverages and family and child-rearing related issues. Pinterest is ready to turn into one of the enormous four top informal communities.

- Over 90% of individuals who use Instagram are less than 35 years old, which makes it an alluring platform for that age group.

- Tumblr is solid with youngsters and youthful grown-ups intrigued by self-articulation. Also, the teenagers that do use Tumblr use it a lot 61% of

13 to 18-year-olds said they use Tumblr a few hours a week or more.

What are the benefits of social media marketing?

Harvard Business Review in an article, 'The New Conversation: Taking Social Media from Talk to Action'[29] said that the exponential development of online networking, from sites such as Facebook and Twitter to LinkedIn and YouTube, offers associations the opportunity to join a discussion with a great many clients around the world consistently.

The important point being made here is that social media is really all about having conversations online. Social media sites try to influence a company to move away from the traditional marketing approach of one-sided statements to a friendlier conversation. The bottom line is to enhance the relationship between the company and its target by creating an atmosphere of trust. This is based on the belief that if a company and its target engage with each other the target is more likely to purchase. Social networking can create a sense of urgency and greater rapport when required. This level of rapport may not happen with a traditional marketing approach. Social networking allows a company to monitor its customers' and prospects' perception of its brand in real time. A company can also react quickly if a negative message about one of its brands goes viral. Social media lets a company reach many people very quickly, help it recruit staff by creating a positive image for the company and is a good way of announcing competitions and promotions for brands. The business benefits of social media may not always be obvious, in much the same way that public relations is often difficult to quantify.

Is there a downside to social media?
There is a view that social media can be time consuming. Companies need to be constantly feeding content to keep customers and prospects interested. Social media can be a low burn and long-term strategy. It can be a long time before companies start seeing a return on their investment in the media channels. If a company has many of its people posting messages on social media sites then this can lead to a lack of continuity and style. If a company is careless with social media management it may have a negative effect on the target. Anything published is open to interpretation by the target and may not come across as intended by the company. Companies can lose money if employees are spending too much time online.
Social networking by terrorists can be used to destabilise governments. Social networking can increase crime and become a place where people carry out bullying. Viruses and software can be specifically designed to damage computers. An unhappy employee can use social network sites to air a gripe against a company. It can cause friction between departments. Employees can show intentionally or unintentionally disagreements with management in public, which can affect the image of the company.

Chapter 7: Email marketing

In the 1998 movie *You've Got Mail* Kathleen Kelly (Meg Ryan) in an email to Joe Fox (Tom Hanks) says that the odd thing about email is that you're more inclined to discuss nothing than something. She went to say that such a lot of nothing has implied more to her than such a variety of something's.

Basic requirements for successful email marketing
- Setting objectives, planning sales targets, improving the number of visits to the website, building discussions on the company's blog posts.
- Building a list of people who have asked to hear from the company.
- Compelling and well-thought-out structured copy and eye-catching design, possibly similar to the company website and encompassing the brand logo.
- Deciding the topics to be included in the campaign, special offers, promotions, new brands, events, news, etc.
- Keeping the content up to date and leaving a call to action.
- Ensuring technical know-how and infrastructure to ensure the company's emails get delivered to the right people on time.

- Setting a schedule for each of the mails. Deciding whether it's needed quarterly, monthly, weekly, or daily.

Most efficient and effective online marketing tactic

Many experienced marketers believe that email marketing is the most efficient and effective way to market brands. It is much cheaper and faster than conventional mail because of the high cost and time required organising leaflets and brochures. Companies can reach many email subscribers who have 'opted in' to receive emails. There are sceptics who believe that an email marketing campaign is a dying art. Not true. Email is still one of the most preferred means of contact by customers. It is believed by many practitioners that the number of customers agreeing to receive special offers from companies is actually increasing. The key is to create the right email content and tone for the target audience, whether the company's objective is to send out a series of lead-nurturing messages, a focused email promoting a one-off offer, a monthly newsletter, or a special update about the company and its brands. It has to consider how the audience will view it among the many other emails they receive each day. The trick is to have the skill to put together emails that bring a positive response from the target market, resulting in sales. Results should come in the form of clicks on the company's website, which has a well-crafted call to action. Ideally readers will share the information with their friends and social media followers.

Well-structured emails

Poorly thought-out or generic campaigns will result in companies' emails being moved to spam folders or deleted. On the other hand, well-structured, creative emails can have the opposite effect, starting with the email's subject line. The key to creating a click-worthy subject line is to make it intriguing so the target will be tempted to learn more. A company can run a series of tests in advance to see what appeals the most to arrive at an optimum subject matter that will create interest amongst its targets. Next the company needs to write compelling body copy. This doesn't mean that it has to be a literary masterpiece. Email text should be brief and to the point, telling the target the basic selling promise of the brand being offered in a convincing way, while also offering them a link to click and learn more about it. A company should use visuals and attachments to reinforce the selling message. It should incorporate graphs, images, brand logos, videos, or whatever is eye-catching and visually appealing. It should use bullet points if the email is mostly text as a reader's eye is drawn to them. Many company email campaigns fall short because those in charge see it solely as a means of nurturing and converting leads, rather than a way of also finding leads. A company should include share buttons on its emails to give readers a chance to show the content to their friends and followers. Companies should make sure every email includes a valuable offer, something their readers will actually want to pass on to their friends. Emailing leads is the best way to turn prospects into customers or casual readers into leads. Whether the campaign consists of several spaced-out email reminders or one single email hit (or both), the company should consider all of these elements before hitting that ever-powerful "send" button. It should consider how its audience would take to its email from every perspective. Emails can be designed to develop relationships with current customers and prospects, to enhance customer loyalty, often resulting in repeat brand purchase. Email marketing can be perceived by some as out of date and overtaken by the more trendy social media options. Some people are convinced email marketing is in decline. Others say that with good content, email is a most powerful marketing tool.

Good content and penetration is key

Persuasive email content greatly enhances the relationship between a company and its target market. Admittedly email is not as sexy as social media, but in reality from an ROI perspective many practitioners view email as the most effective way of contributing to a company's bottom line and helping business growth. Some other reasons include penetration. It is estimated that over 90% of online users use email and check their inbox at least once a day. It is part of most people's way of life. With regard to lifespan, email messages are around much longer than social media, where tweets can be gone in seconds. Emails sit there inside the subscriber's 'inbox' waiting to be acknowledged. Even if they aren't read, they have to be deliberately deleted. Email is a private communication between a company and its customer or prospect, with an 'opt-in,' that makes it a permission marketing vehicle.

2013 Email Marketing Benchmark Report[30]

This report tells us that 60% of advertisers say email advertising is creating ROI, and 32% trust it will in the end. Both email and online networking have costs, the distinction is that most email suppliers have a month-to-month fee or some type of cost while most social platforms don't.

Advantages of email

- It doesn't cost anything; once online, there is no further expense.
- It's an efficient filing system. Incoming and outgoing messages and attachments can be stored for easy reference. It's more convenient than a filing cabinet.
- It's easy to use. Once a company is up and running, sending and receiving messages is simple.
- It's easy to prioritise mails. Unwanted incoming messages can be deleted.
- It's fast and efficient. Message can be sent instantaneously.
- Mails can be accessed almost anywhere in the world.
- Same messages can be sent to any number of people anywhere.

Disadvantages of email

- Once sent, emails with amendments required cannot be retracted.
- People can waste time sending too much information.

- When required it lacks the personal touch that a handwritten letter has.
- Emails can be rambling and badly written.
- Hitting the wrong button and replying instead of forwarding an email with comments can prove embarrassing.
- Having to deal with spam can be time consuming.
- Dealing with a virus can seriously affect the computer.

Dos of email marketing

- Personalise emails, even if it's only the recipient's name. It can make communication more effective and interesting. Where possible personalise content and offers throughout the mailing.
- Keep the content fresh and interesting, with relevant attachments to create interest. Remember customers and prospects will be getting other mails as well and won't have the time to read mails that are unclear or uninteresting.
- If attaching videos etc. do check in advance to ensure recipient has capabilities to open such items.
- It is recommended that HTML graphics be kept small.
- Visitors should not be sent to the homepage, but linked directly to content.
- If prospective customers are a target for information gathering give them something in return.

- Messages should be short and sweet.
- Test to continually improve mailings.
- Segment email hit list based upon their needs, demographics and interests. Targeted emails result in higher click through rates.
- Customise messages and content via segment.
- Offer the option to unsubscribe.
- Give subscribers the opportunity to make choices about the content they receive. Let them pick and choose the type of content they want.
- Use automation to follow up leads.
- Make emails mobile friendly.
- Use social media buttons to give brands an extra dimension
- Add a human element and personality to branded content.

Emerging email marketing trends

We know that consumers are now buying smartphones at an ever-increasing rate and are reading their emails on them. Marketers need to make themselves aware which smartphones their subscribers are using and make their email designs and content relevant to that mobile experience. In the email marketing space there may be a need to redesign emails to encourage a greater number of click-through rates on mobile devices.

Consumers tend to be positive about companies using emails because they can decide if they wish to read them. They believe companies will know it is in their interest not to antagonise them with something they have no use for. Consumers know they are in the driving seat because companies have given them that control. They also know they can 'unsubscribe' if they wish. Another interesting trend is that the industry has become more trustworthy. There is less spam due to Internet service providers being more proactive in putting smarter algorithms in place to block spam and unwanted emails. Consumers view the 'inbox' as something positive that they have control over.

When things go wrong

Email is a much-used digital marketing vehicle. It is fast moving and high-volume, so mistakes will happen. A company will need to have a plan B in place so it can react quickly, just in case. A company should anticipate and define possible mistakes and decide on an appropriate response, recognising that every mistake doesn't warrant a response and that sending an apology email is just one of many possible responses.

Developing an effective email strategy

Due to the growth of mobile smartphones and tablet users increasing the use of emails, companies need to capitalise on this growth area and develop appropriate digital marketing strategies. Companies will be aware of this and will be planning marketing strategies accordingly. Salesforce Marketing Cloud[31] is a resource to assist companies to move their brand forward by anticipating needs. I outline a number of helpful strategies for consideration posted on its website recently.' Build an acquisition strategy'.

- If a company has prioritised audience growth, begin by analysing the places where customers are already engaging with the brand. Then, determine how to enhance those experiences and drive interactive engagement with new tools and techniques.

- Optimising for mobile is extremely important. For brands that do not optimise email for mobile, the penalty is stiff. Offer an elegant mobile experience from the word go, beginning with the initial welcome email.

- Data should always be relevant. Companies should assess current data to make sure its sending targeted communications, not "batch and blast" messages. Using simple data points like gender and location can dramatically improve the subscriber experience.

- Personalise email whenever possible. Subscribers will appreciate messages even more if they're personalised. Adding personalised product recommendations into marketing emails can increase sales conversion rates by 15-25%, and click-through rates by 25-35%.

- Email drives accessibility across channels. The ability to easily archive and access messages at a later time influences consumer channel preferences. Email remains a powerful channel for its ability to bridge the three-device environment of smartphone, tablet, and PC.

- Get permission. Thanks to the good work of author and marketing guru Seth Godin, the email channel is permanently linked with the concept of "permission marketing"— namely, that brands should first seek permission before sending customers email marketing messages. Equally important, the CAN-SPAM Act of 2003 — a law that set the standards for commercial email usage — dictates that it must be easy for subscribers to opt out of receiving emails, and those opt-out requests must be honoured in a timely fashion.

- Email drives deals. If a company is not making deals available via email, it's ignoring the largest direct audience for this content. According to the Audience Growth Survey, 91% of survey respondents reported being involved with email marketing on a regular basis because it's a channel that drives results for their businesses.
- Sharing isn't just for social networks. If a brand is emphasising only consumer's share via social networks, it's reaching just the tip of the iceberg. Private communications are extremely valuable to brands, as a friend's thoughtful personal endorsement will often realise a better response than one broadcast to thousands.
- Did they abandon before they bought? Tailor the frequency and number of abandoned cart emails to the purchase at hand, and that item's typical purchase window. Pay attention to the industry's typical sales cycle, and send abandoned cart emails accordingly.
- Automate post-purchase messages. Automate a re-engagement campaign for a week, a month, and 90 days post-purchase. Determine the point when subscribers typically purchase from the brand again

(or disengage), and start from there to further personalise the send dates. Email, in combination with a strong website and customer experience, forms a stable foundation for digital marketing.

Chapter 8: Video Marketing

Why online video is the future of content marketing.
...Video is taking content marketing by storm.' *The Guardian*.

The Guardian writer Chris Trim[32] went on to say that with online features rapidly turning into a key means for individuals to fulfil their data and amusement needs, organisations that neglect to incorporate it in their Internet showcasing procedures will do so at their risk. In the event that it were five years later on, would you be spending more time perusing this article or would you be viewing it with greater interest in less time on a video? As online proceeds with its incomparable ascent, it's a fascinating thing to consider.

What is video marketing?

Video marketing includes any marketing activity that involves the use of video for promoting a brand, or promoting a specific video, for example, in the music business. Video marketing is growing in popularity; companies now promote their brands on YouTube and other channels using videos. Consumers watch the videos on their laptop or tablet, often sharing them enthusiastically with friends and family. In recent times, there have been examples of videos going viral over the web, often giving global coverage at very little cost.

A company should consider posting corporate and brand videos on its website.
Videos can be used in many ways to promote the company itself or one of its brands. It is often the case that consumers are more interested in watching content expressed in a video than reading it in a newspaper or magazine. Videos can capture and express the culture of the company or its brand more easily and more effectively. It is suggested that videos should be kept relatively short and to the point as people do not have time or patience to sit through lengthy videos no matter how interesting they are.

Benefits of video marketing
Video marketing has many benefits for companies who wish to promote their brands online:

- Marketing using video lets companies promote their brands in an interesting and entertaining way.
- Research conducted by 'Simply Measured'[33] in 2012 showed that visitors to websites found visual content more enjoyable to browse through than plain text and is also easier to share with friends and family. The research showed that visuals were gaining traction in digital marketing with the growing success of Instagram and Pinterest. People will sit through a video as opposed to sitting down and reading a lengthy article or a long blog post.

- Videos assist companies to communicate concepts much better, often with the use of presenters communicating directly to the viewer.
- Articles used in marketing campaigns including PR activities can be easily turned into videos without penalty by the search engines.
- Some companies find it easier to create fresh content regularly using videos to keep their website ranking at the top of the search engine pages.
- Videos enable companies to get their targets' attention, because if the visitors are used to reading about brands in print, using an audio and video concept creating movement will often intrigue them.
- Making a video can be inexpensive.
- Websites such as YouTube give companies the opportunity to show their videos on their sites. This often results in videos going viral.
- When companies use videos, consumers will often help market them by word of mouth.
- Video marketing is on the rise. Videos can result in companies gaining increased traffic and consumer engagement.
- Video websites such as YouTube engage with lots of people who comment on the videos; visitors then read these comments.
- Visitors who enjoy the content of videos produced by companies are more likely to buy from the company.

Making good videos

Research shows that people enjoy watching videos online as long as they are produced professionally, with reasonable production values. To do this, marketers need to:

- Focus on the target audience's psychographics and demographics, as they will dictate the tone of voice and mood of the video.
- Videos need to have good production values and they need to be interesting and entertaining to watch.
- A good video provides value as long as it's interesting and increases web traffic and improves conversion rates.
- Videos should give the viewer a preview of the treat they have in store, while leaving them longing for more. After they have watched the video, visitors should feel the next step is to click on the link to the website.
- The more professional the videos look, the more impressed the viewer will be.

Creating video content that will get views

All the video content to be viewed by customers and prospects represents the company and its brands, so it all needs to be of good quality.

- Google's crawlers will read the word content of the video to decide what it is about, so using phrases that prospects are more likely to use will help to get the content ranked on page one. Google will check the transcript of the video, so it's important to write copy for the video and highlight the key phrases earlier on in the video.

- YouTube, one of the biggest search engines for videos, is the ideal place to post videos in an easy-to-use free space.
- It is a good idea to include a site map so it will be easier for search engines to find it.

A word of caution

Words are important for search engines. It's equally important that professionals are used to produce brand videos with high production values to attract visitors' attention. While moving visuals and eye-catching graphics are essential, text-based content is still very relevant. A combination of good visuals and text is ideal. A company will need to monitor whether its target market is responding positively to its videos. Constant testing of content is needed, as well as knowing the aspirations of the target market, which will help companies to know when to change the videos.

Dos of video marketing

- Keep checking the videos and try and get visitor feedback. Change as necessary. Avoid copy fatigue.
- Make sure video and audio are top quality. Both are important.
- Make sure video is engaging and compelling throughout.

- Share video with customers and prospects on the company's social networks, on email database and on company blogs. Use videos anywhere people are watching. Hopefully, they will in turn share them with their friends and family and promote the company's brand in the process.
- Keep it short, and make sure it's worth watching.
- Show new videos on a regular basis to retain people's interest.
- Be real and authentic at all times, with no waffle.
- Include outside people. Use guests where possible to talk about something related to the business that is relevant and interesting to the visitor.
- Watch other videos to pick up ideas that are relevant.
- Include special offers to increase interest in the website.
- Be budget conscious, even when high production values are needed to reflect the brand values.
- Optimise the page to ensure people will locate video.

Don'ts of video marketing
- Don't use videos to make a hard sell or people will turn off.
- Don't try and go viral deliberately, it seldom works.
- Don't overload YouTube with videos.
- Don't forget to have a call to action in videos.
- Don't forget to measure the viewing results.

Creative Options for video marketing
Using webcam

A webcam video featuring a presenter talking to camera, like a newscaster, will give a company the opportunity to add a personal touch to its product range. It gives the company the chance to introduce itself and talk with conviction about a particular brand. This will give the audience the impression that the company is speaking to them on a one-to-one basis. A webcam presentation can create and build up trust between the company and the viewer. Current top-of-the-line computers or laptops are likely to have a webcam built right in. The ideal thing to do is a test to make sure the quality is acceptable to the site visitor. If the quality of the built-in camera is not acceptable a webcam can be purchased at a reasonable price. A webcam allows companies to make straightforward video that can be recorded while the presenter sits or stands in one place near a computer.

Professional digital video production

To do a more professional video production an actual digital video camera will be needed. When it comes to video marketing, the more money invested in video production the more professional the final video will be and the more impressed the web visitors will be. Professional video production is very labour intensive. Companies who are serious about producing quality videos will need to have access to creative people, probably at an ad agency, which will make the difference between amateur and professional persuasive communication.

YouTube

YouTube is very well known, with millions of viewings every day. A company can set up its own channel on YouTube to promote its brands. If they wish, consumers can subscribe to receive news of upcoming videos. There are other sites that can be included in a video marketing plan, including, amongst others, Viddler, Google Video, Vimeo, Metacafe, Daily motion, Yahoo Video, MySpace and Revver.

Tube Mogul[34] is a free tool that companies can use to register for the sites previously mentioned. The company uploads its videos and Tube Mogul will distribute them to the various channels on behalf of the company. It also has tracking and analytics data facilities which companies can use to find out who and where people are watching their videos. It is an ideal source if companies want to get videos on the Internet quickly. Marketers are aware that they have to create more 'noise' on more communications vehicles than their competitors. Video marketing is one such vehicle

Chapter 9: Blogging

What is blogging? Normally, business websites are a series of pages that are connected through a home page or landing page. Each page is usually dedicated to a particular aspect of the company's business. Visitors to the website can select the pages that interest them. They are usually listed on the home page for easy-click access. Blogs are all about regular updates and usually visitors only read the first page, in other words, the page featuring the latest blogs. They regard other pages as out of date. Blog is a term derived from 'weblog; it reads like a journal except it's online. Blogs cover business and personal matters. Blogging can be described as the online version of a newspaper or magazine. People may read blogs regularly and not be aware that what they are reading are blogs. Such individuals read articles on the homepages of MSN, Yahoo and other sites on a regular basis. Although Yahoo is primarily a search engine, its home page has a blog facility. Many writers, or bloggers, contribute articles on those home pages. In early 2014, there were 172 million blogs in existence. If we look hard enough we will find a blog on pretty much any topic. Some individuals' blog monthly, weekly and daily and others update whenever they feel like it.

Different types of blogs

Blogging operates in much the same way as newspapers, magazines and even TV shows. Each of the communication channels is filled with content that bloggers hope people will be interested in. To start a blog, a company or individual needs a platform. There are a variety of platforms available that are free, while others have a cost associated with using them. Individuals who wish to communicate their thoughts and ideas about a particular topic write a blog. Their posts can be about themselves, the work they do, and their families and friends, and hobbies or interests they wish to talk about. Personal blogs usually do not have extensive readership, since other people aren't interested in the lives of people they don't know unless they are celebrities. Blogs that concentrate on a topic of specific interest to a section of society can over time become very popular. Some companies start blogs to tell people about their brands. By making their content interesting they can get a number of potential customers involved. There are a number of different blogs, which can vary in style and content. The personal blog is like a diary and is written by an individual. Micro blogs are postings of digital content, often involving text, photos, and short videos, with links to other media on the Internet. Micro blogging can be spontaneous and can create large followings. People use blogs to keep in touch. Companies use blogs for business purposes. Blogs can enhance internal and external communications. Some topics deal with specific areas such as politics, health, travel, gardening, music, theatre, fashion, cinema and so on. Recent blogs that are popular incorporate tutorials for specific subjects. Another blog feature gaining popularity is celebrity blogs, which can have millions of followers.

Blogs connect perfectly with social media

Companies have access to many platforms that can create the ideal environment for them to connect with their customers online. These companies understand and believe that there is a need to use every means open to them to communicate information that will make their brands more attractive and desirable to their target audience. The key benefit is that marketers are able to provide much more information and persuasive content about their brands for public consumption. Blogs can include testimonials. The content can be changed easily and updated regularly.

Building loyal communities with blogs

Effective and well-written blogs can create little communities of their own, all centered on a particular discussion that will have been deliberately initiated by the company running the blog. Other social platforms may find it difficult to achieve this. As marketers become proficient in blogging they will realise that when it gets a good discussion going on a topic that is has originated it will be easier and more relevant to introduce the company's brand in a natural way during the course of the discussion. The marketer will be aware that from a marketing perspective the discussion, good and all as it may be, will only be successful if it encourages visitors to talk enthusiastically about their brand both online and later with their family and friends, ending with a sale.

Blogs can increase subscription lists.
When a visitor participates in a blog discussion and is comfortable with the company running the blog it would be usual for the marketer to introduce the visitor to the merits of the company. It may encourage the visitor to become a subscriber to the company's newsletter. The marketer may offer an incentive by way of a discount on a brand to encourage the prospect to sign up. Once this is achieved it would be the marketer's objective to turn the prospect into a customer.

Blogs make companies seem human
Usually people who participate in company blogs will, after a certain period, come to view the company in a more positive light. This will be no accident; it will be the result of a very deliberate strategy by the marketer to put a human face on the company to reel in the prospect. The visitor will soon realise that there are real people in the company they knew very little about and will begin to be receptive to its communications and recommendations.

Blogging is an effective PR source
Blogging can be used for brand enhancement. This can be part of a successful public relations promotional campaign. Companies can connect with different media channels to promote a particular brand. A blog can be an

important marketing tool for branding. It can be a building block for success, especially in competitive markets, where it can be part of a marketing strategy to establish the brand in the marketplace. Blogging can help bring awareness of a company's brand, bring in old and new customers, and start camaraderie between the company and customers.

Major advantages of blog marketing:
- Blogs can be included in an existing website.
- Blogs can reach targeted readers anywhere.
- Blog marketing benefits a company by keeping it visible amongst its target audience.
- Blog marketing is great for getting visibility for company brands.
- Blogs on every imaginable subject span the net. Paying high-quality bloggers to speak about a company's brand is another effective blog marketing technique.
- Blog marketing is a way to move to a more personal level with customers.
- 'Comment' sections can reveal pertinent information about customers.
- Blogs can assist in determining a more focused marketing strategy.
- The more blog posts a company has the better, to engage its audience.
- People may regard blogs as their main source of information about a particular topic.
- Blogging is not complicated.

- Sales people will understand customers' issues better.
- Blogging can show consumers that a company cares about them.
- Blogging helps companies recruit better staff.

How to write a company blog

There usually isn't a problem starting a blog but companies need to know how to write a blog that customers are interested in reading. The trick is to be able to write a blog in a way to keep visitors coming back for more engagement after their initial visit. The impact of a company blog starts with interesting content subject matter, a friendly writing style and nice layout. The most important part of any blog is what you have to say and how you say it. Visitors will return to a blog if they like how something is written about a specific subject. Just as a company defines the target audience, the image and message for its brands, it must do the same for its blog. Does it want its blog to be family oriented or targeted to teenagers or single adults? Does it want its blog to be humorous or serious? How does it want its readers to feel when they visit the blog? These are the types of questions a company needs to consider before entering the blogosphere.

Once a company has defined the image it wants its blog to portray, it needs to create a blog design that communicates that image in line with its brand values. This will include the choice of typeface and choice of colour scheme it uses. The first thing a company should do is to agree the format and elements of its home page.

Blog posts will need to be organised into categories to help visitors access the blogs easily and to help the company find the different blogs in the future. Blogs, which should be updated frequently, can get buried quickly and can be hard for readers to find. One way to avoid this is to archive blogs by month or by category. As blog categories are created, companies need to keep search engine optimisation (SEO) in mind. Search engines typically find blogs based on keywords used on each page. Using a blog's most popular keywords, without overdoing it and becoming spam in category titles, can help boost the search engine results. People seek bloggers who have something interesting to say. Companies need to cajole visitors and convince them they know what they are talking about and that they value their opinions. Visitors look for bloggers whose writing style they enjoy or bloggers who have the appropriate level of experience to write on a specific topic. The company can establish what it represents so visitors can assess the company's input and how it qualifies it to speak on the topic in question. This can be achieved via a link to the 'about us' page or as a short bio on the web sidebar. Though every blog post will be different, there are certain steps a company can follow to make sure it has the essential components necessary to perform well.

Decide on an appropriate tone of voice

A company should decide to whom it is talking and why. Is it relevant advice and information or banter? A company needs to have specific goals for its blogs in order to have better engagement with its audience, with an appropriate tone of voice.

No waffle. Blogs that are written in an honest way with no waffle are usually the most popular. The company needs to be mindful that its success will depend on how well it creates a community around its blogs.

It's not all about adding links. Done properly it can be time-consuming, and companies should be careful not to fall into the lazy trap of just linking lists to other online content. This defeats the whole purpose of a blogging strategy as a means to keep visitors in touch with the company and not have them moving away from the company website.

Use short paragraphs. Companies should use short paragraphs with plenty of space and not reams of copy, which is usually off-putting for the reader, who may move on to something easier to read. As content grows in stature in social media and public relations platforms, blogging is no different. It is a means for companies to create a meaningful dialogue with their customers and prospects outside of the normal online brand transactions. Successful companies will continue to integrate their blogs with other social media sites, which will be accessed through a host of devices. This will ensure that blogs continue to be an essential part of their digital marketing strategies.

Chapter 10: Search engine optimisation (SEO)

What is SEO?

In general, the higher a website ranks on a search engine results page, the more traffic the site will receive. However, sites can improve their rankings on search engine pages on their own by ensuring that their page content is based on what the visitors are looking for. It is fair to say that the practice of search engine optimisation (SEO) is a very complex and often confusing topic. Its task is straightforward. It's all about ways of improving, promoting and optimising the web that will result in more visitors emanating from the search engine searches. The objective of the exercise is to try and get the company site to rank first on the search pages. People clicking on Google, Yahoo, or Bing etc. find most sites by typing in certain words called keyword phrases, which play a very important role in SEO. Once a person has typed in a keyword phrase and clicked on the 'search' button various sites will appear for selection. People do not normally click beyond the first page, hence the importance of getting the site listed here. Sometimes there are sites at the very top of the first page in a slightly different colour, these are sites that the search engines get paid for to guarantee a prominent position. Usually there are two or three of these, but sometimes none. SEO is only concerned with organic sites, which means they are paid for.

Trying to get a company on the first page of search results

The pertinent question is, what sites are displayed on the first page of the search engine listings and what do companies have to do to achieve this? Search engines use their own proprietary ranking algorithms that are confidential and not known to the public. There are some techniques a company can incorporate using keyword phrases to help its site show up on the first page of searches carried out by potential visitors to its site. This emphasises the point that today a company needs to be online, as most potential customers would expect it to be. The theory is that by getting a site to show up on the first page, the company will get more people visiting its site, resulting in a greater opportunity for it to sell its brands to the prospects in the process. By using Google Analytics code,[35] a company can monitor the number of visitors to its site, how they are getting there, the length of time they spend on the site and the type of pages they are browsing. To start the SEO process, a company must refer to its marketing plan to confirm whom exactly it wants to talk to. A company will need to choose the keywords it needs to target that audience. This is the most important, and sometimes the most difficult, part of SEO. There is an immense amount of competition in the marketplace for keyword phrases on the Internet. Some keywords would be difficult to rate highly because of the large number of people also targeting those same keywords. Some competitor sites can be long established and may be already doing SEO successfully. If there is lots of competition in a company's market it means that by targeting those competitive keywords the company may potentially never show up in the top search results. The company could choose slightly different and less used keywords which fewer people may be searching for and still greatly increase its chances of showing up on the first page of the listings. A company can become innovative and try out keywords and phrases by using Google Analytics to see which words or phrases are working best to attract visits from search engines. Google Analytics will also tell a company what Google keywords people are using to find its site.

Optimising a site and measuring success
Using a page title tag, the element that creates the title of a web page, in SEO comes second in importance after the page content. The page title tag will usually be at the top of the browser and in the text of the link in the search engines' link search results. The page title tags give the names of documents. They are frequently used on search engine results pages and give a preview of pieces of information for a particular page. They appear in three main places: browsers, search engine results pages and external websites. They play a major role in ranking and should be kept short and sweet and incorporate the principal page keyword phrase. Brand names should be included in page title tags. If the brand is well known it

should be included at the beginning, for SEO purposes; this will also entice more clicks. Less well-known brands should be included at the end. Title tags should be different on every page. Some sites use the same tags on every page and miss out on the benefits of having a variety of tags for added impact. It should be remembered that page title tags create the link for visitors in search results. Page title tags should be seductive and draw in the viewer to absorb the page content and should be written in a way that will motivate visitors to press the click button. The most valuable keyword phrase should be part and parcel of a page title tag; this will entice visitors to read it. The page title tag should state what the page is about and be relevant to the content within it. The description should be thought of as copy. It should be kept to around 150 characters. Any longer and it will be cut off in Google and other search engines.

Content is king for SEO.
When writing copy, it's important to integrate keywords in a natural way. Duplicate keywords throughout the copy. Use original copy on each page to optimise the website, duplicating copy leads to lower ranking. When linking to other areas of the site, try to link keywords. Make sure copy isn't just full of keywords, but makes sense when read. Use alt tags on any images. Alt text is the little piece of text that shows when an image is covered over with a mouse. It should be descriptive and again companies should try to integrate at least one of the keywords in it. It's important to include keywords in

the page URL or web address. Companies should keep content fresh to easily optimise the website. Google likes fresh content and an easy way to do this is through posting blog updates about new tips or content that's related to the business. Getting others to link to the website also often helps. This ties into blogging. If an interesting article is written, someone may find it and share a link to it on their site back to the company's. The more links to the site from others the better, as long as they are quality links.

Developing keywords
Brainstorming is a good way to start the process of developing a candidate list of keywords. The company should set aside some time to stimulate its thought process with a view to drawing up as many keywords / phrases as possible. A short list of phrases should be agreed when some themes have emerged. The next phase in the process is to create a series of contenders using one of the keyword tools such as Google AdWords or WordTracker.[36] A company should analyse words and phrases that its customers use. It can look at its analytical data to establish the phrases that are currently being used to bring people to its site.

Building a friendly search site
To create a successful site, a company must ensure that the search engines can find its pages. It needs to eliminate any obstacles and not create barriers, such as the title/description being too long, too short or missing, that might prevent the search engine crawlers from finding the

company's content. Sites can be created that will reinforce its keyword themes and assist search engines crawlers hone in on what it wants visitors to see. Anything that helps visitors appreciate the site more is an asset. If many people access a site it will usually be a search-friendly site as well.

Building links to the website

It is well established that growing the link profile of a site is essential to gaining traction, interest and traffic from search engines. From an SEO perspective, building links to other successful sites is essential to increase traffic and improve search ranking. If a company wishes to build trust and authority in its site it can do so by associating with sites, through links, that have a proven track record with the general public. It is the quality not the quantity of the links that is important. It is generally accepted that the easier a link is to organise the less effective it will be, or put another way if it is difficult to secure a link it is fair to assume that the link is good.

Analytics

With all the rather complicated jargon surrounding SEO, how does a company know what works and what doesn't work? One way to find out is by using analytics. There is an old maxim that if you cannot measure it, it's not worth doing. Marketers should be able to measure what SEO is doing and if it results in an acceptable ROI. SEO is an iterative process, things that are tried should be checked out to see how effective they are and this can be taken into account for the next phase of iteration. Every marketer should have an analytics programme set up for the company site. There are a number of resources to choose from. Google Analytics is one and it's free. It's not complicated to set up and it supplies a lot of information so the marketer can observe what is happening on the company site. It will show the amount of traffic emanating from search engines and other sources. Feedback will tell if people are going only to the home page or if they are searching other pages as well. Many things can be done with analytics, but first the most appropriate system needs to be installed. A company needs to know on an ongoing basis what exactly is happening on its website to determine what needs to be sorted out. The company will be able to monitor those keywords/phrases that are bringing visitors and those that are not, and track keyword rankings. Analytics should inform the company what content is doing best by getting the most views – what is attracting the most clicks? It will tell the company who exactly is visiting the site, the browser and operating system they are using and where they are located. The marketer should analyse everything about the visitors to the site so more focused content can be used to attract them.

SEO is not an exact science

As we have seen, SEO is not an exact science. It is just a subset of digital marketing that can be confusing at times. To end with an apparent contradiction, a company may receive very few visitors from search engines and yet have a successful website if it is attractive to visitors. It is the view of some experienced marketers that if they market their brands well, the complicated aspects of SEO will take care of themselves.

Chapter 11: Pay per click (PPC) marketing

What is pay per click (PPC) marketing?

Pay per click (PPC) marketing is used for banner advertising on websites. A company pays a fee every time its advertisement is clicked, as distinct from paying for the number of times an advertisement is viewed organically from the company site. PPC is defined simply as the amount spent when an advertisement is clicked. Search engine advertising is a common form of PPC. It enables marketers to put in a bid to place an advertisement in search engine sponsored links. Manual bidding gives users the most control. They can set maximum bids for individual keywords and also advertisement groups. They should compare price versus volume to determine their bids. It is prudent to start above the minimum to get quicker results and feedback on the effectiveness of the advertisement being used. It is recommended that beginners should use automatic bidding. They can set a daily budget and a cost per click (CPC) bid limit per keyword, and the system will try to provide the most clicks within those guidelines. It will also adjust bid amounts between keywords, advertisement groups and placements based on set CPC limits. If automatic bidding results are not great and the advertisements don't actually appear, bidders can remove or raise the maximum limit, increase their daily budget or switch to manual bidding and a higher bid. Bidding success often depends on increasing the budget, but what is really needed is a clever strategy to get the best placements and beat the competition.

It's very effective when a site visitor uses one of the marketer's keywords/ phrases that are related to the company brand being advertised. Normally if the PPC is benefiting the marketer the cost of the sale will be more than the cost of the click. PPC can be an effective way to get visitors to a company site when traffic is needed urgently, but it can be risky if not done properly. A lot of marketing budget can be wasted generating too many visits that are fruitless and end with no sales. Setting up a PPC campaign can be work intensive for a company. It involves making sure that the right keywords/phrases are selected, which can take time to get right.

What the company (the advertiser) organises

The company is responsible for generating relevant content and deciding on the keywords/phrases for the advertisement. It also has to decide on the maximum amount it is prepared to pay for a click on the advertisement. The amount can be related to each keyword/phrase it has chosen.

What the search engine algorithm organises

The search engine has to make sure that the advertisement is compliant and acceptable to editorial guidelines. It has to display the advertisement for any required search queries. It is responsible for deciding rank or position of the advertisement related to the marketer's maximum bid and the advertisement's relevance to click through rate, content, keywords/phrases and landing page.

A word of caution about PPC
The company is responsible for generating relevant content and deciding on the keywords/phrases for the advertisement. It also has to decide on the maximum amount it is prepared to pay for a click on the advertisement. The amount can be related to each keyword/phrase chosen. The search engine has to display the advertisement for any required search queries. It is responsible for deciding the rank or position of the advertisement related to the marketer's maximum bid and the advertisement's content, keywords/phrases and landing page.

Inflation occurs when a company gets involved in bidding for a keyword /phrase and spends far too much money acquiring it. Inflation can also play a part when a company decides that it has to have a specific keyword/phrase and is prepared to outspend competitors to secure it at any cost. Search engines can impose quality restrictions on some keywords/phrases that can also cause inflation. These restrictions can artificially increase the cost per click rate even if there is nobody doing any bidding. Another issue is that PPC does not scale. If the site increases its traffic the advertiser pays more money in direct proportion to the traffic increase. What actually happens is that the cost per click remains constant but the overall cost increases. It is the complete reverse for search engine optimisation, when a company sets aside a budget to improve its rank but the cost per click reduces as the company increases its site traffic.

On the other hand

Well-thought-out PPC advertising will usually result in visitors going to the site right away. Companies who have large enough budgets will get a top listing on the first search engine page. If an eye-catching advertisement with substance and effective keywords/phrases is built into the text the company should get clicks as soon as the advertisement appears. The response from PPC advertisements can be very quick. It would be usual for a company to get a response from such an advertisement minutes after it opens an account with Google AdWords. PPC advertising can work successfully as a tactical marketing tool, getting responses that are much faster than those generated by search engine marketing and various other forms of advertising. Companies are also able to adjust campaigns very quickly to take into account changing audience behaviour. In certain cases, companies may find keywords/phrases for niche markets where the top bids can be low, resulting in good value for money. Sometimes the final cost of the campaign can be a fraction of the cost that a company would have to pay for alternative forms of advertising. Two significant search engines in use to day are Google AdWords and Yahoo Bing, accounting for the biggest percentage of the sector.

Google AdWords

Advertisements generated in conjunction with Google AdWords[37] appear on the right-hand side of the Google search page under the 'sponsored links' heading. They can also appear in a shaded form at the top of the page listings. The prominence of these text advertisements will depend on how much the company is prepared to pay for them. It would be expected that the higher the budget and the more focused the copy the higher the advertisement will appear on the page. Because Google AdWords is a PPC service the advertiser only pays when a visitor clicks on the advertisement.

Advantages

- It's great if a company wants to drive traffic to its site fairly quickly. SEO takes much longer to work. AdWords is instant.
- AdWords is a simple process. Carry out keyword research, decide on a budget, select a few target groups, and write appealing copy. Advertisements will appear as soon as Google has approved them.
- A company get to run a campaign on Google, one of the Internet's largest search engines.
- AdWords doesn't have to be expensive, unless a company wants it to be. By specifying how much a company wants to spend, and setting a maximum cost per click for its keywords, a company is able to maintain complete control of its budget at all times.

Disadvantages

- A company is restricted to the number of characters it is allowed. It needs to be sure to have an attention-grabbing headline, the right keywords, brand benefits and call to action, all in one small area.
- A company pays for clicks even if a user doesn't stay for long, or doesn't buy a company's brand.
- To ensure a company's campaign is efficient, and has been set up properly, it needs to invest time in monitoring the effectiveness of its campaign.
- A company's landing page needs to be up to par in terms of relevance to the search query. If a company neglects its own website's SEO, and relies solely on Google AdWords to drive traffic, Google will look at the quality of the landing page and determine if it is adequate.

Yahoo! Bing Network

Some companies do not depend on SEO to get visitors to their sites and confine themselves to PPC. They believe that an effective paid search campaign is better when doing business in a competitive environment. Companies who are hooked on paid search tend to use Google AdWords, which is regarded as the top PPC vehicle. Many of these companies will also use Yahoo Bing to extend the reach of their target audience.

Improving PPC marketing efficiency

Since companies have to bid for advertising space, it is important that they use the PPC tools and resources available to them to keep costs down. For PPC optimisation a company needs to conduct thorough keyword research to find those most relevant to its niche. This can take a lot of time and effort, but is essential for a successful campaign. The problem with keywords for PPC marketing is that they are constantly being updated and there is a constant need to stay on top. The traffic generated as a result of optimised PPC advertisements, using the best keywords, is relevant to a company. The people clicking on the advertisements are genuinely interested in what it has to offer so it has a better chance of improving its PPC click-through rate. This can help justify the cost a company incurs for placing its advertisements online. As the cost per click improves a company can generate greater profits. Often, PPC keyword research finds the most relevant and attractive keywords for a company but it does not account for all types of keywords. Changing search engine algorithms means that advertisers have to adapt to different types of keywords, including long-tail keyword phrases of between two and five words, which can be more effective when looking for a specific item. Using PPC keyword research tools like Word Stream, Keyword Eye, Google Keyword Planner ensures that a company has a list of the ideal keywords to use, regardless of their length. Most importantly, a company has to use the keywords which would enable it to expand its campaign should the need arise. Marketers and advertisers should think two steps ahead. This may involve increasing the scope of a PPC campaign. When a campaign grows a company will have to increase the number of keywords it is using. This is where a PPC keyword tool can be useful. Companies should have a constantly expanding keyword list to ensure problems do not arise. A company has to make sure the keywords being used are improving its quality score. Its PPC campaign's success depends a great deal on the quality score it has. Incorporating generic and random keywords will reduce PPC marketing efficiency.

What is a quality score?

A quality score is an estimate of the quality of the advertisement's keywords and landing page. Higher quality advertisements can lead to lower prices and better advertisement positions. The components of a quality score – expected click-through rate, advertisement relevance, and landing page experience – are determined every time the keyword matches a customer's search. A company can get a general sense of its advertising quality in the "keyword analysis" field of its account, reported on a 1-10 scale. The more relevant the advertising and landing pages are to the user, the higher will be the 1-10 quality

Recapping, finding the right PPC keyword tool to use for a campaign will improve its efficiency in the following ways: higher rate of conversions, more targeted traffic, increased ability to expand campaign and a greater return on investment. SemRush[37] is a great resource for PPC optimisation as it enables it not only to conduct research for the best keywords for its campaigns but also to keep an eye on it the keywords its competitors are using. Maximising the efficiency of PPC marketing can help companies to lower costs, improve results and generate higher profits. Using a quality keyword tool can help achieve this.

Planning and setting up a PPC campaign

When considering a PPC campaign, a company should carry out a detailed analysis of the online and offline options available to it. This analysis will include a look at its customer make-up, including relevant demographics and psychographics and the make-up of its competitors. It not complicated to set up a PPC campaign. The company, as it would do for any other marketing campaign, will evaluate and agree its brand positioning, proposition and unique selling proposition (USO). In a PPC campaign a company has three lines to get its message across:

- It needs to know what it is trying to achieve. Normally it will be tactical as opposed to strategic, which is the territory for branding campaigns. This can be a slow burn to achieve its objectives. The amount of money to be spent on the campaign will depend on what it is trying to achieve. It needs to have a sound keyword / phrase strategy.
- It needs to know how best to bid for keywords/ phrases. No matter what, objective, persuasive advertisements will need to be developed. The company needs to display an appropriate URL that should target the landing page with a call to action.
- It needs to agree the maximum amount it is going to pay for keywords/phrases. The financial

investment can be altered as the campaign develops and is tested.

The company will consider if it needs to change the text of the advertisement to improve the click-through rate and consider different landing pages to establish what is best.

The significance of the landing page

A PPC campaign doesn't end when the advertisement appears, the key word/phrase bidding is complete, and the visitor clicks on the advertisement and reaches a landing page. It is essential that the landing page be well constructed to create maximum impact. Sending visitors to a home page is not a good idea. Some will get lost with too many options and may retire from the site in frustration. Whatever page they land on, it must be dedicated to the brand campaign that the company wants to promote. It should bring the brand to the attention of the visitors so that they will hopefully make a purchase before they leave the page.

Chapter 12: Online reputation management (ORM) and public relations (PR)

What is online reputation management and public relations?

A good reputation helps a company to achieve trust in the marketplace, which may help to encourage customers and prospects to accept and use its brands. It will improve a company's dealings with suppliers and retailers. It will help the company's human resources personnel, influence business partners, and assist its dealings with government and trade regulators and communities, as well as enhancing its ongoing relationships with its customers. Corporate reputation is considered to be a fundamental intangible asset, and an indication of a company's perceived competitiveness. There is a view that the reputation of a company only appears on the management board's agenda once it is being questioned. The threat to a company's reputation is one of its biggest strategic risks, particularly from a stakeholder perspective. In this context, stakeholders are defined as any group who with their actions or views can influence the success of a company directly or indirectly. These stakeholders will have different perceptions and expectations of a company, including its innovative capabilities and its responsible behaviour.

Why is a company's online reputation relevant and how is it assessed?

A company's online reputation is relevant when trying to attract and recruit staff, when it is selling a brand, looking for an investor, or trying to influence stakeholders and the media, who will almost certainly click on a search engine to learn what the company is up to if its reputation is under threat and when it is involved in local community activities. Any negatives that may arise about a company and its activities need to be discussed internally by management and dealt with immediately. If necessary, an effective reputation management and PR campaign should be mounted.

A company's reputation is not an end in itself but it helps to achieve its goals.
To properly manage a company's reputation it is necessary to manage its stakeholders' expectations in a methodical and considered way. Synergising the corporate reputation of a company with its brands is a crucial step in doing so. The company mission statement will normally define what it stands for, how it wants to be perceived by its stakeholders and the community at large, thus contributing in setting stakeholders' expectations. The company's brand itself tends to be considered in terms of its advertising image, whereas reputation is regarded as the sum of all the parts of the company, including the public, external images expressing actual perceptions and experiences. On this basis, the purpose of reputation management can be determined. It should aim at influencing the perceptions and expectations of stakeholders in a way that gives them an affinity with the company. ORM and PR is about organising a company and

its brand's publicity in such a way that it will reflect well on its activities, particularly amongst its target audiences. It is the act of endeavouring to share an open impression of an individual or association by creating online data about that entity.[38]

Online reputation management and PR gets involved in putting a positive spin on malicious and negative content that may appear about a company and/or its brand. These negative online comments usually appear in the 'comments' section of a media channel or in blogs. Once a negative comment has been posted it is very difficult to have it removed unless this is done by the source that put it there in the first place. Companies may, as a first port of call, try and move the offending comment from a prominent page to a less prominent one in a blog or other media channel. Because of this, people may view ORM and PR as the business of minimising the effect of negative publicity about a company and/or its brands. It is very important that everybody in a company is aware of the negative side of publicity. The company main players may need to be particularly careful how they are perceived by the general public and the media in their private lives. They need to understand that they can become synonymous with their brand portfolios. Maintaining a positive reputation has to be an ongoing strategy for everybody involved with the company and its brands. One of the problems today is that an online crisis can occur very quickly because of nature of real-time surrounding social media. Not too long ago, it was the traditional media like TV, radio and newspapers that broke news stories often affecting the reputation of

companies. Today, major breakthrough news stories can emanate from blogs and other social media channels like Twitter etc. A company needs to have a structure in place to deal with such eventualities. Its task will be to try and stop a story gaining traction and developing into a reputation crisis. It needs to know how to deal with the impending crisis using the same social media platforms that may have caused the crisis in the first place. The company needs to monitor online brand mentions and be aware if any of the stories have the potential to do damage to the company or its brand's reputation.
It should be remembered that social media stories happen in real time and therefore quick responses from the company will be needed; its customers will expect it too. The company needs to have the resources to communicate relevant information quickly and accurately. If the story reflects negatively on a brand it is essential that the response is rapid, particularly if there are safety issues for the public. Many companies are not up to speed on this critical management issue. They are not aware that the company needs to quickly take ownership of any offending stories that reflect badly on them. ORM and public relations is a key issue, particularly for companies that deal online A well-thought-out ORM and PR strategy can help lessen the impact of a negative story and replace the offending content with a positive spin that will help the brand maintain its good imagery.

What's the difference between offline PR and online PR?
Online PR is about organising campaigns that will influence consumers using online social media channels,

including blogs, search engines and chat forums. Online PR will also be heavily involved in monitoring the reputation of brands online. Offline PR does something similar when dealing with offline media including TV, radio and press. A major difference between online and offline PR is the way the process varies between the two approaches. Normally, the traditional offline approach can be to brief a journalist on a specific story and in the case of a company issuing a major statement it may brief journalists in a group at a news conference. A representative takes questions from the company and afterwards journalists, who may or may not use the media release issued by the company, write up the stories. With regard to online PR, pitching a story to a blogger may require a more considered approach. Press releases are normally not used to write bloggers' stories as they usually don't find them compelling enough — too commercial and company biased. They may, however, point links on their sites to the company's media release in their blog.

PR versus reputation management
Traditional PR is very effective in its own right. The media will publish interesting stories, often created by the company's PR resources, with interesting content for the public to consume. Reputation management has evolved more recently as more urgent with the arrival of the Internet. Both approaches can have an influence on consumers' perceptions. The two disciplines overlap quite a lot. ORM has become more prominent in recent years as a result of the rise in popularity of social media. The

traditional PR approach has an emphasis on both tactical short-term and long-term projects and mainly involves journalists from TV, radio and press. In online PR, there is more emphasis on dealing with companies' brands on a tactical basis rather than strategic. The 'sound bite' is very much part of traditional PR and the trick is to keep the media sweet when they are given an exclusive story. ORM today uses all forms of online media channels. It delivers the brand objectives just as traditional PR does, except it tends to do it more often in real time. ORM tends to focus on the company's corporate long-term identity, which tends to be more strategic in nature. Many believe that traditional PR is blending into ORM; others would argue that it is the other way around. There is a general view that one or the other is evolving into a single marketing discipline. Time will tell.

Combining PR with reputation management is perceived as a more encompassing use of this marketing concept which is better than relying on media for covering tactical issues and separately embracing online platforms to communicate a company's message using online real-time dialogues. The past decade has seen a major shift from the traditional role of PR to one that focuses on communication through online digital content. Gone are the days when PR people consulted to come up with a PR strategy, created newsworthy content and pitched stories to media, resulting in press releases being featured in a range of printed publications. While the above approach is still valid, in today's technologically driven environment it can be perceived as too limiting. Online content is the new panacea for brands, especially when using social media channels. It allows the new service, an amalgam of PR and reputation management disciplines, to reach a much larger audience online at a faster pace and in real time. Most top PR professionals are very much aware of this development and decide which medium and mode to use when promoting a brand by tailoring the content depending on the platform that is regarded as most appropriate. Content is published in the form of blogs and in other social media platforms like Twitter and YouTube etc. and results in interaction with the target audience by anticipating and responding to reactions when required. Content is now available online via blog posts. Promoting content via these platforms requires constant engagement with the client's target audiences, responding to and editing content when required.

In a nutshell, the rise of online social media content has been enormous and the provision of content to these channels has been a major development across the PR industry globally. PR agencies realise how important it is to post content quickly in order to ensure their clients' messages resonate with their targeted online communities. Traditional PR is still used on a daily basis but it needs to be synergised with constant online presence in its daily activities. PR practitioners will continue to involve themselves in leveraging online platforms strategically to create maximum exposure for their clients' brands.

The benefits of having a good reputation
It is argued by many that there is a direct link between a company's bottom line and its reputation. There are many

advantages to having a good reputation. It assists when a company is looking to raise finance from banks, financial institutions and venture capitalists, particularly when times are tough and there is not too much capital about. Customers are more likely to stay with a company and its brands if it has a good reputation. A good reputation is synonymous with trust, which can make a company the first choice of loyal consumers. A company with a good reputation may allow it to charge premium prices for its brands, to create brand extensions and to launch new brands in the marketplace. It can help a company retain key employees and recruit new ones. It should be remembered that ORM deals with a reputation that doesn't actually reside within the company but lies outside it, where it can be based on opinions and beliefs of people outside the company.

Basic rules for sound reputation
- Maintain great brands.
- Establish company core values with a clear mission statement and make sure all employees understand them.
- Be honest and admit faults when they happen and correct them.
- Be sure to draw up a relevant social media strategy.
- Have the correct internal resources to deliver the company's reputation policy objectives.
- Have a realistic corporate responsibility strategy.
- Have a good customer brand portfolio.
- Have good brand positioning and a unique selling proposition.

- Be adaptable and innovative.
- Have an effective intelligence network to anticipate problems to stay ahead in the reputation game.
- Have a fine-tuned crisis management plan. Have effective stakeholder engagement and communications strategies in place to deal with reputation management issues.

Key reputation management tactics
- Organise a search engine results page.
- Develop the brand's social media profiles.
- Set up a blog.
- Get customers to talk about their brand experiences.
- Have an active formulated PR strategy and ORM plan in place.

For a company the most effective approach to reputation management and PR is to promote the company honestly at all times, track and oversee every interaction between the company and its stakeholders and actively engage with customers offline and online in real time.

Chapter: 13 Cloud computing

One of the more recent developments in digital marketing is referred to as 'cloud computing' and surprise, surprise it's connected to the Internet's unbelievable and unquestionable domination of the globe.

What is cloud computing?

In very simple terms, it's all about storing and connecting to data and programmes over the Internet as opposed to using a computer's hard drive. It gets its name from the fact that the network elements provided for the user are invisible, as if hidden in a cloud. When a person stores data or runs programmes using their own hard drive, that is referred to as local storage and computing. The computer industry functioned by working off the hard drive for years. Some people believe that the system is as good as if not better than cloud. Cloud, on the other hand, provides its service via the Internet at a different location to the user, where it shares the necessary data information for the various applications in use The services offered by cloud include storage of online files, social networking sites and a range of other business applications. Cloud is based on the assumption that it doesn't matter to the company where the hardware and software is positioned as long as it works effectively and efficiently. The company is aware that it is there and is available to it when required. Cloud is a new 'trendy' term that covers information technology; others would describe it as a service that is outsourced like any other service required by forward-looking companies.

Examples of cloud computing

Cloud computing can be used by people without them even realising it. When an individual types a query into Google or one of the other search engines, the computer, laptop or tablet they use doesn't have anything to do with finding the answer to the query. The words typed in are immediately transmitted via the Internet to one of the many search engines' connected computers that work together as a single unit which gets the information requested and sends it promptly back to the person seeking the information. When a person does a search engine search, the real work involves finding a computer situated in any city in the world to supply the answers. The same thing applies to web-based email. In its infancy, email could only be sent and received using a programme running on a PC or Mac. But eventually web-based services such as Hotmail arrived on the scene and carried email off into the cloud. In other words, emails are now gathered and delivered through a server in some part of the globe, which can be accessed without any trouble from a web browser wherever the user happens to be. For people on the go, cloud is ideally suited as a convenient way for sending emails.

Another example of cloud computing in action is the preparation of documents. Google Documents[39] facilitates individuals and companies by allowing them to log in and create a host of documents including spreadsheets, presentations or anything else it uses in its normal activities. Apart from Microsoft Word, the company can use similar type software stored at one of Google's global data centres. Any documents produced can be stored on a web server that enables it to be accessed from any computer connected to the Internet anywhere 24/7/365. In other words, individuals and companies are outsourcing their computer needs to search engines.

What is different about cloud computing?
Cloud computing is a third party providing a service for an individual or a company. It does away with a lot of unnecessary hassle. For example, Google Documents cuts down considerably on the number of licences normally required for word processing software that a company needs to hold. What it does is always up to date. Viruses are no longer the threat to companies they used to be. There are no worries about backup files, which Google Documents looks after. A company needn't bother itself with how the service it gets is provided; it is free to concentrate on the end results and can leave the rest to someone else. A company can buy whatever service it needs on demand or if it wishes it can pay as it goes. In actual fact, the system is no different to purchasing any other utility service like gas, electricity or the phone. There are cases where cloud computing is free and subsidised by advertising. Another great advantage is that a company does not have to tie up a lot of its cash in an elaborate computer system. As we have already seen, with cloud computing a company can get information from anywhere in the world, at any time. Companies do not need to have computer storage facilities in their

offices when all they want is stored elsewhere, often thousands of miles away. This is ideal for companies that cannot afford the types of systems bigger companies have in their buildings. There is only one basic requirement to access cloud and that is access to the Internet. Whatever documents the company wishes to access, it can do so by a simple click on the computer screen.

Advantages and disadvantages of cloud computing
There are advantages attached to cloud computing. If a company is small it doesn't need to invest in an expensive system and only pays for what is uses. It avoids having its sales people using valuable selling time tied up in computer maintenance, running anti-virus software or upgrading word processors. Cloud computing allows a company to concentrate only on its services when it wants them, resulting in lower upfront costs and reduced infrastructure costs. It avoids the need to upgrade computer systems and the hassle of computers crashes and hacking. Additional services can be added or discontinued very quickly as the company's needs change. New applications or services can be added immediately without the hassle of waiting for new computers to be delivered and set up onsite.
Here are also some disadvantages. Instant convenience can be expensive, resulting in increased operating costs, which can often work out more costly at end of financial year. Another requirement is the need for a permanent, reliable, high-speed broadband service to ensure high efficiency. Some company reports have strict deadlines and cannot wait for inefficient printing methods. Another

factor that has to be taken into consideration is that a company buying ad hoc services may be limited in the extent of services available to it. Outside supply companies may discontinue a service, which may leave the company high and dry. Critics maintain that with cloud computing companies are locked into unsuitable, long-term arrangements with large, inflexible companies. There are also potential privacy and security risks of putting valuable data on someone else's system in an unknown location.

Different types of clouds
There are different types of clouds that a company can subscribe to, depending on its needs. Small business owners are more likely to use public cloud services.

- Public Cloud - Any subscriber with an Internet connection and access to the cloud space can access a public cloud.
- Private Cloud - A private cloud is established for a specific group or company and limits access to just that group.
- Community Cloud - A community cloud is shared among two or more organisations that have similar cloud requirements.
- Hybrid Cloud - A hybrid cloud is essentially a combination of at least two clouds, where the clouds included are a mixture of public, private, or community.

Choosing a cloud provider

According to Appcore[40] there are three types of cloud providers. To paraphrase its views, a company can consider:

- Software as a Service (SaaS) – For this, a supplier gives subscribers access to both assets and applications. A company does not have to bother with having a physical copy of software and can install the same software on all company devices at once by accessing it on the   cloud. In this case, the company has the least control over the cloud.

- Platform as a Service – This framework goes a level above the Software as a Service (SaaS) setup. Here the provider gives subscribers access to components that they need using applications over the Internet.

- Infrastructure as a Service (IaaS) – This choice, as the name infers, deals principally with computational structure. The user totally outsources the capacity and assets, for example, equipment and programming that they need.

With regard to these three options, the company ends up with greater control over what it can do as it moves from option one to three, or, put another way, the provider of the service has less control in the IaaS situation than with the SaaS agreement. The great advantage here is that the company can choose the type of control it requires for the supply of its requirements from the cloud provider. The bottom line for the company is that it needs to evaluate its current computer resources and future requirements, the level of control it needs and where it sees its future growth before deciding on its cloud computing resources.

Security

A company need to bear in mind that with cloud it will be sending confidential information to an outside source, namely, cloud. The company will need to examine carefully the security arrangements, such as encryption methods, the cloud provider has in place to protect the company's secure data. This can be easily done by demanding to know the security measures the provider has currently in place. If the company is contemplating joining a computer cloud for cost reasons it will need to ensure that the company's information is kept secure from all other users. A read of the provider's standard terms and conditions would be prudent. The Catch 22 situation is that in order for the company to take advantage of the benefits of cloud it will knowingly have to give up direct control of its data to an outside source. At the end of the day, like many business relationships, the arrangement entered into will be based on trust.

Conclusion

The company has a number of options when considering cloud computing. If it goes ahead it needs to review carefully the type of information it will be releasing to the provider to go into the cloud. The company will need to be happy that access to its information is outside its direct control. It will need to ensure that it is protected. The company has to decide the type of cloud that is best for the company. In the end, it will all be down to a matter of trust between the cloud provider and the company.

Chapter 14: How do customer-purchasing models work in the digital marketing arena?

The Purchasing Funnel
The Purchasing Funnel is a business model, which describes the theoretical customer journey from the moment of first contact with a company's brand to the ultimate goal of a consumer purchase. This model is relevant when marketing a brand/product as it provides a method of understanding and tracking the behaviour of an average customer throughout the sales process. It can help with planning marketing campaigns, highlighting areas that can improve a company's conversion rate from prospects to actual customers, assist in the sales process and help with designing better relationships with customers. The shape of the funnel is ideal to explain the natural loss of potential customers at each stage of the purchasing process. There are many versions of the purchasing funnel, which are basically similar in content and process. To outline a version produced by 'marketing-made-simple.com':[41]

The stages of a modern purchasing funnel
1. Pre-awareness. At this stage the prospect is not mindful of the company's image and has no previous contact with its brand.

2. Awareness. At this stage the prospect is mindful of the company's image through advertising messages, in-store presentations or word of mouth comments.

3. Purchase intent trigger. This is the moment a prospect starts thinking about a purchase. It could be activated by an adjustment in the prospect's circumstances through a pay rise, for example, or seeing a companion using the brand.

4. Researches and Familiarity. At this stage the prospect has decided they need an item like the company's brand. They will read reviews, taking in the item highlights, asking for opinions, requesting sentiments, and search the Internet to research for alternatives. The length of this stage will depend on the cost of the item. Considering a washing machine will take longer than a tin of soup.

5. Sentiments and Shortlist. The prospects settle on a choice of items similar to the one being offered by a particular company; this could be a written note of choices, or bookmarked websites.

6. Consideration. Prospect begins the procedure of deciding between the most likely purchases.

7. Choices and Purchase. Prospect settles on a definite choice of brand.

8. Brand Advocate (or saboteur). When the prospect has purchased, a view will be formed about the brand. For

instance, were there concealed expenses? Did it match up to expectations?

9. Repurchase Intention. It is a simple fact of life that current customers are essentially simpler to draw in than another prospect. This ought to be borne as a primary concern when planning marketing activity.

10. Previously established inclinations and experience. Did the previous purchase give a phenomenal client experience, or break in the blink of an eye a while later? In the event that it breaks, clients may abscond to competitors. If the prospect was previously satisfied, they might re-enter the pipe at Stage 4 - Researches and Familiarity.

11. Recognition. Despite the fact that the prospect is likely to have a good feeling about the company's image, they will need to acquaint themselves with the company's present image range, and with its rivals.

12. Assessment. Should they upgrade to the next item in the brand range or stay where they are and repeat the purchase at a future date?

Alternatives to the funnel model
Some digital marketing practitioners believe that the funnel model is no longer relevant in a mobile age, particularly because consumers are more informed through social media and the buying process no longer

progresses from one stage to another in sequence. They believe prospects don't just enter at the top of the funnel. In fact, they can enter the funnel at any stage, jump stages and move back and forth if it suits them.

The Consumer Decision Journey model

A popular alternative to the funnel is McKinsey's 'Consumer Decision Journey' model,[42] that explains how purchasing decisions are made. It believes that consumers are moving outside the purchasing funnel, changing the way they research and buy a company's brand. Like the purchasing funnel, it believes that the objective of the model is to reach consumers at the moments that most influence their decisions, often referred to as 'touch points'. As we have already seen touch points have been understood through the metaphor of a 'funnel'. Prospects start with a number of potential brands in mind at the wide end of the funnel through the influence of marketing activity directed at them. They reduce that number and proceed along the funnel and finally decide on one specific brand they have chosen to purchase. McKinsey and others argue that, particularly in the era of digital marketing, the funnel concept fails to capture all the touch points and key buying factors. This results from the rise in brand choices and digital channels. This coincides with the growing numbers of educated and online consumers. What is needed is a considered and systematic approach to assist companies better understand this new paradigm, which tends to progress from one stage to the next in a more systematic way than the funnel suggests. McKinsey called this approach the

'Consumer Decision Journey'. Examining the purchase decisions of almost 20,000 consumers across the globe led to the development of this approach. Their research showed that the increase in choice of media and brands requires companies to find new ways to get their brands included in the initial consideration period that consumers develop as they begin their decision journey. They also discovered that because of the shift away from one-way communication from companies to consumers towards a two-way dialogue, companies need a more systematic way to satisfy customer demands and manage social advocacy. The research also identified different types of consumer loyalty, which stimulated companies to examine and improve the way they manage the customer experience. Finally, the research reinforced the importance of not only aligning all elements of marketing with the journey that consumers undertake when they make purchasing decisions but also of integrating those elements across the company. When companies understand this journey they direct their spending and messaging to consumers in the right place, at the right time, with the right message, at the right price.

The significance of 'touch points'
There is not a day that goes by without some people forming a view of a brand from one of the many 'touch points' like advertising, social media, news commentaries, TV specials or conversations with friends and family members. There is a growing view that much of traditional advertising is wasted (remember the old saying, "50% of my spend on advertising is wasted, the

problem is I don't know which 50%") because people are exposed to a lot of advertising messages when they are not in the market for it or they are not in a buying environment. The argument that they will remember the advertising at a later stage is becoming more dubious. The view is that with all that is going on nowadays consumers will not recall the messages that are broadcast each day. This activity is known as 'push' advertising and has been around for some time. McKinsey's research would suggest that push advertising is becoming less effective because nowadays people are inclined to take in advertising on their own terms and not be dictated to by persistent advertisers; this is known as 'pull' advertising. McKinsey tell us that things are changing and the communications process is now a more 'circular journey'. This involves stage one, when prospects go through an initial brand evaluation of a range of brands available to them; stage two is when they actively evaluate their options, ending with a shortlist; stage three is when a decision is made and a particular brand is purchased. The final and most important stage is post evaluation, when the prospect decides if the brand will be purchased again at a later stage.

As we can see marketers used to 'push' their brands on consumers through traditional above the line and below the line advertising. This is giving way to 'pull' advertising, where the consumer decides when and where it will consume advertising messages. At the end stage of the purchasing funnel as prospects reduce their choice of brand options marketers will continue to actively engage the consumer with relevant and persuasive advertising to influence their buying decision. With the growth of digital marketing the emphasis on advertising messages is based on real-time, when the advertising can be more effective as it happens much nearer the consumer purchase. Astute marketers are au fait with all the changes in the communications process and also realise the importance of retaining first-time purchasers by adding new 'touch points' almost daily, reflecting the growth of digital marketing.

So what about the future?

The Purchasing Funnel and the Consumer Decision Journey will continue to be used by companies when analysing consumer-purchasing patterns, but digital marketing with its many facets may require a new model to deal with the ever-growing changes that are taking place in the area of consumer purchasing. It will come as no surprise that consumer behaviour keeps changing and a model may be needed to reflect the changing market environment. Marketers will need a new process to reflect what is happening around them. A critical part of the model will be to address the changing ways of social influence, the non-linear paths to purchasing, the role of the prospects who have been recently converted into customers. Another significant influence is the advances in web coding and design. Consumers have an array of goods to choose online that they didn't have before. Purchasing can now be done in the comfort of people's homes, 24/7/365. The growth of digital channels is changing the commercial environment. In the next one or two years it is estimated that the Web will account for 50 per cent+ of all retail sales.

Chapter 15: Forces that drive consumer behaviour in the digital age

What do we mean by consumer behaviour?

Consumer behaviour can be explained, as the behaviour that consumers show when they are searching for and purchasing brands that they hope will satisfy their desires and needs. It's about how consumers allocate their resources, including their time and finances, acquiring goods and services. In the context of sales and marketing, it's about companies who convince consumers to avail of their brands in exchange for money. Consumer behaviour incorporates elements from psychology, social anthropology and economics. This involves the study of behaviour and mental processes; the study of people in relation to their culture; and the study of people's consumption of brands. Research shows that consumer behaviour is difficult to predict. Being able to understand consumer behaviour helps companies to develop focused marketing plans based on their analysis of how consumers behave in their choice of brands and retailers from which they decide to purchase.

Today consumer purchases are being made to a greater extent online. This process involves the psychology of how consumers are influenced by their environment through their culture, family environment and their social status in the community. Consumer selection will differ in its level of importance and interests Lars Perner of the Marshall School of Business University of Southern California[43] describes consumer behaviour as the investigation of people, gatherings, or associations and the methods they use to choose, secure, utilise, and discard items, administrations, encounters, or thoughts to fulfil needs and the effects that these techniques have on the customer and society.

The significance of culture in relation to consumers and their choice of brands

A company needs to understand the significance of the role played by culture in shaping consumers' thoughts and ideas, especially about brands. Understanding the significance of culture is helpful to companies who are interested in what makes the consumer tick. Throughout their lives consumers will be influenced by their environmental surroundings, which will have an effect on their values and desires. Their families and friends will also influence them. A company focuses on the role communication plays in this process. It is important for the company to take on board the cultural issues to help them develop an appropriate brand strategy to suit specific environments. This thinking involves the study of consumers' habits and behaviours and issues that motivate the consumer. This can include everything from the arts, fashion, literature, music, newspaper articles, TV coverage, YouTube videos, TV commercials, blogs, Twitter, Facebook etc., all of which helps a company to understand how the world is changing, how people are changing and will predict what they will like, need and eventually purchase to satisfy their desires. It will be up to the company's marketing people to understand these changes and ensure that its brand offerings will be more relevant than its competitors.

Subcultures are important in the communications process

The various societies are made up of a number of subcultures that consumers can relate to and be affected by in many ways. Consumers make up these subcultures by sharing similar values based on similar lifestyles and experiences. Subcultures can include such things as different nationalities, religious groups, ethnic groups as well as different age and gender groups of consumers. Marketers will often segment markets by various subcultures so that their brand promotions will suit the make up of the different subcultures in the marketplace. Companies will sometimes develop a specific strategy to go after a particular age group or gender or a specific subculture grouping.

It is essential that consumers are more open to brands that are actually aimed at them. Companies can target brands at specific social classes, which are usually described in terms of social status and hierarchy. Some of the social groupings can be large in number but members of each social group will have similar values, social interests and display similar lifestyles. It is usual for companies to segment these groupings into four categories: lower class, middle class, upper class and farming class, usually designated ABC1, C2, DE, and F in market research terminology. Each will have different tastes, interests and consumption patterns that reflect their buying powers. It would be unusual for the four social groups to buy similar brands like foodstuffs, holidays, watch similar TV programmes or read similar newspapers and magazines. They wouldn't have similar hobbies and would not visit similar department stores. Purchases on the Internet would tend to follow a similar pattern. Companies will find that people from the middle and upper classes will consume healthier foods than those from the lower classes. In other words, common consumption trends are usually found in the same groups. Families can exert a lot of influence on each other. The home is where consumers normally develop their personalities and their tastes. It is here that many consumers develop perceptions of brands that will stay with them for most of their lives. The exception will be when people improve their social standing, possibly as a result of education and work. The marketer will monitor all these consumer traits to get a better understanding of particular features such as values, lifestyles and mindsets so they can better focus on their target markets and the brands that attract them.

Consumer and cultural insights

Consumer insight is critical for identifying what consumers require right now. Cultural insights enable a company to understand how these desires and needs will change over time and eventually affect future consumer preferences. Consumer insights will help identify changes that have occurred, and help companies to monitor changes as they happen. Cultural insight has a down-to-earth basis and assists in identifying emerging changes in consumer interests that are not just passing fads. Companies can predict how these shifts may evolve over time and take them on board to keep up with innovative thinking when planning future brand strategies.

The author Grant Mc Cracken tells us how important it is to use cultural knowledge in the right way. He defines culture in two ways: fast and slow. Fast culture is the more prominent. It involves the latest fashion fads, music trends and popular movies, current jargon usage etc. Slow culture is more understated, to the degree that it is often forgotten about. Slow culture is about longstanding values and traditions that underscore how people live. He says that fast culture is similar to all the watercrafts on the surface of the Pacific. We can spot them, number them, and track them. Moderate society is everything underneath the surface, less charted and substantially less obvious.[44]

Marketers need to understand both fast and slow culture in all its forms to make sure they have a comprehensive forward-looking framework of the consumer to provide a meaningful and accurate prediction that can be put to use when marketing a company's brands. Cultural insights tell what consumers are thinking about, what subcultures are up to and what they are likely to do in the future. Ultimately they help a company influence consumers to think about its business and brands in a way it wants them to.

Trendsetting

Cultural trends are defined as trends widely followed by people and which are increased by their popularity and by conformity or compliance with social pressure.

The more people follow a trend, the more others will want to follow it too. Cultural trends affect behaviour and shopping habits of consumers and may be related to the release of new brands or become a source of innovation for brands. Social pressure can create a desire to conform or belong to a group. It can create a desire to follow fashion trends due to the high visibility provided by media, and consumers will be influenced by these trends. Facebook has become a cultural trend, becoming a must have, especially among young people. It is the same with the growth of the tablet market. Tablets such as iPad and Galaxy Tab have become a global cultural trend, leading many consumers to buy one. For a brand to create a new cultural trend from scratch is not easy. Apple did it with its iPad, but this is very unusual. The bottom line is that a company should know what direction a brand should move in before its competitors have moved there. It will know what opportunities to take advantage of. With this knowledge companies will ensure their brands lead the way. By understanding the significance of culture, companies better understand and create the future by making the decisions today.

When nurturing customers and prospects, developing customer bases is not all about making contact on social channels like Facebook and Twitter. It's much more than that. It's about creating a dialogue and eventually a relationship between the company and the people who purchase its brands. In this way trust can be created not only between a company and its customers but also with prospects. A company will need to delegate someone internally or recruit externally to coordinate this engagement activity on an ongoing basis. This person will also be in a better position to deal in a planned way with any surprise threats to a company's brands by a competitor. Another development that is now commonplace are customer forums that are set up by companies. Consumers mix in these forums to get information and ask questions without contacting the company directly. This can often lead to a discussion that can be tied into one of the brands. A company can use forums to help it develop new brands or tweak existing ones. Today, customers are engaging with brands online. Because of this, online channels are playing a critical role in setting perceptions of the various brands available to them.

A consumer's purchasing behaviour may change as they get older. Usually a consumer does not buy the same brands when they are in their teens and when they are retired. Their lifestyle, values, activities, interests and buying habits evolve throughout their lives. American Demographics – Advertising Age[45] recently highlighted these behaviours amongst the five age groupings, 6-12 year olds, and 13-17 year olds, 18-34 year olds, 35-54 year olds and 55 years+. To paraphrase its conclusions, it says that each of these business sections exhibits distinctive buy propensities because of differing backgrounds and increased knowledge of new technology. It is critical that companies have the ability to communicate with consumers of all ages and different geographic locations As we have seen, consumers can change, for example, from unhealthy to healthy diets, and the marketer needs to monitor these changes in lifestyle. There are issues relating to purchasing decisions that may also alter over time. The social benefit of brands are normally more important to consumers when they are in their 20s and 30s than when they are in their 60s and 70s.The geographic location of a consumer's home can have an effect on their purchasing decisions. It is imperative for companies and retailers to analyse the issues that influence the shopping behaviour of their customers in order to maximise the effect of their marketing strategy. The financial standing of consumers will have a major influence on their purchasing behaviour. This affects what they can afford to spend and the type of retailer that they frequent. We have seen how important it is that companies fully comprehend the issues that influence customer behaviour when considering their marketing strategies for their brands.

Chapter 16: A matter of privacy

Very few do anything to protect their privacy on the Internet.

The ever-growing practice of digital marketing brings a lot more interest concerning privacy issues than was the case with traditional marketing. Because data is part and parcel of digital marketing it is important that consumers' personally identifiable data is protected. Consumers in modern societies are now engrossed in a world of digital data, generating a digital footprint trail as they get more and more involved with anything digital through email, using loyalty cards, surfing the internet and making wireless calls on their smartphones and tablets. As the technology gets more and more sophisticated the issue of consumer privacy is gaining more prominence. Key issues include what step governments are taking in monitoring and controlling search engines, ISPs and web companies. It would appear that online there is little control over much of the type of information consumers might prefer to keep private. We already have a situation where anyone, anywhere can find out what our homes look like through Google Streetview. Many consumers are not happy being tracked online but do nothing to protect their privacy. It is their fear that companies in their desire to get profiles of their target audiences will get to know many things about them that heretofore were considered private. Targeted advertising by companies is driving this phenomenon. This may change as the media takes greater interest, resulting in a more digitally informed consumer. On the other hand, many Internet companies have agreed to follow voluntary guidelines and, anticipating consumer concerns, they are taking the high ground and initiating education efforts to allay people's fears about their privacy.

Europe is much more concerned than the US about privacy issues. The EU is looking at legislative and technological solutions for improving consumer privacy. As privacy becomes a greater issue for concern amongst consumers it will be important for companies, and high-tech companies particularly, to become more transparent and to give consumers a greater say and more control to avoid a growing fear factor. Some researchers will make the point that a great deal of companies and consumers think the Internet is a good thing and are happy with the way it is developing to benefit them. A number are, however, concerned about online privacy issues.

'Marketers from Mars'

To paraphrase from its report entitled 'Marketers from Mars', Exact Target[46] says that privacy concerns differ between marketers and consumers. Marketers fear there is too much data available online, consumers fear their lack of knowledge about privacy issues.

The report goes on to state the way to meet consumers' need for privacy is about permission. In other words, if a company wants information other than the consumer's name, address, phone, email it should explain why they want the information and what they intend doing with it. It advises that companies should give consumers a chance of supplying detailed information about themselves so they don't feel they are being exploited. Exact Target says that instead of side-stepping privacy issues, companies should tackle them head on and clearly articulate the benefits consumers can expect in exchange for their personal information, and companies will continue to build trust-based consumer relationships with their brands.

Another concern is the marketer's lack of transparency about how some of the websites collect and use their users' private data. This happens when a website collects and shares any kind of data about its users with another party without the user's consent. Consumers can also get wary about online behavioural targeting advertisements. This is where companies engage in collecting information about consumers online from the web pages the consumer has visited and use it to show them advertisements or content they believe is more relevant to them.

Securing data from the Internet

Many consumers are now seeking information online about medical issues and possible treatments. Most of the major pharmaceutical companies continuously adapt their digital marketing strategies to reflect their customers' requirements. Successful digital marketing can depend in part on understanding consumer behaviour online and giving consumers information in the form of advertisements, blog articles, social media posts and other media that's uniquely directed at them. Pharmaceutical companies secure data from consumers' online activities. Needless to say, pharmaceutical companies are not the only type of business securing data from the Internet to better understand consumer behaviour and attract them with more targeted and effective ways. Companies in a range of industries set out to answer many questions relating to their customers and prospects, including the type of media channels they use, what types of programmes they are influenced by, what topics interest them, and what brands they're most likely to want or need in the future. Pharmaceutical companies are particularly aware that consumers have become increasingly worried about the privacy of their online information, which can be very sensitive as it relates to people's personal health. In addition to providing consumers with the most secure experience possible when purchasing pharmaceutical products or signing up for health services online, pharmaceutical companies have to consider how they use, store and analyse the data they secure from their products. Other industries will follow suit.

Consumer privacy and data protection

Consumer data protection laws have evolved over the years, resulting in greater compliance and risk management issues that need to be addressed when executing advanced advertising campaigns and consumer relationship management programmes. This can be done effectively only if a company carries out impact assessments before launching new brands, services, campaigns or programmes that could have an effect on consumer privacy or data protection. These assessments can also incorporate analysis of traditional consumer promotional and sales laws, and analysis of intellectual property. Companies would be wise to obtain legal counsel when preparing digital marketing campaigns. Companies are increasingly relying on innovative and edgy digital marketing campaigns to promote their brands. Campaigns can be made up of content created by the consumer, viral marketing activities, the company website and social media content. Companies can also accumulate data through loyalty programmes and consumer tracking to better understands and serves their customers. The tech-savvy marketing professionals who are entrusted to implement these programmes are often unaware of the complex legal implications involved and the repercussions for their companies' failure to comply with applicable laws. We are seeing how technology has changed and how companies can target consumers in ways hardly imagined before. Beyond the privacy issues, regulatory and intellectual property issues need to be considered. Companies need to weigh the benefits and risks of proposed advertising, customer relationship management, and sales schemes and be aware of the changing regulatory landscape that is evolving as technology advances.

Protecting consumer goodwill is important.
The most important asset a brand has is its consumer goodwill. New marketing, customer relationship management and sales approaches that consumers appreciate can create an atmosphere of goodwill but any activity that consumers perceive as unprofessional or unethical can do a lot of harm to the company and its brands. A company can avail of legal counsel to allow its

marketing people to analyse and evaluate the impact of promotional concepts to ensure that they don't impact negatively on the consumer. Consumers are now living in a world where information about their behaviour is collected (often referred to as mined information) analysed, used and shared. Banks and credit card companies have been doing this for decades. This issue is more significant in the digital world when data and information are used in near real time to deliver better services, improve target marketing and the quality of advertising. In most cases the use of data is not visible or known by the consumer because it is delivered by cookies or snippets of code. There is a growing concern of how to ensure the fair use of the data that is generated from digital marketing activities. There is an ever-growing lobby advocating greater education so consumers understand the issues, risks and dilemmas involved and protection of consumers online.

Data is becoming more available everywhere and anywhere.
The Internet can be an instrument for creating good in society, making information and services available to all by allowing people to communicate with each other around the globe. This has to be balanced with people trying to use the Internet for antisocial purposes. Keeping the Internet in the control of people who have the common good in mind is not always entirely possible but it needs ongoing work and vigilance. What is needed is public global discussion about when and which kinds of privacy are important to us to protect online activity and

how exactly it can actually be done. It is an important issue for everybody, not just a select few 'experts'. Education is needed so consumers understand the privacy issue risks and dilemmas involved. One thing is for sure, data is becoming more available everywhere and anywhere. As consumers' lives become more digitised, more and more of what they do is leaving a digital footprint.

Interestingly, research suggests that Facebook and Google are not generally seen as sinister and untrustworthy, but rather as innovative and inspirational brands that consumers trust. Consumers tend to be more concerned about viruses than data theft. Most consumers would prefer to use the Internet anonymously. Many believe governments or other institutions should give more protection. There is also a clear sense the individual consumers have to share some responsibility for privacy themselves. Some try to maximise their privacy by deleting cookies from their browsers. Use of 'private mode' in browsers is also fairly widespread; others will encrypt their communication. Others believe they bear the responsibility for protecting themselves rather than relying on others to find solutions. People who use social media eventually accept the trade-off for their free account by accepting they no longer solely own or control any of the contents it has shared. These people realise that search engines can predict their every move. They know the type of reading matter they are interested in, type of movies they like, the football club they follow, their age and education and family background. It doesn't take long for consumers to realise that things that seemed a coincidence are far from it. They realise that particular advertisements are tailored to them. For many this is not something to be concerned about but something that makes life easier for them when their favourite brands come to their attention when they go online.

The Irish experience
In Ireland, the Office of the Data Protection Commissioner is responsible for upholding the privacy rights of individuals in relation to the processing of their personal data. These rights are contained in the Data Protection Acts. The Acts state that information about consumers must be accurate, only made available to those that should have it and only used for specified purposes. Consumers have the right to access personal information relating to them and have any errors corrected or, in some cases, have the information erased. If consumer information is being held for the purposes of direct marketing, people can have their details removed. Data protection rights apply to information held on computers or in manual or paper files. If a person suffers damage as a result of a breach of their data protection rights, they may sue for damages through the courts. The Commissioner also maintains a register, available for public inspection, giving general details about the data-handling practices of many important data controllers, such as government departments and state-sector bodies, financial institutions, and any person or organisation who keeps sensitive personal data.

The future

Consumers need to realise the implications of all of this. They now live in a world where information about their behaviour, activities, interests, bobbies etc. is collected, analysed, shared and used for the benefit of third party interests who have their own agenda. What is very obvious is that we need an effective and sustainable regulatory framework for privacy and data protection to ensure the future success of individuals and companies in the growing information economy. The information society has evolved in ways that were not remotely anticipated just a few years ago. Attitudes and expectations concerning data protection and privacy are changing rapidly and what is required is a global regulatory framework to keep pace in the ever-changing digital age. It is obvious that we need to fundamentally re-think the data and privacy framework, which needs to be in step with the well being of both consumers and businesses.

Chapter 17: Digital assets: Who owns them?

What are digital assets?

In the old days, people would have filed away photographs in an old shoebox in the attic, kept their music on a cassette suitably labelled and kept correspondence in a metal filing cabinet. People had hard copies of what was clearly their property and possessions. Today, the Internet has altered the way people keep a record of what they want to keep. These are referred to as digital assets. A digital asset is basically anything that is stored in a binary format in which file information is kept in the form of ones and zeros, or in some other binary (two-state) sequence. This type of format is often used for executable files, which are computer files that run a program when they are opened, and numeric information in computer programming and memory. It also incorporates people's right to use them. Files that do not possess this facility are not considered digital assets. Digital assets can be made up of but are not limited to: brand images, lifestyle photography, logos, illustrations, animations, audio and video clips, presentations, office documents and spreadsheets, including their metadata. Metadata is the embedded descriptive information generated by technology that stays with files. It allows assets to be catalogued, searched for and retrieved for permitted usage. People don't physically possess their photos, music and imported documents anymore and this raises the fundamental issue of ownership and value. Apple's iTunes[47] agreement states that people lease the assets from Apple and that they can't transfer them to someone else. Many photo services state that a person's account should not be considered a permanent photo album and that the account and the photos included can be deleted after twelve months' inactivity.

Digital asset management

So the fundamental question is, are digital assets really an individual's assets? Do people have them in their possession? If they don't will the person's heirs be able to recover them after they have passed away? This has become a major issue and there are legal developments underway to give a person's heirs access to their digital accounts. The important point is that heirs have to have information about a person's digital accounts in order to gain access with a view to getting possession of them. Without possession it is hard for a person to truly claim their assets. 'Possession is nine tenths of the law' comes to mind. Therefore if possession makes something an asset then the best way to make sure it continues to be is to document what one owns, name of website and login details to gain access. Once that information is documented it can be passed to heirs, who can use it to gain access. This is digital asset management, representing an intertwined structure incorporating software and hardware and/or services in order to manage and organise and retrieve digital assets. Companies are often surprised to learn how little control they have over data that will determine how successful or comfortable they will be in the future; data can be worth its weight in gold in building a sustainable business. Ownership of digital assets can give control and help a company to respond to developing trends and market forces. Being able to understand how customers are finding and dealing with digital assets is vital to planning where to allocate resources. Return on investment is more accurately calculated and reported when people have the big picture. Direct access to data enables customised reporting and the ability to allow data to lead companies to minute details that often provide the greatest insight. The moment a company or individual approves the design and content of its website that is created on a custom platform, content management system, or hard-coded by an individual or programmer they basically hands over the keys to someone else and is permanently locked into that decision.

Investing in custom website development
Some companies have specialised needs and generic services may not be appropriate, in this case custom web development is necessary. This means that the company will only have to pay for features that are unique to the system being considered. There are often very good reasons to invest in custom development to address complex business demands or integration with proprietary databases and/or applications. A proprietary database is a database that is privately owned and password protected. It is usually unavailable to the general public, and a person who wishes to access its contents must first purchase rights from its owners. Even when a user gains access, it usually come with strict conditions and restrictions. For example, users may lack

the ability to copy, modify, share or redistribute the material.

Custom development can be used in conjunction with open source or licensed solutions, offering the best of both worlds. However, the ability to upgrade to the most up-to-date version of the platform must be maintained, or the company or individual will have opted out of the benefit of continual upgrades in security, features, and response to evolutions in technology that open-source platforms, as well as related plug-ins and widgets, now provide. When the website code is created and owned by a third party, every business using that code is under the control of the creator's interpretation of best practices. If a company later decides to make the transition from a privately developed website or platform, the likelihood that it will be able to export related assets into a format that can be simply plugged into an open-source platform or another content management system are very unlikely.

Regaining control of the company website and data and assets

Companies that decide to discontinue using the creator of the custom platform will have to face recreating or manually transferring data and assets that they will have control over. This operation can be extremely time consuming and costly. Lack of data creates a distinct disadvantage to companies who rely on data as opposed to gut feeling and intuition to make informed decisions on website design and content, SEO, social media, advertising, reputation management and PR, and other connected digital marketing investments. Data is the lifeblood of a business and enables it to continue without any ill effects. If a company doesn't own the data, it is no longer in control and is at the mercy of others determining what data it can see, the interpretation of that data, and how it acts upon the insights that data provides.

It is often difficult to assess if a social media campaign combined with an email and SEO campaign is creating a presence for a brand resulting in clicks on the company website that converts visitors into paying customers. Google is very strict about Google Analytics ownership and doesn't get involved in the transfer of ownership.

Google Analytics is one of those assets that freelance web designers and developers can seize away from a brand they have been tasked to work with. They can easily replace the Google Analytics (UA) account code that was running on the website when they inherited the project with their own account code so they will have control over its workings. Some website vendors deliberately assume ownership of the account without granting administrator access to the analytics. Vendors can be reluctant to release ownership of client analytics accounts, often forcing companies to abandon historical brand data and start from scratch with a new account. Whenever possible, companies should use a generic company email address rather than a personal email address. If a personal email is required a company needs one that it feels will be secure in the long term; this will prevent someone leaving the company with sole control over vital assets that should belong to the brand. A company should only grant 'administrator' access to those it trusts. Rarely in a company does one individual manage all the digital assets throughout the life of the organisation. This can result in historical data and related insight being lost.

Define ownership of data as a company policy
When possible, define ownership of data as a company policy, and stipulate in service agreements and contracts with vendors. The email address of data@ followed by a company's name will stand the test of time better than various people using a personal email and taking ownership with them when they leave. The brand must assert ownership over data from the beginning and professionally manage it.

Access-based consumption may reduce the relevance of ownership
With regard to, for example, Netflix and Spotify, ownership becomes unimportant when consumers can access them whenever they want. Customers may hold the right to use a product or service while multiple parties may hold rights to the same product or service simultaneously. This activity is increasingly complicating ownership. In acquiring, using and accessing digital goods consumers have to agree to terms set out in end-user license agreements and/or terms of use agreements. Service contracts can include a range of restrictions on ownership. Research shows that consumers can form a deep attachment to digital goods they may never own. Therefore, if consumers hold only limited rights to digital

goods this restricted ownership may inhibit their meaningful possession.

Restrictions are usually placed on the use of digital goods, as in the case of the eBook market. It is now pretty common to employ digital rights management (DRM) technologies to control the use and distribution of intellectual property in digital form using techniques like data encryption, digital watermarks and user plug-ins. This raises the question of whether consumers can pass on their iTunes libraries and other digital content to others. In the past, a person was able to pass down their childhood toys to their children. In the case of digital purchase the terms of use insisted on by the provider may prevent this practice from taking place. As we have seen, subscription-based models such as Netflix and Spotify clearly position access to digital goods as temporary. In the case of content hosted online, consumers may have a perception of permanence but no guarantee of continued access. Accounts can be terminated in the case of consumers violating the company's agreement and terms and the service may be discontinued, while data loss is another potential risk.

Apart from fully owned digital goods and clearly positioned access models there is an array of more complex and limited ownership structures, which may have significant consequences for consumers. It is difficult to image a situation where a consumer has purchased a particular coffee table and then to find that it cannot be transported to a new abode or given to a family member or friend. Yet in some cases this is what is happening with digital goods. This becomes particularly problematic when research would suggest that digital good 'terms of service' contracts are rarely read. As well as this, some contractual agreements are very confusing, resulting in the consumers being unsure of what rights they hold. The fundamental point here is that the company sees it's offering as access to a service but the consumer perceives digital goods as possessions. The real concern is the existence of digital goods with platforms owned and controlled by companies who are able to change the terms of contractual agreements at any time to suit them. Public policy needs to get up to speed on this issue to clarify how consumers might regain rights to their digital possessions.

Chapter 18: Permission marketing

Invading people's privacy and personal time

Companies who are trying to sell their brands are constantly trying to grab the attention of their target audiences. In today's marketing environment with the invasion of new media this has become more difficult to do. Consumers no longer feel they have to give their attention when requested. Today, companies wishing to attract consumers need to be aware of the different types of marketing approaches there are and which one suits a particular business and its marketing strategy the best. For a long time, marketing was exclusively focused on bombarding customers with promotional messages designed to persuade them to buy a particular brand. The growth of the Internet, the development and growing popularity of mobile communications and social media has provided companies with an easier and more affordable way of spreading their key marketing messages to target markets. On occasion, this approach has also led to invading people's privacy and their personal time. This approach can include online pop-up banners, the email and SMS spam that many consumers may ignore and some may even find annoying. At it's most basic this sort of marketing practice interrupts the viewer's attention and is called interruption marketing. Interruption marketing covers traditional methods of advertising such as TV and radio commercials, display banners, print advertising, outdoor, cinema advertising and telemarketing and direct mail. Even though this type of marketing has been extremely successful, modern day consumers are increasingly indifferent to certain types of it. They have become more sophisticated and aware of the brands out there and therefore are more likely to be turned off by the invasive and unsolicited promotional messages constantly bombarding them from when they get up in the morning until they go to bed at night.

Interruption marketing

Interruption marketing is still widely used and some types of it can be successful when dealing with specific marketing issues. Digital marketing provides an easy and affordable way for companies to interrupt people and invade their personal space. However, it has also given consumers a platform to choose and search for what they would like to see and for companies to engage them in an intimate and personal conversation. There are too many high quality 'me too' brands, all competing for the consumer's money. Consumers are bombarded with hundreds and hundreds of messages each day, more when they visit supermarkets. Many are happy with the brands they use and have little interest in knowing about alternative ones. This has forced companies to move from mass marketing to interactive marketing. It is possible to do this today with the new cost-effective technologies available.

Interruption marketing covers traditional methods of advertising such as TV and radio commercials, display banners, print advertising, outdoor, cinema advertising and telemarketing and direct mail. Even though this type of marketing has been extremely successful, modern day consumers are increasingly indifferent to certain types of it. They have become more sophisticated and aware of the brands out there and therefore are more likely to be turned off by the invasive and unsolicited promotional messages constantly bombarding them from when they get up in the morning until they go to bed at night.

What is 'permission' marketing?
Companies can ask the prospect for permission to sell them brands. This has resulted in a new approach called 'permission' marketing, often called invitational marketing. Seth Godin,[48] who coined the term, says that permission marketing is the ability of delivering anticipated, personal and relevant communications to people who actually want them.

It indicates that the prospect is in control, including when to ask the company for more and when to tell the company it has enough. The busier people are, the more difficult it is to get their attention. Permission marketing is aware of this and concentrates on treating people with respect in order to earn their attention. Marketing to a target audience has become a privilege that requires first seeking permission from the customers. Permission here is the crucial word, because if prospects haven't given the go ahead, the company's marketing messages are more likely to fall on deaf ears. Seth Godin points out[49] that genuine consent works like this. Consent is generally given when an organisation makes a guarantee, e.g. 'I will give you valuable data in the event that you issue me your consent by listening to what I need to say (e.g. issue me your email address)'.

Real permission works like this, if you stop showing up, people complain, they ask where you went. Permission is usually given when a company makes a promise, e.g. 'I will provide you with useful information if you give me your permission by listening to what I have to say (e.g. give me your email address).' A company needs to be very careful when they do that. It needs to make sure that it delivers exactly what it has promised, no more, no less. Buyers know how to opt out, so companies shouldn't oversell or over claim. If a company has promised gardening tips it should stick to that and not try and bombard them with advertising messages about their gardening brands. If a company breaks the initial agreement with its customers they will simply stop trusting it and start ignoring its messages.

Not all forms of marketing activities need permission. A company can blog, post free white papers and e-books on its website and since it is not pushing content in its customers' faces, it doesn't need their consent. It's recommended that a company should add as much relevant content to its website as possible as that will influence its SEO and credibility and if its content is shareable, its key messages will reach a lot more people than just those stopping by on its website. Permission can be informal and can be explicit when a prospect has actively agreed to be listed by the company by signing up to a newsletter and supplies their email address. It's implicit when a prospect relationship has been established and there is an implied understanding that the prospect is happy to hear from the company with promotional messages.

Getting permission marketing right

It takes patience and hard work. Companies should realise that by giving their permission, prospects let them know that they will listen and pay attention to the company's brand communications, which makes their marketing efforts very relevant. The role of permission marketing is becoming more prominent in online and direct mail campaigns. Social networking sites like Facebook and Connect encourage different applications and websites to swap information with the user's permission. In this way, the user doesn't have to repeat giving the same information every time an application is made. A good example of permission marketing in action is when a user adds a new app on Facebook. Immediately Facebook will notify the user that the app requests their permission to access their information. Other examples of permission marketing opportunities are when a user subscribes to an SMS newsletter, blog or loyalty card. Some people are more than prepared to allow companies to gather information about them, particularly if the customers are looking for a specific brand that the company has on offer. Just like any other two-way dialogue, permission marketing is more effective when the prospect or customer has no problem in sharing information about them. There are consumers who are willing to share very private and confidential information about themselves to gain better deals and better service from companies. This is particularly true of young people who are computer literate and are used to the online way of things, including the growing mobile marketing scene.

Five levels of permission marketing.
From the lowest to the highest effectiveness, the five levels in permission marketing are:

- Situational Permission: The prospect permits the business to come into contact by providing their personal information.
- Brand Trust: The prospect permits the business to continue supplying their needs.
- Personal Relationship: The prospect's permission is granted because of a personal relationship that he/she has with someone in the provider organisation.
- Points Permission: At this stage, the customer has agreed to receive goods or services and has allowed the business to collect their personal data. This is usually because they are provided with incentives, such as exchangeable points or an opportunity to earn a prize.
- Intravenous Permission: The supplier has now taken over the supply function for a specific good or a service; the customer is completely dependent on the business.

At each consecutive phase of the permission structure the company becomes more efficient, with a corresponding reduction in the cost of marketing. The company's objective should be to arrive at the 'intravenous permission' rung of the ladder. In reality, it is not necessary for the five phases to be reached consecutively. This is because more than one could be a reality, depending on the make-up of the company's business. A pertinent example of permission marketing is YouTube, where companies and individuals can upload and share videos. This is an effective way for companies to promote their brands by using the channel's subscribing features, where they achieve a permission-based connection with their customer base. This arrangement is usually arrived at on the basis that when a consumer signs up for a subscription they are giving the company the go-ahead to market to them.

Benefits of permission marketing

- Cost efficiency can be achieved if the company uses low-cost online tools. As well as this, companies can lower their costs by marketing to consumers who have expressed an interest in the company's brands.
- Because the consumer has shown interest in the company by giving it permission to have a dialogue with them, a higher conversion rate is usually achieved, resulting in cost savings.
- Permission marketing is all about sending information to consumers who have shown interest in the company, unlike Interruption marketing, where consumers can face a constant stream of messages, which can be unacceptable and expensive.

- With the use of social media and emails, companies can communicate and build long-term relationships with their customers.

Permission marketing is perceived as being successful, articulating the view that consumers now wish to be in control of what advertising messages they want to consume. In the past consumers were told what programmes to watch or listen to; today they decide when and what they want to watch or listen to.

Getting consumers to spread the word about a company's brands can be more effective and cost-efficient than advertising their brands.
Although permission marketing has really existed for a long time it is more significant today because it takes greater advantage of new technologies than any other form of marketing.
Today, Facebook, Connect and others are helping to redefine the concept of permission marketing. Using these technologies, companies, retailers, publishers etc. can create relationships based on permission with consumers on their websites. Now websites can promote honest and open policies and be upfront about how the data it collects is used and how it benefits the company and the consumer. Today, we have a new generation who are confident using social media sites and are more than happy to share confidential information with interested companies as a trade-off for better value for money brands. It could be that this relationship between company and user may become the norm.

Advocates of permission marketing basically reject the concept of mass marketing and mass communication. They argue that these concepts are outdated in today's highly competitive world. They say that consumers are more discerning than previous generations. They are much more demanding and much less patient with untargeted marketing communications, coupled with other technologies and business digital marketing innovations enhanced by modern technology such as mass customisation. Permission marketing is one of the tools that can protect consumers from a lot of nuisance sales efforts but will make a company's marketing efforts a lot more challenging. There is a Catch 22 situation, however. Permission marketing can go hand in glove with interruption marketing. To develop a permission-based relationship with a prospect, the first step a company may take can be in the form of traditional marketing, where the marketer has to win the prospect's attention before moving to a permission marketing strategy.

Chapter 19: Agile marketing

The 'waterfall' approach to systems design and development and what marketers can learn from it

While it is not usual to go too much into the technical side of a business in a marketing text, nevertheless, on this occasion, it may be helpful to understand where agile marketing had its roots, adapting a management concept from the IT world.

The IT industry for many years approached its development of software design systems by progressing from one stage to the next in a sequential manner. A separate team of experts in their fields was assigned to each stage of what was called the 'waterfall' approach. This resulted in the teams having greater control of the project and ensured that the system would be delivered on time. The management approach meant that each stage of the development had a certain process as follows.

Firstly, the project team carried out a detailed analysis of what was involved. They then prioritised their business objectives and requirements. Transforming the business requirements into IT solutions followed this and then there would be discussions and debate about the best type of technology to be assigned to the project. As soon as the various series of actions were defined and agreed online layouts were constructed, followed by code generation and implementation. When this process was complete it was followed by the conversion of computer data and encoded in a variety of ways, finally being converted into a solution to be fully tested for overall evaluation by the end user. The final stage in the process centered on making a final judgement on the project's merit. A major difficulty with this process was that if a glitch was found, changing or amending the software was not practical, resulting in the project being scrapped. This meant that the company needed to go back to the beginning again to develop new coding from the start.

The Agile Development Manifesto

In 2001, seventeen IT programmers got together and developed what they called the Agile Development Manifesto, which sought to unite a number of alternative views to overcome the hindrance of more traditional software development methods and be able to adopt quickly to unexpected changes. The agile philosophy in software development embraced detailed and disciplined planning and execution processes that created dedicated teams that were customer focused and had clearly defined roles and responsibilities. They were fully accountable for their sales targets and performance and were expected to adapt quickly to unexpected changes in the marketplace.

Faced with all the changes we have seen in marketing practice over the last few years' companies have increased pressure to produce results within shorter time frames. Marketing campaign planning had to be re-evaluated against the quickening pace of change of business and the need for companies to respond more quickly and frequently to market forces. It was agreed by many that marketing campaigns took too much time to organise and by the time they were ready to implement market conditions and requirements had changed, often by the arrival of a new competitor. The rapid evolution of digital marketing and technologies with its new prospect engagement techniques put complacent companies at risk of being overtaken by more flexible and competitive companies coming into the market. The plan for a positive response to the new business paradigm came from the world of software development. Certain progressive companies adapted this business model to their marketing plans. At a time when consumers' requirements were changing and market demands accelerated by digital technology, companies found the agile framework helped them keep up to speed with their target market. These companies were aware that agile's basic principles were relevant to the marketing scenario that was being disrupted rapidly by digital technologies. Companies traditionally connected and progressed from one stage to another in a sequence of steps, often defined by the familiar purchasing funnel. In reality marketers realised that the path to purchase can be fraught with difficulties as customers interact with various groups within an organisation. Today many consumers follow brands through social channels. They can ask for assistance and request information in support forums. They can download software and other digital content from the company's website. They can give their verdict, positive or negative, on company's brands on their own social networks. Customers are redefining the brand purchasing experience by ensuring they get consistent quality. These customers are leaving behind a trail of important data that can be picked up by companies and analysed for consumer insights.

Transforming marketing into the agile concept

Transforming marketing into the agile concept is a major challenge. Agile marketing needs to be able to anticipate change, execute quickly and efficiently and create value for the company that will contribute to its ROI. Today agile marketing has become an accepted methodology. Passionate marketers who have produced some interesting agile marketing case study successes support it. In 2013, a number of brands moved fast during the Super Bowl blackout. Tide ran a tweet "We can't get your black out but we can get your stain out." Oreo cookies tweeted, "Power out, no problem. You can still dunk in the dark."

Agile philosophy puts the consumer at the centre of everything. The common goal of the agile model is to agree a framework for dealing with complex issues and break them down into smaller, more manageable units. A successful agile model follows four key steps:

- Assesses the current state of core marketing functions, including processes, tools for marketing planning, execution and measurement. This is done in tandem with assessing the current structure and skills of the existing team.
- A key element of agile marketing is the use of cross-functional teams who are given windows of

opportunity, known as 'sprints', to plan, define and execute defined tasks. Team members have specific roles and responsibilities: a) The brand owner represents the customer's voice at team level, drives workshops and determines the release of 'sprint' items; and b) the 'scrum master' tracks the budget and progress of the project, runs planning meetings and removes' blocks' who hinder progress.

- The delivery team consists of remaining members who are responsible for executing the tasks. Basically agile marketing maintains a consumer focus and uses fast iteration across disciplines to complete the development of a better campaign in less time. It frequently returns to the customer's point of view, enabling the direction of the campaign to be reset along the way to reflect changing trends and market forces. The important thing is to realign based on feedback and changing objectives. This is where the agility concept comes into play.

We have seen that consumers have undergone a major transformation over the years. They are more demanding, more vocal and more connected than ever. Their attention span is decreasing. They want to be recognised no matter what channel they visit and this means that marketers need to be much sharper. Old marketing approaches that were set up often twelve months in advance will no longer work. Consumers will have moved on and will require more up-to-date dialogues with companies based on their changing tastes and not what marketers want to sell them. Agile marketing has strong consumer and quality focus. It works in short, iterative steps. It stimulates face-to-face dialogue and collaborations between empowered cross-functional teams and is based on delivering on an ongoing basis. It encourages continual measuring, review, feedback and ongoing adaptation. Agile marketing is process driven and methodical, allowing marketers to respond and adapt quickly. It encourages companies to react in a flexible manner to changing market conditions. Marketers must know what really works and what does not. They must know it on an ongoing basis because what was effective last month may not work next month.

Agile marketing is big on testing and measuring, not just after the project like traditional marketers do, but also during the entire marketing engagement. A company has the capabilities to methodically analyse most of its efforts, even in real time. We are in an era when web tools can show companies how prospects come to their website, how long they stayed, where they went to before leaving the site and if they bought anything. Companies can learn more about social media sentiment analysis to learn how consumers really feel about a company and its brands. Agile continues monitoring and measuring how a company's efforts influence prospects, allowing it to keep learning what is working and what it should change.

It is argued that traditional marketing in many cases lacks the elasticity and innovative mindset to act upon up-to-date information in a timely fashion; this is one of the major plusses of the agile marketing approach. Traditionally marketers intuitively wait until everything is right before they move with a plan, but agile encourages them to move and not wait for 100% perfection. Having total control of an approach can be an illusion in marketing conditions that move very fast these days. Agile marketing encourages a group of people to connect as teams.

Implementing an agile marketing approach
How easy is it to implement in practice an agile marketing approach in a major company where top down planning using the previously mentioned 'waterfall' methodology results in success moving steeply downwards through the company. Although agile may eventually be seen as beneficial, getting there may be difficult due to cultural, political, organisational and social reasons. A lot will depend on the CEO persuading his key managers and team to take ownership of it.

As we have seen, there are two different types of software development, 'waterfall' and 'agile', which marketers observed and applied the principles to the marketing concept. Waterfall is essentially a model that progresses from one stage to another sequentially. In the development of software design there are different stages in the process, which were applied to the marketing function.

- The creation of the idea.
- The start of the make-up of the idea.
- A detailed examination of the make-up of the idea.
- The development of a plan to show the look and function of the idea.

- The actual building of the software programme.
- The functionality of the software programme.
- Putting the plan into effect.
- Presenting the programme.

Agile is totally different to the waterfall approach. Here the approach is incremental, suggesting that the process consists of a series of regular consecutive additions approached separately. It is suggested that this approach came about because of the perceived limitation of the waterfall model. It was felt that the agile approach gave more freedom to designers to experiment. The design process is broken into separate models for the designers to concentrate on. With the agile method the entire process of arriving at the end result is not decided on in advance. Instead the design team can experiment and make changes to the design as the project develops. Although relatively new, the agile approach has become very popular in certain quarters. Before a typical consumer-orientated company considers an agile digital marketing approach instead of the traditional marketing approach it needs to be aware of the advantages and disadvantages of each model. The agile model can be altered as the project progresses to adapt to changing circumstances and therefore promotes breaking a plan into smaller sections so that each stage can be managed more efficiently. The software team concentrates on small modules and they can incorporate customer feedback and results from testing to amend anything if necessary. The great advantage is that the project team can respond quickly to issues as they arise. Agile can be very helpful at times when the final outcome of the project is not clearly defined and understood. In the agile situation the company's requirements will become clearer as the project progresses. Agile is very appropriate when a company is dealing with experimental design issues. Agile is more about communications and getting colleagues to interact more with each other, leading to greater teamwork. Different teams work on different modules as the project progresses and eventually will come together with a common goal to create an effective end project. On the other hand the agile system, though highly flexible, does have some downsides. Because it doesn't have a clearly defined end product, adapting as it goes on, the end result can be difficult to predict and without a definite plan from the start there is often a certain vagueness that can creep into the project.

Waterfall versus Agile

As we have seen, agile requires the whole team to be on the same page, with significant collaboration required throughout the process. This approach can raise certain problems. It can be far more time consuming than the waterfall model. It also requires the entire design team to be continually committed to the project from start to finish. With the waterfall model there is no great problem if one of the design team decides to leave the company as the project is based on a plan that doesn't change from start to finish. New recruits can easily fit in when they understand the end goal. Because the waterfall model is all about a start-to-finish detailed plan the company can launch software quickly. Its budgets and timetables tend to be a safer bet because they are so plan-based. On the other hand the waterfall method cannot be changed as market conditions change. If a change has to be made the entire project has to be scrapped, which can be very expensive and time consuming. In contrast, agile would appear to be more relevant to a company's marketing function as we have already seen it is a model that allows the marketing team to respond quickly to frequent changes in the marketplace.

Chapter 20: Viral marketing

What is viral marketing?
Viral marketing is a model that involves using people as opposed to media campaigns to communicate brand values. Companies running digital marketing campaigns often use this tactic. The term 'viral' reflects the biological virus as it too relies on 'carriers' to spread the brand message. The main objective of viral marketing is to encourage people to pass along brand promotional messages to others, who themselves pass it on. The interesting thing about this process is that it is all done for free, apart from the initial costs to produce the promotional material for whatever is being marketed. A definition given on the web reads, viral advertising is a technique by which an advertiser makes a battle focussed around the objective of bringing about viewers of that advancement to suddenly spread it by sending it to companions.

It is suggested that the earliest known use of the term 'viral marketing' goes back to 1989, when a City Bank executive is reported to have first used the term. Jefferey Rayport[50] also used the term viral marketing. The Harvard Business School professor wrote concerning getting a message out with little time, insignificant spending plans and maximising effect nothing on earth beats an infection. Each marketer hopes to have a dramatic impact on thinking and behaviour in a target market. Every successful virus does exactly that.

To paraphrase the main points of his findings:

- Marketers seeking new approaches to their profession view the virtual world of information with enthusiasm. They realise that viruses can be used to get into the consumer's mind under the guise of another unrelated activity.
- Marketers have to be patient with viral marketing as it can take time to catch on in the online world.
- Viruses can be carried into new areas by consumers' behaviour on social networks.
- Viral marketers can fashion their messages so the target consumer will take them on board as part of their core interests. This tactic will work even when no one individual is leading the campaign.
- Viruses can avoid being rejected by humans and computer systems because they can masquerade as something they are not. The trick is for the marketer to be aware of this and be in control of the situation.
- Consumers with any casual social connections have a bigger influence on connections than do consumers with fewer strong connections.
- Viruses do not become an issue until they reach tipping point, when they can be problem for marketers.

Viral marketing can be described as being like word of mouth marketing that has the effect of a communication spreading quickly amongst a lot of consumers. Viral marketing first got noticed when email provider Hotmail.com used it in their marketing campaign. When the company went live online, each email message sent carried an advertisement for Hotmail, along with a link to its website. As individuals were sending emails to relatives and friends, they were also sending out messages that promoted the email service. After clicking on the link, recipients could easily sign up for a Hotmail account, and as they send out messages using their new account, the advertisement spreads throughout the world in a short time, with very little input by the email provider. Viral marketing projects are successful when a communication expands quickly based on a planned strategy. One of the problems with viral marketing is that its outcomes can be unpredictable and risky. The low costs involved, however, make the model very popular with some marketers. The main goal of viral marketing is to send out viral messages that can be passed along rapidly from person to person without investing a lot of time, money and effort.

The tools of viral marketing

Viral marketing activities are included in company blogs and social media channels like Twitter and Facebook. The greatest impact of a message going online is that it can spread very quickly across many consumers, much faster than traditional advertising methods. While there are various strains of viral marketing, they all use the same basic principles. Incentive-driven opt-in pages can sometimes offer free items for providing an email address. Pass-along messages can come in the form of interesting emails and funny video clips which people share and forward to others. Buzz marketing or gossip creates controversies about something, which gets people to start talking anonymously. Viral marketing is spawned by strange or entertaining news items and spread by word-of-mouth, transmitting the virus like an uncontrolled epidemic. Many consumers have taken advantage of viral marketing successfully by using the likes of Facebook and other social networking channels. Viral marketing is much more effective than word of mouth because it uses the high-speed impact of the Internet. Viral marketing has recently been in the crosshairs of consumers, marketing experts and privacy rights defenders due to spam emails. However, those who have mastered the game use this strategy prudently to avoid drawing fire on themselves.

There are two types of viral marketing approaches:

1. Organic viral campaigns take off on their own with very little input by the company. These types of viral messages can spread like wildfire. The interesting thing for the company is that outside its control the message about its brand can be negative as well as positive. When the viral message is positive it can result in increasing the brand's value and the company has to be agreeable to allow the viral activity to run its course so that it doesn't become restricted in any way. This is critical if it wishes the viral campaign to be successful.

2. Viral campaigns that are placed by the company. They are not created by accident. They are based on the normal marketing process disciplines, including goal setting, brand profiling etc., which form the basis of planning and implementing a well-thought-

out mailing campaign. Viral marketing can assist companies in many ways with well-thought-out planning. A viral campaign can be linked to the company's website and its SEO strategy. The normal marketing principles will come into play in viral marketing, including increasing brand awareness and ensuring the right target consumers are reached. Companies will be aware that viral marketing can assist in driving direct response via newsletter sign ups. Viral marketing normally reaches its customers faster and can be either offline or online. This can have a positive impact during promotional campaigns or brand launches and it doesn't require a lot of money to finance a campaign.

Here are some reasons why viral marketing is important for the survival of a business.

- Viral marketing creates a buzz. Getting consumers talking about a company's brand can create a real sense of anticipation with some potential customers. The louder the buzz, the farther the campaign can spread. Messages that become popular and create great public interest will definitely help the campaign.
- It builds more credibility as the more people across the network talk about and recommend a brand, the more credibility is built. This is because more and more people endorse a company to their friends and close associates as the message goes

viral, adding points to the company's credibility rating.

- It is inexpensive. Viral marketing costs a lot less to launch but is very fast and effective in getting messages out to prospective buyers. It is the least expensive way to market a business because it doesn't require a large advertising budget. Blogging, newsletters, and email marketing are some of the ways to go viral inexpensively.
- It keeps a business in the black. Viral marketing helps to keep a business afloat. If a business has already earned more credibility, people will continue to patronise its brands and ensure business stability.
- It can launch a business globally. Its reputation as a reliable company can reach potential clients across the globe, enabling the company to branch out internationally.
- Viral messages are easy to share. Attention-grabbing videos can be easily embedded into blog posts, web pages and social networking sites.

What viral marketing is not

Many people erroneously believe that viral marketing requires a huge budget to work. Not so. A traditional marketing campaign promotes a brand, singing high praises about its merits, and giving it a lot of exposure and expensive movie star endorsements. With today's consumers being sceptical about nearly everything, this may appear like a hard sell for a weak product. All those big advertising dollars for so little gain. This is not viral marketing.

What your message should be

The key here is to create an interesting viral message that will appeal to the market. Viral marketing can be phenomenally successful for a company when an innovative idea catches the eye of the consumer and it can be a cheap way of getting massive publicity for a company's brand. Consumers can feel compelled to share the idea, promoting a brand with their friends and family. After this happens the company can harness the excitement surrounding the innovative idea for maximum impact with its customers and prospects. Viral marketing can be easy to use, starting with the company's website, including blogs and videos. There are a number of ways a company can make its message more engaging with consumers:

- Make consumers an appealing offer. Free online webinars, video tutorials, eBooks, and relevant reports are examples of low-cost but attractive offers.
- Make sure any information offered can be communicated with a simple click on the company website.
- Hook into existing networks to reach more people.
- Make a lot of noise around the brand offering to draw people in.
- Keep the message short and simple at all times. People do not have time to hang about trying to

understand what they have to do to get the brand's message.

- Know what consumers want and give it to them in an attractive package.

Chapter 21: Affiliate marketing

What is affiliate marketing?
Affiliate marketing at its very core is about relationships, a relationship between the advertiser, the publisher and the consumer. An advertiser can be a company or an individual, selling anything from airline tickets to caviar. Advertisers are ready to pay other people to help them sell and promote their business. A publisher can also be a company or individual, promoting an advertiser's brand or service in exchange for earning a commission. Advertisers form a contract and agree to work with a publisher, provide the publisher with creative content in the form of links, banners or text advertisements or even unique telephone numbers that the publisher incorporates into their website. The final piece of the jigsaw is the consumer, who sees the advertisement and takes action by either clicking or completing a form online that moves from the publisher's website to the advertiser's site, possibly ending with a dialogue.

What are Cookies?
A major technology used in this process is called a cookie. It operates with web browsers to store data such as users' preferences, login information and the contents of relevant shopping carts. One specific task cookies fulfil is to recall the link or advertisement the user clicks on. Cookies can file away the time and date of a user's click. Cookies can record the type of website and content a person likes. There are many different types of cookies

but as far as affiliate marketing is concerned it's the first-party cookies that are important. By default first-party cookies are permitted in every web browser. If a user disables first-party cookies, a website would not be able to keep track of the user's activity as they move from page to page. As a result of this the user would not be able to buy multiple items online in the same transaction. In other words, every time something is added to the checkout cart from another page on the site it would be regarded as a new order. The financial risk for a company to use affiliate marketing is extremely low and the rewards can be high. Companies only need to pay affiliates when a prospect converts, not when they drive people to the website. Affiliate marketing can be thought of as outsourced hired affiliates who are paid to bring in customers. While companies are trying to generate traffic, as a marketer the main goal is to increase the number of prospects to paying customers.

Affiliate marketing relies on performance.
The company only makes money when the advertisement performs well. Performance-based marketing enables a company to promote its brand on others' websites, but to only pay when the advertiser in question initiates an action. Traditionally, companies have been allowed to advertise on certain spaces on the web. This might be a banner advertisement within certain websites or email messages. It might also include investing in advertisements at the top of search inquiries for the popular search engines like Google or Yahoo! The problem with buying space like this is that the company

may have no experience of the medium and pay more for the advertisement than it gains back in sales. However, with affiliate marketing, the exposure that the company gets stays intact, just as it would for advertising through something like a banner advertisement. The difference, however, is that instead of paying the affiliate up front, the company only pays the affiliate when a user does something by either clicking the home page or landing page or completing an online form. The significant point here is that affiliate marketing is a strategy based on referrals and increase in traffic that means extra cash for the affiliate. In this way, the affiliate has an incentive to promote the company. There are certain kinds of models that are used to perform affiliate marketing:

There are three models that affiliates use in affiliate marketing:

- Cost per 1000 impressions (CPM). This means that a merchant pays a flat fee for every 1000 views or clicks the advertisement attracts through the affiliate.
- Cost Per Action (CPA). Similar to the CPM model, it operates on the same principles. The difference is that the amount of money a merchant hands out to an affiliate is directly related to the response to the merchant's advertisement. The prospect's response is related to things like website clicks, filling out forms on the web, downloading videos or buying an item. The merchant only pays when the

advertisement works well as opposed to paying a set amount for a specific number of clicks as in for example a banner advertisement, or visits to a URL that is provided.

- Cost Per Click (CPC) – Similar to the CPA model, it is dependent on performance, but the factors that determine how much a merchant pays to an affiliate include clicks. This may refer to the number of times a banner advertisement is clicked, as its name suggests, or the number of people who visit the URL that is advertised.

The marketing strategy behind the three options is about performance. Amazon.com created one of the original affiliate programmes on the web. It was a programme that allowed websites to become affiliates of the main Amazon.com website. The affiliate would place some kind of link on one of their web pages and allow users to connect to Amazon.com. The point of the link was to entice users to visit Amazon.com for all their literary needs. This was very beneficial for Amazon's affiliates because they received a commission every time one of their users was sent to Amazon.com. Proctor and Gamble was another of the original websites that offered affiliate-marketing programmes in the early days of the Internet. Affiliate marketing today is a reminder of the fall of click-through banner advertisements that saw a sharp decline in actions taken. This is why affiliate marketing, which exists as exclusively performance based, is essential and beneficial to an Internet marketing strategy.

As we have seen, merchants are the companies that sell brands and pay affiliates for their marketing campaigns. Affiliates are the companies that own the website or have blogs that a merchant can use to advertise. They get paid whenever an advertisement performs by triggering an action. The affiliate is always motivated to deliver traffic to the merchant's site. If traffic is delivered the affiliate benefits by getting the kudos and financial rewards for the resulting sale or lead. The merchants benefit by getting potential customers by taking advertisements on the affiliates' websites. As already mentioned the great bonus for merchants is that it only costs them money when they successfully sell a brand through an affiliate's website. For it to work merchants have to plan effective and eye-catching advertisements So when a company thinks about who it wants its affiliate to be, this is one of the factors to consider. A merchant must be diligent in his approach to making an affiliate marketing strategy work. The affiliates have to deliver. This is another great benefit for merchants. They have a choice in who they want as their affiliates. A smart merchant will be able to gain an affiliate relationship with websites that are in line with their brand strategy service. Affiliate marketing allows merchants to target specific demographics on the Internet.

To develop effective marketing strategies the affiliate must know the make-up of the company's target market, where they are and where to find them, so they can pitch the advertisement to them. Affiliate marketing, like other marketing disciplines, is about contributing to the company's ROI. A great advantage of affiliate marketing is that click-through and view rates can be monitored. It is also a way for the merchants to know if the affiliate is performing well on their behalf. if not, the merchant can look at other affiliate options. It will help the merchant to develop an effective marketing strategy involving different marketing tools such as banners and link placements. This will help the merchant to allocate the marketing budget more efficiently by investing in the right advertising to maximise results. It's all about exposure. The merchant can use affiliate marketing to help build positive brand imagery. By doing this it will leave a good impression with customers, who are more likely to make repeat purchases.

Affiliate marketing is catching on as a marketing tool.
There are a number of conditions a company must meet before venturing into affiliate marketing:

- Sufficient profit margins to accommodate the affiliate's commission.
- A first-class brand that affiliates will be enthusiastic about and will promote.
- Good commissions to enthuse the affiliates.
- Brand should be in demand and easy to sell.
- Have sufficient stocks to meet demand.
- Be able to train affiliates about the brand's attributes and usages.
- Be able to fund a system to rack affiliate's sales.
- Have the resources to monitor affiliate's sales efforts.

- Remind affiliates that they are also the public face of the brand.
- A merchant needs to clearly state the benefits that it offers an affiliate without building too much hype:
- It needs to ensure that the brand it offers is high quality.
- It needs to inform affiliates about how the brand is relevant them and their traffic.
- It needs to show them what is on offer compared to the competition.
- It needs to explain to them the tracking system for sales and their earnings.
- It must make sure they know about the company's reputation and credibility so there is nothing to lose by partnering with them.
- It needs to explain to its potential affiliate how they are going to be able to make money by referring some of their traffic to its website.

Affiliate marketing is a serious business venture for any company or affiliate doing business online. Like every other marketing option it requires careful consideration and SWOT analysis before making a commitment to proceed with it as part of a marketing strategy.

Chapter 22: Real-time marketing

What is real-time marketing?

There is a view held by some marketers that if consumers are nearly always online the brands they are interested in should be online so that they retain a presence and relevance for the customer. Nowadays, with the growth in popularity of social media, brands have an affinity with consumer interests and reach the target audience quickly, often costing less than traditional broadcast advertising. The growth of brands engaging with consumers through interesting content, advertising and at times product placement related to a topical event can be very appealing to digital-conscious marketers. With the ever-growing technologies in the digital world companies can have real-time dialogues with prospects and customers, providing interactive services and establishing long-term relationships with their target markets. Real-time marketing required marketers to replace their broadcast mentality, which for many years had dominated marketing, with a desire to give the consumer access to the company and to create ongoing dialogue that would keep the brand relevant in accordance with changes in consumers' tastes. Real-time marketing requires companies to concentrate on giving the consumer a satisfying brand experience and to provide help and support by responding to their enquiries to win their long-term loyalty. Real-time marketers need to understand how the consumer relationship with the company's brands is changing and to think of the new role marketing could play in the company. They used media to broadcast advertising messages, advertise brands and process transactions. Their mindset was that they would decide what the consumer needed to know, not the consumer. The bright and more marketing focused companies like Apple and Levi Strauss led the way and saw the new media channels as a way to involve the consumer in the brand development process. They realised that the past practice of selling mass-produced brands to brand-homogeneous markets would no longer be enough.

Traditional marketing connections no longer sufficient.
Traditional marketing connections with the consumer were no longer sufficient in the real-time world. Marketers began to realise that focus groups and market surveys amongst a very small sample of their target market were no longer viable to reflect what was really happening in the marketplace. More regular connections with consumers produced information the focus groups could not. The new interaction between companies and the consumer gave marketers new insights into their own and competitors' brands. The new technology created ongoing communications between the company, its brands and the consumer. The only difference is that today this dialogue happens faster electronically in real time. The information revolution means that a company and its customers know more about one another and work more closely together than they could have ever done in the past.

For marketers to move from broadcast to sustained dialogue was a challenge. They did so by opening themselves to consumer access. They sustained it by involving consumers in an iterative process as partners in the business model going forward. In the US many companies did this initially by using the 800-digit numbers on their packaging. This eliminated the need for warranty cards as it encouraged the consumer to connect with the company and drew them into the new iterative process. It was a start and today website companies can connect 24/7/365 with their customers. Real-time marketing is not really a new concept. It's about recognising an opportunity and responding to it, which marketers have been doing for quite some time.

Social media has had a major impact on real-time marketing.
It did this by changing the marketing goalposts. Social media has opened direct contact between consumers and brands, which encourages them to connect directly to one another. Social media marketing is about sharing information with the consumers and not talking at them. Real-time marketing brings discourse to a new level by encouraging consumers to share their experiences with the brand so that it becomes a relevant part of the conversation. Information is moving faster than ever before. Major stories are breaking in social media in real time, often before the broadcast media have the story. Consumers have got used to up-to-date news and they're using social channels to get it. They want to discuss news as it happens, not days later. A story or an idea can go viral or become a non-event within 24 hours, which is why timing is now crucial for a company's social marketing messages. It only has a small window within which to

reach people. People come together to bond over a hot topic and then that bonded audience dissolves very quickly. If you engage with them at the perfect moment what will remain is your reputation as a brand that's timely and relevant, a brand that "gets it."

Real-time marketing efforts are about responsiveness and capitalising on something while it is still relevant. It's about delivering a relevant message to a relevant audience at a relevant time. According to a recent study Americans spend one out of every four minutes online on social networks. Integration with social media and more traditional channels of advertising has also increased. 40 per cent of adults surf or participate in social networking while watching television. So what does this mean for the social marketer? The target audience is turning to multiple channels for news. A critical part of this phenomenon is real-time marketing, which creates relevance and value on an ongoing basis. It's about more than posting a one-off cartoon for a quick notice of attention. It's about long-term engagement; it's about participating in a person's life. It's about being culturally aware and taking leads from society. It's about participating in a 'newsy' conversation in a way that meets the consumer's needs as opposed to the company's brand needs. New marketing options like real-time marketing don't mean companies should get rid of all their traditional advertising. It means they have to add a certain element of connecting with people and being part of what they care about as opposed to constantly telling them what to do.

In this way real-time marketing allows the company's other marketing efforts to be more effective. When real-time marketing is added to the mix, there is a significant lift in the consumer's likelihood to seek out the information offered and connect with the company and its brands.

There are basically two forms of real-time marketing available, depending on the budget:

- Content-based real-time marketing involves creating content, often video, images, etc., that reacts to the conversation around it. The content has to be changed 24/7/365 as the story in question develops. It can involve a lot of time and can be quite expensive. It wouldn't be feasible for a small brand. It is possible for a small brand to create content on the cheap but doing so in real time involves a huge time commitment.

- Conversation-based real-time marketing does not involve content but rather pure participation in the conversation. This is essentially real-time engagement, listening and reacting to current conversations. Conversation-based real-time marketing can also involve pre-planned engagement, which involves being online and ready to interact during certain events, whether it is a public event or a live chat session the company has organised with a media channel in advance.

Hosting a chat around a live event, where a company can guide and participate in the conversation, allows it to get involved with its target market and be an authentic part of the dialogue. The company needs to ensure the event is relevant for its brand imagery. If a company decides that real-time marketing is right for its brand and has the right people on board for its efforts to be successful the company has to be reaching the right people and needs to determine the best way of reaching its target audience.

Establish where dialogue relevant to the brand is taking place.
Does the target audience use Twitter, Pinterest or Instagram? Do they like to dive into longer topics? Research where they go online. Why do they go there? What do they like to talk about? Who do they talk to? Once a company picks its platforms, it can research what has been most successful for a brand on those platforms. If a company gets to know what topics work in particular circumstances and if it gets to know more about its target market it will be able to give them what they want and when real-time content or conversations are relevant. In preparing a real-time marketing strategy a company can introduce a schedule of interesting events or topics for discussion; these could be anything from product launches to interesting news releases. The idea is not to create content about the event itself but rather the conversations that are happening around it. If a company is planning to create content, it should have a large collection of visual elements, brand images, logos, etc. ready to use. That way, when an opportunity presents

itself, you're prepared with the initial groundwork so creating content will be that much faster.

The events calendar is just a guideline for when a company should be on high alert. It also needs to be prepared for the unpredictable. It should always be monitoring social media in general for any breaking news. On top of that it should be vigilant to the dialogues and issues that are occurring around the type of products it produces. A company should also be on the lookout for organic conversations around its brand and any customer service opportunities. The best way to make sure a company doesn't miss anything is to set up an alert system to monitor online activity. This will allow it to have a constant eye on mentions of its brand and its competitors so it knows when its brand has an impromptu window to act. Once a company chooses what topic or conversation it's going to target, it needs to make sure its content is of good quality. Choosing the right opportunities and the right content will ensure that its real-time marketing efforts have long-term benefits instead of just being a quick-hit attention getter.

The tone of the content should be appropriate for the situation and the audience. The company should spend sufficient time monitoring the conversation to ensure it knows the overall sentiment of the piece and responds accordingly in the right tone of voice.

Real-time marketing is most effective when it's consistent and faithful to the company's brand.
Real-time content should not be any different to a company's existing content, but rather a natural

extension of other marketing efforts. All content and conversations should align with its established brand position and voice. This means that the audience must be able to tie in the content with a particular company. There's no point in creating great content if a company doesn't get credit for it. This creative exchange is a great example of how brands can participate in social conversations to gain some attention rather than just pushing out standard marketing messages. When done right a company can still incorporate a plug for its brand. Sometimes marketers incorporate a 'newsroom' style in their real-time marketing communications to introduce a spokesperson for the brand. The company's copywriter or PR executive uses the theme as a guide to messaging, drafting and issuing real-time content of current conversations and determine and guide the social channels' distribution strategy for its various messages, which may be targeted at different audiences. The company's legal people may also be in the loop to oversee and sign off on any contentious issues being covered. The ultimate goal of real-time marketing is for the company to generate attention for its brand, both among its current audience and prospects. Real-time marketing can help give a brand a personality and establish it as relevant, of the day, and worth listening to or watching. The important thing is that the company is relating to its audience rather than forcing them to relate to it. Companies may have to organise multiple agency partners to create and develop marketing campaigns and the world of real-time marketing is no different. Very few companies have the human resources to provide the amount of content that the website publishers require 24/7/365. That is the challenge for the future as the Internet expands as well as real-time marketing.

Chapter 23: E-commerce

What is e-commerce?

One of the many explanations cited for electronic commerce (e-commerce) is that it's about that aspect of a company's operations which relates to the exchange of goods electronically and incorporates everything which directly or indirectly is involved in that activity. E-commerce marketing is defined as a business tool that helps a company or consumer to carry on business over the Internet. In e-commerce there may not be a retail outlet as we know it. In a lot of cases the sellers and buyers do not ever see each other. The Internet, as well as information and communications technologies including voice, data and video communications, is a major force in e-commerce. Although e-commerce and traditional commerce are similar in many ways, when it comes to selling brands to generate profits they do it differently. Traditional commerce communicates brand data by using traditional advertising media including TV, radio, newspapers etc; e-commerce communicates by using company websites and online catalogues. Traditional commerce still avails of regular mail to communicate; e-commerce does it by electronic mail. In traditional commerce potential customers often check out brand availability by phone, fax and letter; e-commerce checks brand availability through email and websites. In reality, today, most companies use a combination of traditional and e-commerce to carry out their business activities. It would be fair to say that almost every large and medium-sized company uses e-commerce in its activities. E-commerce is basically about doing business over the Internet. Sometimes we can come across the terms e-commerce and e-business. While many people use the terms interchangeably, they aren't the same. E-business is broader than e-commerce and includes transaction-based e-commerce businesses and those who engage in traditional commerce but cater to online activities as well. An e-business can run any portion of its internal processes online, including inventory management, risk management, finance, and human resources. For a business to be e-commerce and e-business, it must both sell products online and handle other company activities.

Some companies set out to do away with the middle person by using the Internet to deliver brands directly to customers. The theory is that by taking this approach the company may be able to offer brands at a cheaper price and in some cases provide better service to their customers. The ultimate objective, apart from maximising profits, would be to differentiate its brand from its competitors, increase its market share and improve customer loyalty.

Companies have ways of creating profitable activities online.
This is achieved with traditional commerce and e-commerce or a combination of both:

- Purchasing and selling brands with appeal.
- Creating effective customer service.
- Promoting internal company communications.

- Getting involved with other interested parties.
- Monitoring competitors' activity.

Electronic Data Exchange (EDI) came about in the late 1970s. Companies wishing to deliver data from one entity to another used it. The World Wide Web and the Internet arrived in the 1990s, providing a whole new way of doing business. The Internet increased the accuracy and speed of communications between all parties in the buying and selling process. The Internet reduced cost for companies to do business and enabled them to exploit value chain integration. E-commerce improved the value chain by creating new opportunities to reduce costs. Email was used instead of regular mail. Companies were able to sell to customers far away by using their websites. The merchant model moves the retail models to the e-commerce environment using the Internet.

There are various types of merchant models.
The most common one is similar to the traditional business model that promotes the sale of brands over the web. A good example of this model in action is Amazon.com offering good value for money and speedy service. Amazon.com is able to sell well-known brands directly to consumers anywhere in the world. Traditional companies also use the merchant model to sell brands over the Internet, including companies like Dell, Cisco Systems and Compaq. By making a major part of their overall sales over the web, their businesses are able to operate without the middle person and they are able to connect with out-of-the-way customers.

Another system used is the brokerage model, where businesses drive the buyers and sellers together over the web and earn commission. A good example of this model in action is eBay, which is very popular with consumers. Companies can also create extra revenue by offering banner advertisements on their sites. The advertising model is an add on to traditional advertising media, including television and radio. Various search engines and directories including Yahoo and Google offer content just like TV and radio. They offer the content free to consumers. By generating major traffic they can charge a fee to advertisers for organising banner advertisements on their site. With the mixed model they create revenue from subscriptions and advertising. Examples of this system are AOL and SuperOnline.

There is also the infomediary model, which involves the gathering of information on companies and consumers and selling the information to those who want it for marketing purposes. An example of this system is bizrate.com.

The subscription model is where a customer pays a subscription price to have access to a particular brand. The model was pioneered by newspapers and magazines but is used now by many businesses and websites. Examples are the *Wall Street Journal* and Consumer Reports.

Major types of e-commerce

E-commerce includes electronic data interchange on the Internet, email, shopping online, brand sales and services online, Internet banking, and transferring funds online. There are a number of types of e-commerce used today, depending on the type of deals being done between different groups. We have business to business (B2B), referring to e-commerce being carried out between companies; B2C is defined as e-commerce between business and consumer; and C2C involves e-commerce between individuals or consumers.

The main benefits of e-commerce to a company are:

a)   Ease of market expansion at home and abroad.

b)   Technology usage reduces the cost of creating, processing, distributing, filing and retrieving paper-based information.

c)   Use of technology reduces costs of storing raw materials, work-in-progress goods and finished foods due to its 'just in time (JIT)' approach to business.

d)   Automated business processes contain or reduce costs.

e)   Involves less paperwork, with more cost-effective document transfer.

f)   Speeds up delivery time for finished goods.

g)   Reduces time to complete business transactions.

h)   Results in improved customer service.

i)   Creates greater productivity.

j)   Can reduce transportation costs.

From a consumer point of view the benefits of e-commerce are:

1. Transactions can be done 24/7/365 from most locations in the world.
2. They have more choices and can get an array of options by using search engines.
3. With the use of emails interpersonal communication is extremely fast and there are many information points to access online.
4. There is a wider access to assistance and to secure advice from experts in the field.
5. Purchasing goods online saves time and in some cases money.
6. Servers like Amazon are extraordinarily fast and efficient.

Technical limitations of e-commerce include:

1. There can be a lack of security and reliability, particularly purchasing from an unknown source.
2. Insufficient data transfer speed online at times.
3. Frequent changes in software tools can be costly and inconvenient.
4. Not everyone is online.
5. Possibility of credit card theft.

A web browser is used by the consumer to open home and landing pages of a company website on the Internet. The consumer looks for brands displayed on the web pages and often makes purchase selections. The purchased item is put in a shopping cart and the sale is completed when the credit card and the address have been confirmed as valid. The Internet introduced the concept of e-commerce that is now the mainstay of many successful businesses.

Chapter 24: Native advertising

What is native advertising?
Although the concept of 'native advertising' is becoming more prevalent in advertising and marketing circles, many people are not quite sure what it actually is. With company brands, agencies, publishers, social media channels and technology vendors venturing into new and sometimes uncharted territory, it's important to know precisely what the concept is all about.

Native advertising is the integration of marketing content with a website or service in such a way that it is not distinct from the rest of the material presented there in terms of its content, format, style or placement. Although native advertising is often informative rather than overt marketing material it is reckoned to be valuable for a company's brand. The concept is the complete opposite of 'interruption marketing' in that it is presented to the consumer along with other content that they are freely viewing; the consumer is not coerced into viewing or reading it; they will do so if it appears to be useful and interesting to them. The integrated form native advertising takes depends on the media vehicle being used. On publisher sites, native advertising placements are deliberately made to look and read like the accompanying editorial. On Facebook, this could be sponsored stories or page post advertisements, or promoted tweets on Twitter.

Earned media is publicity achieved through promotional efforts other than advertising. This is in contrast to paid media, which is about publicity achieved through advertising, like social sharing, which provides websites with social media sharing buttons. Although earned media is not an essential part of native advertising, it is an important aspect of many native campaigns. The explanation of native advertising clearly overlaps with existing definitions of sponsored/branded/custom content, as well as advertorial. The goal of native marketing is not to disrupt the user experience and to offer information that is helpful and similar to the other information on the site so the content is engaged with at a higher level than a banner advertisement.

With regard to native advertising the company needs to identify an audience and their interests, create content that matches the interests of the audience, locate a channel of distribution that matches the audience consumption habits, pay for added distribution, make use of targeting and measure results and iterate the process. The benefits of native advertising for companies are higher advertising effectiveness and less advertisement blindness, increased brand perception, and better engagement. The benefits for publishers are seamless user experience not disrupted by advertisements, new revenue stream with better results, and engagement with messaging intended to attract rather than interrupt consumers. Paid placement for attractive content is reckoned to be much more effective than banner advertising, which many marketers regard as an ineffective way to get the consumer's attention.

Aspects of native marketing

- EMarketers predict that spending on native advertising will increase as the concept becomes more popular and brings with it opportunities for the entire ecosystem, for publishers; for social platforms with new advertising brands; for brands, new opportunities for attention and consumer engagement; for agencies with benefits from creative and media opportunities; for technology with its new solutions to facilitate the creative aspects of native advertising.

- Native advertising serves as a growth component to mobile smartphones and tablets where display advertising is highly limited and more disruptive to the consumer. A number of social networks like Facebook and Twitter are well geared up for native advertising. Native is becoming part of that conversation more rapidly because of the growth in mobile.

- Publishers, social networks, companies and their brands and agencies stand to benefit from new revenue streams created by native advertising with its inherent benefits to their target audiences because of the opt-in nature of the medium. Companies promoting their brands and their agencies need to be well versed in the use of native advertising, with an emphasis on maintaining the authenticity that consumers expect from the publisher.

- Some publishers don't clearly distinguish native advertising from the more commonly used terms 'sponsored content' or 'promoted content'. Many publishers will argue that they've been offering native advertising solutions for brands for some years, they just weren't using the term. It's just a new way of describing something publishers have been doing for years.

- While the overall concept of native advertising as sponsored content may not be new from the publisher perspective, the digital complexities do make native advertising much different from the standard advertorials that have been used in the past. The native advertising relationship between publishers and brands can be positive. Publishers offer not only copywriting facilities but also full creative resources to synergise with existing imagery, including videos and website banner advertisements to create a total campaign package. The best native advertising campaigns are collaborative, where the publisher helps brands tell their best story without making a sales pitch. The publisher wants the content to resonate with their audience and get them involved. The more collaborative it can be with brands and their partners the better all round for all those involved, including the publisher, the advertiser and the always important consumer.

In the main, social media platforms are gravitating towards advertising as a viable product to offer brands that wish to heighten their customers' experience in a way that is relevant and non-intrusive in comparison to traditional online banner ads. Community building, lead generation and awareness are cited as the most common goals of native advertising campaigns on social networks like Facebook and Twitter and Tumblr, who themselves are very proactive in promoting ways to improve the way advertisers can use their facilities to gain greater traction.

For a native advertising approach to be successful content is key.

Andrew Gorenstein, Chief Revenue Officer for the Gawker Media Group,[51] said Native is simply a container, a wrapper for content that recounts a brand's story in a manner that bodes well for the publisher or the platform's audience. It's just the container we serve our brand content in. At the same time, regardless of the fact that it is served in the most fashionable way possible it'll fall flat if the substance isn't solid.

There are conflicting views about the future of native advertising.

The difference between editorial content and advertising is shrinking. The *New York Times'* first foray into native advertising recently through an attractive eight-page advertisement for Shell could herald a broader industry acceptance of long-form native content. Traditionally, advertising has been clearly separated from editorial, with companies purchasing advertising space alongside relevant content. That's what the biggest spending brands could do with the limited number of marketing options available. With the rise of native advertising, some companies are attempting to integrate their brand messages directly into content to give them an editorial look and feel. Today's native advertisements are significantly better and more effective than the advertorial advertisements of the recent past, as a new concept to engage with consumers.

Native advertising is still in its infancy.
Given the novelty and aesthetic quality of native advertisements, they're generating significant attention in the publishing and advertising worlds, but native advertisements are still in their infancy and won't overtake the more prevalent advertising approaches for a number of reasons. First, the analytics for native advertisements haven't happened yet. Advertisers will expect this analysis as they expect with traditional campaigns. Second, audience targeting isn't sophisticated enough for native advertising to steal the budget allocations dedicated to digital. And third, consumers are sceptical about the native concept because they are not comfortable reading oblique pieces about brands in editorial stories. Having a clear dividing line between editorial and advertising content intuitively helps people trust the publisher's integrity in the content they are presenting. Publishers will want to protect their profits as well.
While many believe the future of advertising hinges on companies' ability to seamlessly integrate branded, relevant experiences into publications, native advertising needs to be significantly refined before gaining the trust of consumers and advertisers. Native is certainly here to stay, but publishers need to strike the right balance to address these concerns and help it evolve to the next

level. As an idea, native advertising makes sense. Some research suggests that a US citizen is more likely to complete Navy SEAL training, get into MIT or get a full house while playing poker than click on certain banner ads. Publishers have woken up to the fact that they desperately need an alternative. Native advertising feels like a good replacement. Storytelling is very relevant for companies using a native advertising approach. It works well with social media, where a native advertisement more or less means one which is engineered to be a watchable product in itself, something that sits seamlessly on a user's timeline or news feed and doesn't scream product placement. We have seen that native advertising is an online marketing strategy, which plans and distributes advertisements to ensure they are seamlessly integrated into their channels of distribution. A native advertisement looks more like all the non-ad content that surrounds it. This distinguishes it from a banner advertisement, which is clearly separate and could not normally be mistaken for non-advertising content.

A common form of native advertising is similar to old-style advertorial content in the press. A news or entertainment website might publish a sponsored post, paid for by a brand, which looks similar to the site's other content but was created with the intention of marketing that brand's product. However, it is a misconception that native advertising is simply the modern equivalent of advertorial. Native advertising on Facebook and other social media is a whole new art. Most native advertising is relatively innocuous, but it is true that native advertising in newspapers and other trusted outlets could feel a bit underhanded. It can be a controversial topic among news journalists, who feel native advertising is an attempt to deceive the consumer by trying to camouflage advertising as news. Journalists will argue that marketers can talk all they like about content and story telling but they are hawking advertisements around trying to convince consumers to buy stuff they don't need.

Media culture has been split for years.
There is editorial and there is commercial content, and never the two shall meet as they say. With the popularity of native advertising, that may change. A development in the implementation of native advertising by publishers is to allow advertisers to create and post content themselves on dedicated platforms rather than, for example, including a post in the main section of the site. Both viral cat video distributor BuzzFeed and Forbes use variations on this model. It's unclear how much time editorial personnel, as distinct from commercial content managers, currently spend on this area but there's no reason that editorial shouldn't become quite heavily involved in commissioning and editing content. While critics deride such innovations as selling out and allowing advertisers to dictate editorial choices, this strategy might well empower publishers with a greater say with their advertisers.
On an informal level, money has always affected editorial. Papers and magazines have toned down negative coverage of big advertisers or changed around the order of an issue on occasions too numerous to list, and they will continue to make similar small concessions for as long

as they are commercially funded. However, by inviting brands to create content on a platform controlled by a user the tone and nature of that content can be more attuned to the style the readers like. In the US, nobody has any idea how native advertising is going to be regulated. The Federal Trade Commission recently organised an industry workshop on the topic that brought up a larger number of issues than it answered according to Mary Engle[52] the FTC's associate director of the advertising practices division. She argued that if governments can't work out exactly how best to regulate the sector, they are likely to come down on the more draconian side rather than give the industry the benefit of the doubt. Agencies and publishers are struggling to find an efficient way of working together, and to get the relatively large number of brains required to create a native campaign in one room at one time.

Chapter 25: Digital display advertising

What is digital display advertising?

They say digital display advertising is the powerhouse of most businesses. In the age of the Internet and its many ramifications companies who use marketing technologies successfully are more likely to increase sales and revenue. Companies have a number of ways to communicate their marketing messages. Digital display advertising is one effective method and its value shouldn't be underestimated. Digital display advertising is located on websites and can be seen in a wide range of different formats. Its main purpose is to deliver brand messages to people connected to the Internet. It is said that the first banner advertisement was displayed for AT&T on 27th October 1994.

Traditional offline display advertisements are much less cost effective than online marketing channels, like SEO marketing, affiliate or email marketing etc. Display advertising is used as a branding tactic. It is not usually expected to result in immediate purchases, creating an immediate ROI, but is more for creating long-term awareness and recognition of a company's brand. Many start-ups do not have the luxury of spending their limited budget on brand imagery, given the longer-term payback. They need to plan accordingly, based on their available cash resources and desired timeline for customer engagement.

The Internet and the Web allow companies to use online advertising as part of their marketing promotional strategy. Online advertising is used to communicate different marketing messages to appeal to consumers. There are a number of online advertising methods, including targeted advertising, where the content of the advertisement is in direct correlation to the content of the web page the consumer is viewing. Other examples are banner advertisements, email marketing, online classified advertising and web pages that use advanced technology including viewing video streaming that alters when the user's mouse passes over it. Sponsored links on websites like Google are an effective way for a company to promote a brand by attracting pre-determined target consumers.

Digital display advertising uses the Internet to communicate messages.
Display advertisements come in numerous shapes and sizes and locations. Most publishers that offer display advertisements offer them in the leader board at top of page, the skyscraper on the right side of the page and the big box either in the right column or interior of the page. Other popular display advertisement placements include pop-ups in a new window over the page being read, pop-unders in a new window under the page being read, interstitials inserted in between two pages being read, within an email, and within or around a video player. The creative technologies that can be deployed within these ads can be as simple as a static image, to moving parts, to expandable size when rolled over with

the user's mouse to data-entry forms for sign-ups, to videos in motion. There are also technologies that can be deployed that drop a cookie on the user's computer when they first visit a site, and then push the advertisements on third party sites after they leave the site to try and get them back. The more complex the creative part is to execute the more costly it will be to run. Creating a video is more labour intensive than creating a static image advertisement.

Online advertising campaigns are usually less expensive and easier to produce than traditional television advertising. Online advertising is usually more flexible and can be changed at the last moment if market conditions dictate a change in consumer behaviour. Online advertising gives quicker, real-time feedback. The great thing about online display advertising is that the marketer has many ways to target the placements of its advertisements. The marketer can either run advertisements run-of-site (ROS), on any page of a publisher's website, or, preferably, they can target their advertisements based on demographics of the user, subject matter of the content (or behaviour of the user), or time of day/week etc. However, although the performance of deep targeting is materially better than run-of-site ads, publishers will always charge more for each stage of the targeting required by the purchaser.

There are basically two ways to purchase display ads. One is on a pledged basis, resulting in the order securing a guaranteed placement in the time period desired. The other is on a remnant basis, which means the order will be run only if there is unsold space available in that period, which means it is not guaranteed to run if there are committed advertisers willing to purchase the space. Committed placements create a higher CPM than a remnant placement. But when a marketer can get it, remnant advertisements are definitely the way to go for a start-up, given the material cost savings. Publishers should be content to think about remaining buys because getting some business is better than getting none. Rates are tied to expected click performance of these placements, where clicks can be 0.05% for the cheap remnant ROS advertisements, all the way up to 5.0% for a targeted email inclusion. CPMs and clicks also rise for using various technologies or targeting placements. As an example, a static advertisement may get a 0.2% click rate and a moving/expandable advertisement may get a 0.6% click rate. Or an ROS advertisement may get a 0.2% click rate, and a deep-targeted advertisement could get a 0.6% click rate. Marketers should be confident about the level of expected clicks from each insertion of the advertisement for any higher CPMs to be considered reasonable. They should ask for CPC (click), CPL (lead) or CPA (acquisition) advertising opportunities, which is always better than CPM (impression) formulated placements, since the visitor has carried out an action that is on the marketer's site.

The best thing about online display advertisements is the ease of tracking the results they achieve.
Marketers should be using unique tracking codes for each specific placement they buy, to track that

sites/placements are performing better or worse than others. They should then optimise the bulk of their remaining budget/campaign into the best performance vehicles from the initial test. Where possible, tracking should be implemented at the click-on, lead generation and buying/selling level, to decide which clicks/vehicles do a better job of leading to customer engagement and conversion.

The advantages of digital display advertising
Digital display advertising can be described as a concept that uses graphics on the web. The advertisements are called banners and are used in a variety of sizes and apart from graphics can include copy and logos. Companies can also concentrate on rich media, which as mentioned earlier is a term for a web page advertisement that uses advanced technology that interacts instantly with the user. A company can often use digital display advertising like it does traditional magazine or newspaper advertisements, with the option of moving from static to interactive.

Digital display advertising can offer a distinct advantage over traditional display advertising in that it is easier to focus in on a specific target consumer and the campaign's performance can be tracked and measured daily using metrics like clicks and impressions to calculate the company's ROI. The proper placement of digital display advertisements is very important. Placing advertisements on sites that are popular with the company's target market can be very advantageous. This can assist in developing an impactful campaign.

The advantage of online advertising is that the marketer can easily do advertising testing. The campaign is usually less expensive than traditional advertising. The advertisements can run 24/7/365. Companies can alter online advertising much more conveniently than in other media, and marketing can target the audience. Digital display advertising doesn't just concentrate on clicks as a measurement of campaign success. It's all about getting a significant number of impressions from the targeted audience, who hopefully will become impressed with the brand's imagery and eventually purchase it. Digital display advertising creates excitement around a company's brand by its sheer display of the brand's imagery. A 2013 Harvard Business School Study[53] came to the conclusion that digital display advertising has a major positive impact on search conversions. To paraphrase HBS, both enquiry and presentation promotions display critical elements that enhance their adequacy and ROI over the long run. Marketers' customers can see the advertisement, shop, and buy all without leaving home. Smart companies target their audiences comprehensively.

But there are some disadvantages to online advertising.

- Sometimes the marketers are not sure if they actually get what they have paid for. They have to trust the website owners that the advertisement has appeared in the proper section etc.
- Marketers have to trust the traffic profiles given by the website owners.

- Surfers may not look at a company's advertisements if they are too focused on their searches.
- Surfers may notice advertisements but not click them.
- The research on the effectiveness of websites is not comprehensive.
- Incorrect keywords may be used due to a company's inexperience.
- May get many clicks but not many sales.

Good online advertising strategies
- Check out what competitors are up to.
- Plan pertinent web content.
- Check customers' demographics and psychographics.
- Ensure brand can be delivered on time.
- List prices of brands.
- Post interesting content to relevant news groups.
- Exploit competitors' weaknesses.
- Ensure SEO is well planned.

Campaigns that are badly managed can be costly and ineffective. The key is to constantly iterate the marketing strategy and change or adapt in line with changing market conditions and consumers' preferences.

Chapter 26: Digital ecosystem planning

What is digital ecosystem planning?

The new digital ecosystem is a set of platforms, tools, people and companies that classify people's lives and that have significantly changed the way companies do business. The digital world as we know it has became somewhat complicated for companies trying to market brands successfully. With the proliferation of media options including smartphones, tablets, desktop applications and a host of social media platforms it is becoming very difficult for marketers to know where to focus their efforts. To try and offer some clarity it is suggested that marketers think of these elements as being part of a broader ecosystem of their business, as being a combination of all relevant touch points that consumers can engage with when using the Internet. Today, the web is very much centered on the likes of Facebook, Twitter, YouTube and Tumblr. So what has changed? Consumers (users) took over the web and the Internet marketplace and moved from a model based on clicks to a model based on engagement, often referred to as fan based. Clicks are not the be all and end all for the advertiser. Today they want fans, they want to be followed, shared, mentioned; fans are the new click. A lot has changed since the introduction of the Web and Internet, including the way we communicate. Very few consumers are using traditional mail anymore. Email is easier and much quicker, with less formal writing. People are also using Facebook messages and a host of other digital mobile apps. The content business has undergone a major change, especially the music business, where CDs are fast becoming a thing of the past as consumers purchase music digitally.

Digital ecosystem is about how a marketer manages:

- Paid media i.e. print advertisements, radio, TV and online campaigns.
- Owned media i.e. website, Facebook page, mobile apps, storefronts, ad brochures.
- Earned media, including forums, social media and word of mouth.

The paid media involves prospects. The owned media involves customers and the earned media involves advocates. These are interrelated. Content is fed into marketers' owned platforms and distributed via paid and earned media; this can take place across many channels and should bring people back to the company's owned media platforms. Ecosystems are an interrelated web of owned platforms that collectively deliver the consumer a super service. To operate the ecosystem, understanding the audience and media channels is key to engaging with its customers. To recap, the trick for the marketer is to make the three layers work together. Use interactive marketing to lead the brand strategy and execution. This doesn't mean using one channel over another, it means organising all channels into a multilayered brand ecosystem. Engage the users with an owned media core, distribute the campaign via social and mobile media. Reach a broader audience using paid online and offline media.

Marketing communications has changed considerably.
In recent times marketing communications has changed considerably. Consumers now require greater choice, greater service and personal recognition in their business dealings. Newly introduced technologies examine and highlight the desires and needs of various markets and the personal shopping habits of individual consumers in great detail. As the media scene changes, advertising also changes and is becoming more interactive by going online. The marketing mix is expanding to include social media, which has become very prominent in marketing. At the same time, new tools have been developed to measure the results of the new media channels. The marketing paradigm has been changing and the traditional dividing lines between marketing organisations, advertising agencies and media companies are gradually changing. Today this change is referred to as the marketing and media ecosystem. When we examine the ecosystem and how the various marketing entities are adapting to the new era the results are interesting. It is obvious that marketers and advertisers appreciate the value of online activities. However, not every company possesses capabilities to prosper in the new ecosystem. It is essential that marketers, advertising agencies and media owners came together to develop strategies to deal with the new order of things. It is indeed an interesting time to be a marketer. It is a time where interesting platforms are being introduced to help capture consumer interests, providing marketers with new ways and means to communicate their brand messages and to

engage in interactive dialogues with customers in real time. As a result of this change companies have a greater grasp of the effects of targeted advertising.

Almost every industry is analysing and redefining its desired marketing mix. This change in marketing practice that the ecosystem brings with it in a much more competitive environment results in a situation where only the best get to the top. The social media ecosystem is all about the experience of the consumer when a company is able to secure reach, one-to-one relationships and dialogue through the integration of its marketing communications strategy, embracing the connection between online social media and traditional media practices. Some companies, however, make the mistake of looking at these media channels as if they are different platforms that work independently of each other. Instead, marketers should consider social media as a coordinated strategy that concentrates on the consumer's experiences but also acknowledge that Internet-focused media is not a replacement for traditional media.

As we have already seen, Internet-based media makes it possible for companies to change consumers from phase awareness to an engagement phase, ending with consumer loyalty. The great advantage of using social media is that it has the benefit of achieving consumer reach and engagement, while traditional media is really confined to consumer reach. Basically marketers require both individual and community platforms to create the environment for consumer attention and influence. The marketing process today is very different to some twenty years ago. Today the consumer takes a much more active role in the marketing process. Their views can influence the choice of brands developed by marketers. These views can be picked up by marketers in dialogue through company websites and in the 'comments' pages of newspapers and magazines. The information elicited can create ideas for new brand concepts and brand line extensions. Learning to understand the ecosystem is a novel but important skill in today's ever changing marketing environment.

The ecosystem is divided into three media segments:
- Owned media, controlled by the company website.
- Paid media, bought by the company through sponsorship advertising.
- Earned media, not controlled by the marketer, could be word of mouth.

The situation we now have is that although media channels transmit messages, the real power is with the consumers who engage in dialogue about a company's brand on the same channels. Companies have to appreciate this change and learn to use the multiple platforms and understand the different ways consumers behave in the various media. In other words, not all people who are part of the social media ecosystem interrelate in the same way and their actions can be open to interpretation. Increases in social media expenditure would suggest more and more companies are taking an interest in the social media phenomenon.

While many companies' marketing plans include the obvious Twitter, Facebook and YouTube, few fully understand and have a carefully thought-out approach to managing a proper social media strategy. Because of this, they tend to go for individual standalone platforms rather than going to the trouble of understanding a coordinated integrated social media plan. The concept of a social media ecosystem teaches a company to consider first its overall strategy. Using the ecosystem encourages marketers to ask fundamental questions. What is the target audience? Which social media platforms are relevant to them? What content does the company want to communicate? How can the marketer expand the content throughout the ecosystem? A fundamental step in the creation of a social media strategy is the social media ecosystem. This approach enables marketers to have a clear picture of how each media platform interacts with the others.

Five categories of social influences
As part of this approach there are Creators, Critics, Collections, Joiners, and Spectators. These categories help marketers to decide the sort of message that they need to focus on within the ecosystem. As we know, companies have for some time tried to identify and track core performance indicators available to measure the success or otherwise of a campaign. It is the same for social media strategy. Marketers should have this approach when using traditional metrics as a measurement of success. Companies using social media should concentrate on measuring downstream metrics like sales, increases in

brand acceptance and consumer involvement with it. The key issue is to agree the key outcomes with a specific ecosystem. The story could be about the introduction of a new brand or a new line extension. Like most communications strategies a company needs to be focused on the exact story it wishes to tell in the marketplace. An interesting aspect of the use of social media as a strategy is that marketing a reasonable campaign doesn't have to be expensive, unlike some tactical campaigns. Marketers can plan campaigns that do not require large media budgets or expensive creative development. This is closely connected to the need to analyse media in terms of what is already owned, what is free and what has to be paid for. If budgets are limited the company can concentrate on owned and free media. Social media is all about having a relationship with other users and is not about elaborate costly production values. Social media like Twitter, YouTube, Facebook and many others are frequently used. These platforms are not just about information but can influence people to relate to brand choice. Because of the amazing growth in popularity of these channels social media marketing is now considered as mandatory when managing a marketing campaign, bearing in mind that social media should be incorporated as part of a successful ecosystem where all elements can be marshalled to launch a new brand or update an existing one.

Chapter 27: Web analytics

What is web analytics?

Not too long ago, marketers had no idea who was visiting websites and why. Web administrators incorporated number counters on web pages so that the site owner could find out the number of times users clicked on a web page, or downloaded a particular file. That was all the information the company or individual had on the site visitor at that time. Today, things have changed.

Regardless of a company's requirements for its website it should be viewed as another important customer-focused medium that requires a significant investment to ensure it is working efficiently to maximise the company's business potential.

To ensure that the company is maximising its marketing budget it is important that it has a web analytics programme running on its home page and any other landing pages it may have. The role of web analytics is to help quantify the company's input and it will tell it how its website marketing campaign is delivering results against a set of key performance indicators (KPIs) that it will have set itself prior to the start of the campaign. Companies who are not used to web analytics can often find the term somewhat overwhelming in the beginning. After a while most companies, including those who would not regard themselves as tech savvy, will soon realise that the analytics concept is easy to understand and operate. Essentially web analytics is about the collection and measurement of data and reporting the behaviour of traffic visiting the company's website. The objective is to optimise the success of the website as a marketing tool. With web analytics a company can learn very useful information that will help it increase its e-commerce business, improve its brand awareness, and help find more 'leads' that it can turn into sales. Most importantly, it can accumulate relevant information about its customers and prospects. Today, a company has a wide range of web metric tracking and measurement tools to choose from. While some of these applications can be costly there are a number of free ones that can be very useful. More and more companies are using web analytics because they are more affordable and easier to use. A company can now gain important insights into what consumers like and dislike about its website so it can adapt its content to suit it site traffic.

Should a company pay for analytics?
The question of whether a company should pay for analytics will depend on a number of factors. There are free programmes like Google Analytics and Yahoo Web Analytics that are no problem to use and are free of charge. These tools are suited to small businesses and allow people who have no knowledge of web analytics to learn the game. These companies have the opportunity to experiment with tracking and reporting at no expense. Companies with a good knowledge of web analytics can invest in more elaborate system like Adobe Site Catalyst, WebTrends, ClickTrends and CoreMetrics. For these services companies can pay up front or monthly to suit their cash flows. These services can offer a more

sophisticated tracking and reporting which can be adapted to provide the information a marketer needs.

Considering a web analytics programme

The following list of metrics will provide a company with everything it needs to be aware of when considering a web analytics programme:

- Visitors: The number of users recorded will tell a company if it is well known amongst its target audience.
- Page Views: Will tell the company what content is working best.
- Referring Sites: Will give the company an idea of the type of people visiting the site.
- Bounce rate/Exit pages: Will tell the company why people are leaving the site without buying anything.
- Keywords and Phrases: Will tell the company what consumer terminology the prospects are using.

When a company starts a web analytics programme it could discover that it is getting many visitors but with no corresponding sales. Unfortunately, analytics will not tell the company what to change to get more visitors buying but it may give some clues as to what to change to improve the effectiveness of the site. If the company finds that the number of visitors is low, marketing may need to do something about promoting the site, possibly through PR activity or an advertising campaign. It may have to look at the content again for search engine optimisation. If a marketer notices a large number of visitors bouncing away from the site this may also indicate that the content is not catching on. Marketers may need to know if there is too much text and not enough graphics, photographs and videos to help increase interest levels. The marketer needs to check if the content is relevant to the brands being promoted. The text may need to be rewritten and visuals may need to be more appealing to make it more engaging for the visitors. The objective of the exercise is to give visitors relevant and persuasive information so that the visitor will add the brand to the checkout cart and complete the sale.

Unfortunately, analytics will not tell the company what to change to get more visitors buying but it may give some clues as to what to change to improve the effectiveness of the site. . Good content, easy to understand navigation with attractive design will impact favourably on the site's metrics. One important aspect of all of this is security. Because many visitors are experienced in online security it's important the company website gives them confidence in this crucial area. These visitors will look for certain signals that the site is security conscious. One way for a company to deal with this area is through the widely known security indicator, secure SocketLayer (SSL)[54] This secures the connection between the visitor's browser and the company website. Protecting the company website with an SSL certificate can be a very effective way to persuade visitors to remain on a site and complete their purchase. Many visitors may not fully realise that to get an SSL certificate companies have to undergo a strict vetting procedure to ensure the company in question is legitimate. Once a company incorporates SSL on its site business transactions between the company and it customers will be encrypted or scrambled so that the wrong people cannot intercept the data and steal it. Companies should let visitors know what SSL is about and make a virtue of it.

A word of caution!

There are a vast number of analytical tools that are available online. Many are free and offer to track or measure social media performance. Some marketers and academics will argue that the analytic capability these tools offer is limited. Before marketers consider the benefits of web analytics they should ask themselves what they want from a website or an app. They need to be able to answer this question clearly before considering the use of web analytics. Before consumers consider the benefits of web analytics to their purchase they should ask themselves what information are they giving up in order to receive the brand. Chances are they do not read the terms and conditions before they click the 'agree' or 'proceed' button, and therefore unknowingly give up a lot of information about themselves to a third party.

Web analytics is fast becoming an essential web optimisation tool for online business activity. By providing detailed consumer insights web analytics can assist the company improve the usability of the web and help keep improving sales and increase the company's ROI in the process.

Chapter 28: Mobile marketing

What is mobile marketing?

Simply put, mobile marketing is about the marketing interaction between companies and customers and prospects using a mobile device with various technologies to communicate by creating a connection between the company and its brands. There was a time when emarketing was seen as the cutting edge of marketing activity. It offered many benefits and had almost altered the existing make-up of traditional marketing and how sales and marketing-oriented companies practised it. With the explosion in the use of portable computing devices connectivity with consumers is now 24/7/365. Portable computing devices include tablets, laptops, portable media players and some other portable computing devices. A run-of-the-mill mobile phone can accommodate text messages; other devices can run additional programmes including mobile access, video messaging and have the capability of interacting with consumers or initiating advertising communications. The popular use of portable computing devices, especially tablets and smartphones, creates an amazing opportunity to devise new ways to communicate with people. Mobile marketing is now probably the most effective way for a company to increase its capabilities to retain its current customer base as well as attracting prospects and turning them into loyal customers.

A company with a clear and effective mobile marketing strategy will create a number of ways to communicate with its prospects and customers to move more brands There are many systems available in the marketplace. Apple (IOS), Google (Android), Microsoft, Windows and Blackberry are the main players; new ones are being developed as we speak. A mobile browser allows consumers to search on the Internet. There are many types to choose from depending on the device and operation system you want. There are several HTML compatible systems available such as iPhone (Safari), Android, Chromo, Opera, Nokia, and Blackberry. HTML5, which was updated in 2014, is a key technology for managing the structure and presentation of web content. Statcounter, an established web traffic analysis tool provider, carried out research in 2013 and estimated that 93%+ of searches made by mobiles use Google. The most popular categories installed are Google Maps, Facebook and the weather channel. The most used categories are news, maps, games, music and social networking. Almost every individual has a convenient mobile device which is used daily and is usually connected to the network it uses 24/7/365 and when not in use is usually in standby mode.

The big loser to mobile devices is the desktop computer. Studies carried out recently suggest that mobiles are overtaking desktop computers for online purchases. Tablet sales will soon overtake desktop computer sales. Time spent by consumers on mobile devices is growing at a phenomenal rate and will soon surpass the time spent with TV, radio and print media. People are using mobile devices to book theatre and cinema tickets, restaurant reservations, airline boarding passes and social media messaging. In the buying process, over 80% of people who have smartphones do their purchasing research on a portable computing device. Mobile electronic vouchers are being used at an ever-increasing rate and are expected to outgrow paper-based vouchers. Mobile devices are very flexible. A company can send reminders of special offers by SMS, or can tweet a voucher. It can use the normal text messages to communicate with its customers. It can get its customers to log in via Facebook or Twitter. A company can optimise its social media presence and launch a dedicated app, where the opportunities are limitless.

When a company is considering a mobile marketing strategy it will need to bear in mind that the mobile website is a very important tool in the mix. A company can consider many themes, website templates and content management systems that can improve the efficiency of mobile devices. A company can develop a range of landing pages depending on its requirements and whether access is achieved by using a mobile or desktop computing system to communicate varied messages to users. If it wishes, it can create an instant and direct interaction. It has a choice from a host of mobile messaging options to expand store traffic and increase sales, sending electronic vouchers to drive online or in-store sales. A company can use 'push' messages to give its customers something they will appreciate, including interesting content or brand offers, resulting in growth in its apps' usage. A company can increase its customer service by keeping its website visitors informed of what is of interest to them. It can send its customers special offers, rewards, and electronic vouchers to make them feel the company appreciates them.

A company can use SMS text messaging to promote its brands but it needs to be careful, as people do not generally like unsolicited messages. Texts should only be sent to customers and not prospects that they have no relationship with. The company and its brands need to be very obvious and up front from the start of the communication. It should be clear that the message is an advertisement and the receiver should easily understand it. A company can embed electronic vouchers in its SMS messaging using a system, which ensures what it is sending, can be traced and verified if necessary. The company should also be able to measure the results of the promotion.

A company can and should use opt-out facilities from its promotion. It needs to remember that it will be charged for the service irrespective of results in sales terms. It can use email as more and more consumers are accessing their emails on mobile devices. A company can use push messaging with a compatible app. It allows it to send brief personalised messages to its customers and prospects for very little cost. Subscription services enable companies to communicate with all their subscribers. This is usually done as an 'opt-in': the customer or prospect decides if they want to subscribe to the company's channel. A company can also expand its blog usage in this way with an RSS server. Any content can be sent by RSS, texts, videos links, images etc. Mobile devices incorporate

Twitter as a direct channel for a company to talk to its customers and prospects. Some communications can be planned to go viral.

One of the most used and popular download apps in the world is Facebook. It should be remembered that a 'like' is not necessarily a 'follower'. A 'like' is a very simple way for an individual or company to promote its web page or brand page, while a 'follower' works in the same way as Twitter. The recipient receives the company's message like a subscription service.

Mobile advertising is about the promotion of brands using mobile devices.

It uses advertising channels such as Google AdWords to reach a specific and predetermined target audience. Here the company cannot personalise its messages into a one-to-one style conversation like it can do with brief messages (SMS) depending on the channel it is using. The channel it uses can dictate the way the company's advertisement is presented. Usually a company has the option of running a pay per click (PPC) model or a cost per impression model and can agree a maximum daily budget, or a price per click cost. It should be the company's objective to change its banner advertisements frequently to achieve as many clicks as possible without affecting the price. It should remember that the higher the click rate the more often it will be shown. Companies will be aware that some people view the use of banner advertisements with some scepticism. However mobile advertising is not just about Google, a company has other mobile sites and app options to advertise its message, including for example the BBC range of apps covering news and sport.

Mobiles can deliver vouchers/ coupons online.
People who have mobiles can be alerted to use a coupon/voucher in a specific area when they are in the neighbourhood through apps like Passbook (iOS) and Passwallet (Android). Companies can use beevou.com to send electronic coupons/vouchers in Passbook format to consumers in much the same way as if they were sending an email message. A company can set up its own app and with a widget show its coupons/vouchers based on the global positioning system (GPS) location. One of the most effective tools in mobile marketing is electronic digital coupons/vouchers. This tool enables a company to issue coupons/vouchers electronically to consumers via SMS, email and Twitter. There are studies that show that electronic coupons/vouchers have a more successful redemption rate than paper ones. This is because customers can store the vouchers in their device, making them easily accessible.

The company can source a lot of information that can be useful in future marketing activities. Magnetic or smart cards support most loyalty programmes. The company can use loyalty plans to target individual customers under a number of headings: brands they purchase, dates of transactions, amounts they spend, etc. The advantage of loyalty programmes is that they can give the recipient a feeling of receiving preferential treatment. Cards are often used as a method of payment or as a private credit vehicle. Basically, customers use mobile devices as a loyalty card. Through mobile apps a company can use Passbook-enabled loyalty programmes. A company sends its customer base its digital card in Passbook format. Its loyalty card will be added to the other ones held by the customer. A company can utilise the system to remind customers of offers and to visit a store when out and about.

The use of games has given those involved in digital marketing a new set of marketing tools. Online and mobile games have become very popular. Games marketing can be used to deliver standard marketing objectives like raising awareness of a brand to drive brand loyalty. Basic mobile and online games enable marketers to engage consumers through owned gaming media where the major online games like Cityville and Farmville enable integration into successful existing platforms. While a company can use existing games or develop its own for marketing purposes, developing an exclusive game can be expensive. Usually it is more effective for a company to use an existing popular game to promote a brand or if it wishes it can advertise its brand on a series of games using one of the mobile systems available. It needs to ensure it keeps the videos short and sweet. A company needs to remember that video networks like YouTube and Vimeo can be used to connect with its customer base with interesting videos that may one day go viral and create a global reaction to a company and hopefully its brand.

A company can use customers' mobile devices to research their brands in real time.
Any problems encountered can also be dealt with in real time. Another interesting point is that research shows that the response to surveys is higher using mobile devices than traditional computing devices like desktops, or paper-based surveys. Surveys can be efficiently organised using SMS. The advantage of mobile is that questions can be quickly changed based on feedback in real time. A company can build its own apps to drive its Internet marketing programme. This will allow the company to develop a one-to-one relationship with its customers. Although mobile marketing is one of the more recent categories of digital marketing, as we have seen it has many of the elements of the older and historically proven methods. The rules that apply to mobile marketing also apply to the many other kinds of marketing communications models.

The benefits of mobile marketing:

- It is almost instant communication as people nearly always have their mobile phone with them during the day or when they retire at night. Messages can be received 24/7/365. If the consumer's mobile is on standby messages can be retrieved when the mobile is turned back on.
- It's easier to work with. Creating text, images or video content is easier to organise and cheaper to use in comparison with desktop or laptop computing devices.

- It's easily adaptable. Content can be suited to the smaller sizes of the mobile screens. Messages can be kept short and simple.
- It's a more consumer-friendly version of direct marketing. Companies can interact directly with consumers. It facilitates personalised communication. Companies can start a two-way communication with consumers, getting quick feedback using SMS. The users' responses can be monitored at the same time. This assists companies to study human behaviour first hand and use the information to improve their brand offerings.
- The system has a lot of viral opportunities because mobile content is easily shared amongst users. It would be normal for people to share good news with their friends and families, which benefits the company, with very little extra input.
- It's fast becoming a major source of total communications. Mobile marketing enables a company to achieve a bigger reach of its potential audience because of the growth of mobile phone ownership and usage.
- It allows marketers to gain access to people who live in the more remote areas of the world. Mobile marketing gives entrepreneurs the benefit of assessing people's location using GPS and Bluetooth technology.
- It's marvellous for blogging. People are using mobiles for blogging in greater numbers and are using various platforms, including the popular Twitter.

- It's excellent for paying bills from anywhere in the world. Consumers can be offered a safe and secure payment process to pay bills online. It means the user can get by without using physical currency every time they want to complete a purchase.

Drawbacks of mobile marketing:
- Mobiles do not have a general standard like PCs, Macs, and laptops do. They arrive in many forms, with a range of shapes and sizes. Mobiles use different browser and OS operating systems. Therefore, a marketer may have difficulty creating one campaign for all mobile consumers.
- Privacy online is a major issue. Companies need to be conscious of this and respect users' wishes. Therefore, they should only organise promotions when they get the users' permission.
- Navigation on a mobile can be a nuisance for the user due to the size of the screen and operating keys, even if the mobile has a touch screen facility. The downside is that they may not go to the trouble of viewing an advertisement due to the constraints.

Mobile marketing in a nutshell
Mobile marketing has the greatest potential of all the digital marketing tools available today. The growth of mobile has been extraordinary and demonstrates an unprecedented way in how people use media. Its growth has been so rapid that many marketers haven't really got up to speed on its many uses to maximise their marketing toolbox. A company can create mobile portals that can

aggregate content for various sources and can offer personalised services and content to targeted mobile users, including unified messaging, search facilities and directories. These portals can be dedicated to the company's brand, resulting in advertising to their most valuable customers with brand imagery, uploaded applications that can create further involvement with the brand and a host of other opportunities that create an exclusive brand message.

The technology chain is not complicated. The company is offered the opportunity through a mobile server to create a mobile brand. The new mobile brand communicates with loyal customers who have an affinity with the sponsoring company and the brand as well as gaining new audiences attracted by a simple value proposition and a better service at reduced prices. The outcome of this approach is greater relationships and brand new revenue opportunities. We now have a new generation of mobile devices, including the iPhone, with everything consumers could possibly need, including high-speed connectivity. Mobile marketing is really only in its infancy, with major opportunities ahead for marketers and their customers.

Chapter 29: Online communities from a business perspective

What is an online community?

It is a community of people that forms on the Internet. It consists of people who come together to share information to achieve a common goal. Those who wish to be a part of an online community usually have to become a member via a specific site.

Usually people converse in groups or on the telephone but online communities use social media such as Facebook, Twitter and Google+. They can also share information and engage with other people in chat rooms, forums, and email groups or in the 'comments' sections of blog posts or newspapers and magazines. Their conversations online tend to be about specific topics.

The marketer is interested in getting a community to discuss brands, and specifically the brands represented by the company. They can do this by promoting the brand on Facebook or YouTube. Online communities are seen as the ideal place to get a discussion going about a particular brand and get feedback, resulting in successful word-of-mouth activity.

Jenny Preece in her book *Online Communities*,[55] she describes online communities are individuals who collaborate socially as they endeavour to fulfil their own needs or perform special roles that give motivation to the group.

Developing an online community

Marketers interested in developing an online community to help promote their brands need to create a forum that is in line with the interests and social needs of the community. The main objective for the online community being set up is to be the focus for people who have similar interests and desires in life. People can have different uses for the online community idea, such as a diary to keep abreast of local events. Online communities can be interested in hobbies, or education development. Marketers will need to be aware of what makes people tick to be able to be relevant to their prospects' needs and get feedback to help them to adapt their brands and introduce new ones. Marketers need to be aware that online communities have become a major force for change in people's buying habits. The growth of online communities has changed the goalposts for marketers, forcing them to adjust their marketing strategies. This is because consumers are getting used to interacting and engaging in becoming more au fait with the different brand choices on the market. Marketers know they have to constantly monitor what is being said about their brands and make adjustments when necessary.

Creating a positive relationship between a company and the consumer is developing into a science with the growth of online communities. Most marketers know that this is a new market to be exploited when they get to understand how relationships are built in online communities. As we have seen, they encourage a person to participate around common interests that often includes brands. Shrewd marketers know that they have an opportunity to reach a new breed of consumers. Companies have the opportunity to connect with a new group of prospects to secure information about them. Marketers can find out a lot about consumers in their secure environment. To bond with consumers a company must seek to have an affinity with individuals and know how they interact with the online community that they are part of.

The use of online community software
There is a well-known maxim that it takes a company more time and expense to get new customers than it does to keep existing ones. It is in a company's interest to get to know its customer base in every possible way by building up a relationship with them online. Today, many companies use online community software to solve an array of business problems. Some larger organisations use local private networks to improve employee communication and increase efficiency. Others create online communities to create better customer engagement with their supply chain management of goods and services from the point of origin to the point of purchase by the consumer. Other companies create online communities to improve the management of their supply chain.

In recent times there is a new development called the management of 'customer communities', which are web-based gathering places organised by a company for its customers, experts in their field and employees to engage and collaborate on topics of mutual interest and post reviews. While these groups may have different agendas and responsibilities they can help the online community to bring more benefits to company brands through brainstorming new brand ideas. The information gathered in these discussions can benefit the company financially.

Online customer communities have made great headway in recent times.
This is mainly because of social media technologies, mobile devices and the Internet. These technologies have improved communication, making interaction with companies more efficient and faster. As a result, consumers now have more success when selecting their choice of brands. In the past, marketing-oriented companies commissioned research companies to help them get a take on consumer insight to guide their marketing strategy. Today, customer communities are fast becoming the trusted sources for more relevant consumer data delivered in real time. This is an example of the customer playing a major part in the development of company brands. As customers are permeating the company's business they are forcing the company to listen to their ideas and incorporate them in their strategic marketing planning. This is leading to greater collaboration between companies and consumers. Online customer communities are part of a company's customer relationship strategy and social media strategy. They can touch the sales, marketing, customer services, partner relations and brand management departments.
Since the tools, resources, and discussions are a benefit of doing business with a company, online customer

communities are 'gated' communities or private social networking platforms, where customers must log in to access the community. Most often, online customer communities are accessed through a single sign-on with the organisation's existing customer-facing systems. To paraphrase a commentary on Arthur Armstrong and John Hagel's article in *Harvard Business Review*,[56] 'The real value of online communities', published over twenty years ago, he said that by providing customers with the opportunity to engage with each other as with the company, organisations can foster deeper buying relationships by customising products and services to consumers' demands and interests. After twenty years, nothing has really changed in customer communities.

Chapter 30: The Internet, a force for good or evil, or both?

Who runs the Internet?

Some would say that the Internet and the digital world are a reflection of the real world that we live in. There is good and there is evil.

Who runs the Internet? No one organisation, but thousands and thousands of companies are involved in the running of it. It is organised as a decentralised network of networks, thousands of companies, universities and colleges and governments and other entities that operate their own resources and exchange traffic with each other based on voluntary interconnection agreements. The Internet Society is a worldwide organisation run by a board of trustees. Its aim is to ensure that the Internet continues to be upfront and honest in its communications with users, and is there to promote the well being of users worldwide. To help it achieve its objectives the Internet Society[57] set out its mission as follows:

- Facilitates open development of standards, protocols, administration, and the technical infrastructure of the Internet.
- Supports education in developing countries specifically, and wherever the need exists.
- Promotes professional development and builds community to foster participation and leadership in areas important to the evolution of the Internet.

- Provides reliable information about the Internet.
- Provides forums for discussion of issues that affect Internet evolution, development and use in technical, commercial, societal and other contexts.
- Fosters an environment for international cooperation, community, and a culture that enables self-governance to work.
- Serves as a focal point for cooperative efforts to promote the Internet as a positive tool to benefit all people throughout the world.
- Provides management and coordination for on-strategy initiatives and outreach efforts in humanitarian, educational, societal, and other contexts.

Ian Leslie and his book *Curious*[58]

The distinguished journalist Ian Leslie, states that our future depends on developing a deep curiosity about the world about us, and he is not talking about the Internet; far from it. He makes the point that while the Internet gives us deeper and faster access to more knowledge than ever before there is evidence that easy access to search engines is making people lazier, not smarter. It makes people less curious to develop fact into understanding. He goes on to say a person's life will become less stimulating and people will be less inclined to fulfil life's full potential both at work and at home. In the Internet age an amazing amount of data that is simply a click away is being created and disseminated and Leslie feels that due to this, individuals' philosophical comprehension of its results languishes a long way behind. He contends that there are two noteworthy classes of curiosity:

1. Diversive interest, the appreciation for everything novel, is shallow and effortlessly fulfilled. It's little more than what he portrays as "a brief fix for weariness" that can be discovered on the Web.
2. Epistemic interest, then again is a more profound craving to comprehend everything about a subject. It may take a lifetime to make a significant discovery.

It is clear that Leslie does not believe that the Internet alone can provide a stimulus to satisfy a person's curiosity. Epistemic curiosity depends on friction, on uncertainty, on being aware of our own ignorance. This is the very opposite of the quick fix, knowing everything from a visiting a search engine. This, he says, will not enable people to see life as a mystery to be patiently explored rather than accumulating a whole lot of facts and figures from the Internet. Leslie reminds us that being able to look up something on our iPhone doesn't make us smart. He refers to a question raised by someone on Reddit, a well-known entertainment, social networking and news website. To paraphrase the response to the question, on the off chance that somebody from the 1950s abruptly showed up today, what might be the most troublesome thing to disclose to him or her about today? The most prominent answer was that they would have a gadget in their pocket that was capable of accessing the whole of data known to man and is used to look at pictures.

However, the Internet, with all its information would not be of much use to a budding student of philosophy coping with the question, "Why is there something rather than nothing?"

Positive aspects of the Internet

- It is more convenient and easier to do personal or business research from the office or home using search engines as opposed to visiting libraries.
- It is easier and quicker to engage with business colleagues, family and friends.
- It can create opportunities to earn income by working from home.
- It can save money by cutting down on business and personal travel.
- Free emails can improve the efficiency of the workplace.
- It can be more convenient for shopping for goods that are not available locally.
- People can study for educational qualifications and have access to top university lecturers online.
- Social media can be used to get support for working causes.
- Companies can gather information about Internet users to fine-tune their digital marketing strategies.
- Forums on the Internet allow teachers ands students to discuss and share ideas on a host of topics.
- Message boards where people can discuss ideas on any topic and get a wide range of opinions. People

can find others that have similar interests.

- Broadcast news and analysis is available from a host of channels 24/7/365.
- People can take action and avoid potentially dangerous situations like hurricanes, storms and accidents.

Negative aspects of the Internet

- People can become addictive to gambling and games online.
- Pornography is very easy to access for all age groups.
- Illegal and inappropriate material can be accessed.
- It can result in people not meeting each other face to face.
- Can be a platform to share copyrighted or illegal material including music and videos.
- Can disturb peoples' privacy
- Can exploit peoples' privacy.
- The addiction to online social networks can disturb a person's way of living and professional activity.
- Criminals can use the Internet to spread computer viruses or intercept credit card or bank details for illegal purposes.
- Can make people vulnerable to criminals, stalkers and paedophiles.
- Terrorists can use it to spread their evil ideology. Recently it has been used to show public executions.
- Companies can be very vulnerable to negative

stories, some true, that appear online unanimously.
- It can promote and propagate misleading or false information.
- It cannot guarantee the accuracy of encyclopaedic sites.

Andrew Keen, an entrepreneur and well-known author, is well known for his very critical views of the Internet. He has written extensively on the Internet and questions whether it has lived up to its own espoused values. His book *The Digital Vertigo*[59] makes for interesting reading. He presents a damning indictment of the Internet and digital technology. He argues that it fails to deliver on its promises of creating greater democracy and openness. To paraphrase him, it hasn't changed the part of either influence or riches on the planet. Instead we are seeing a developing imbalance of riches and opportunity.
He is critical of the Internet because of its destructive impact on jobs, making the point that the private sector is employing fewer and fewer people. The new technology and the Internet impacts on profit margins by cutting out the middleman, as is the case in retail sales. The Internet is creating few new jobs. While Keen concedes that the Internet is not all bad news, in his view, the negatives outweigh the positives. He claims that at present the Internet is not an effective operating system for the twenty-first century. It is destroying the music and newspaper industries. Keen believes that most people do not fully understand what's happening in this space. The search engines are beginning to know more about people

than they know themselves and the significant thing is that people are giving this information for free while the search engines use it to benefit the effectiveness of the brands that are marketed on the Internet.

Max Du Preez, the South African writer[60]

Du Preez says that the world needs to be educated about what is good and what is evil on the Internet, which can be full of contradictions. He goes on to say that the Internet is the most exciting thing that has happened in his lifetime. It can save lives, can be used against tyranny. On the other hand it is unreliable, a vehicle to create hate and intolerance. He says he cannot see anyone controlling cyberspace but decent people can decide to use the Internet for the common good. He reminds us of a point made earlier, that it is important to realise that Internet data is generally untested for accuracy. It is important to remember that anyone can put what they wish on social media or on a website. The objective should be to discover, by trial and error if necessary, which sites have a history of authenticity and balance and if necessary to check out the established traditional media for confirmation of facts elicited online. Max du Preez says he avoids websites, even the major ones, where comments and discussions are not controlled by strict guidelines and where participants do not have to be vetted or register before engaging in debates and discussions.

Incapsula research study 2013[61]

Incapsula, a reputable website security company, presented a research study in late 2013 which makes interesting reading. It states that most Internet traffic happens between machines. In other words it's a bot – short for robot – not a person examining a web page and downloading data at a much faster rate than is possible by humans. When the 2013 report is compared with the 2012 one, it highlights a 21% rise in total bot traffic, accounting for 61.5% of website users. The major part of the growth is accounted for by increased visits by good bots, which are certified agents of legitimate software such as search engines, whose presence increased from 20% to 31% in 2013. Good bots are used as web spiders that move backwards and forwards over websites all over the Internet to collect and analyse information for the major search engines.

However, bots are also used for malicious purposes. What is interesting and alarming is that the survey shows that a staggering 31% of bots are still harmful, but there are fewer spammers about. Another interesting aspect of the 2013 study is the 8% increase in the action of other 'impersonators', a group that is made up of unclassified bots with unfriendly intentions. The common theme for this group was that people behind them were trying to steal someone else's identity. Unfriendly bots try to pass themselves off as legitimate search engines or agents of other legitimate services. The aim of these bots with unfriendly interests is to gain access surreptitiously by evading website security systems. "We now live in one world, one network, one technology," says Bruce Schneier, security technologist and chief technology officer of Co3 Systems, "which means we can't create technological systems that distinguish legality or morality.

What this means is that we need to choose between security and surveillance. Technologies can only be built that are secure for all users, or are vulnerable to all attackers."[62]

The number of people on the Internet worldwide continues to rise. The fact that websites allow individuals to secure information on almost any topic by simply tapping an image and the desire to share information with the whole world is truly amazing. But as we have seen it has its good and bad points. No matter what we think, however, the Internet is not going away.

Chapter 31: Big data

What is big data?

Big data is a popular term used to describe a huge volume of both structured and unstructured data, which traditional database tools cannot store, manage and analyse. Big data is changing the way business is done, is very relevant to digital marketing and impacts on everybody's lives. It could be as important to business and society as the Internet has become.

It leaves digital traces that people leave, which can be analysed by companies when planning marketing activity. There is an assumption that more data leads to more accurate analysis. While big data can tell a company what it is doing right it also helps companies understand which of its customers are unhappy with service, what has caused the dissatisfaction and which customers may change their purchasing arrangements. Billions of loosely structured bytes of data in different locations may need to be processed until the cause of a problem is found. This analysis enables management to address faulty processes or people and retain their 'at risk' customers. Big data technologies can do analysis much faster than traditional data warehousing approaches.

Although technologies and market conditions may cause big data content to vary from business to business, all companies using it are able to benefit from extracting value from data that would have previously been considered useless. It could be argued that big data is an extension of business intelligence, which transforms raw data into meaningful and useful information for business analysis. However, business intelligence is typified by what can be done with data that is understood and can be quantified, whereas big data uses unstructured and general data. By grouping these data sources, unidentified patterns, correlations and trends can be identified to help drive more effective marketing activities.

Historical background.

From the earliest forms of writing people have always gathered information in one way or another. The rise in technology led to the overflow of data that resulted eventually in more sophisticated storage systems. The first documented use of the term big data appeared in 1997 in a paper by scientists at Nasa.[63] In 2008, a number of American computer scientists popularised the term when they predicted that big data computing would transform the activities of companies. Although the term is contemporary, the foundations that it was built on were laid some time ago. Long before computers were commonplace the idea that an ever-increasing body of knowledge was being created was discussed by the academic world. The start of large data centres goes back to 1965 when the US Government planned the world's first data centre to store tax returns and fingerprints. In 1989, the writer Erik Larson in an article in Harper's magazine[64] referenced the term big data (without capitalisation). He wrote "the keeper of big data say they are doing it for consumers' benefit, but data has a way of being used for purposes other than originally intended"). Business Intelligence, a popular concept since the 50's saw a surge in popularity with the introduction of big data. In 1996, digital storage became more cost effective than paper. In 1999, the term big data appeared in an article titled "Visually exploring Gigabyte data sets in real time' published by the Association for Computing Machinery[65].It refers to storing large amounts of data with no way of adequately analysing it. Richard Hamming said 'The purpose of computing is insight not numbers'.[66] In 2007, the modern use of the expression big data emerged. In 2100 Eric Schmidt, of Google told a conference that as much data was being created every two days as was created from the beginning of human existence to 2003.What all this tells us is that big data is not new but that it is part of along evolution of capturing and using data. Big data brings change to the way businesses and societies are run.

Big data defined as the three V's
In 2001, Doug Laney, a research specialist, communicated the now mainstream definition of big data as the three V's of big data, volume, velocity and variety.[68]

- Volume: Very large data volumes measured in terabytes or petabytes
- Variety: Variety of structured, unstructured and semi-structured data
- Velocity: High velocity, rapidly changing data

How does big data work?
How it works is quite an interesting question and it really depends on the technology being used and what is trying

to be achieved through the use of big data. It is a concept that is applied to data that does not conform to the normal structure of a traditional database. It consists of different types of technologies that work together to achieve the end goal: extracting value from data that would have been previously considered useless.

Some of the key technologies / concepts associated with big data include Hadoop, HDFS, NoSQL, MapReduce, MongoDB, Cassandra, PIG, HIVE and HBase, and R. (See appendices).

Big data today

Today, big data generated at very high speeds involves information collected from millions of daily operations that support web retailers and service providers, sensor devices or streaming video from cameras on the go 24/7/365. As we have seen, big data is not a new thing, but its definitely a differentiating issue in today's businesses in order to gain competitive advantage The differentiation relates to getting the right information and relevant insights through analysis of volumes of data. In the digital era big data plays a much more significant role across most businesses as today's digital devices, social networks, mobiles and sensors captures enormous data. It very much about playing with data and gaining relevant insights.

Through Facebook, Twitter and Linkedin, mobile phones obtain user data from millions of people every day. Companies can now interact with their customers in real-time that was unheard of a few years ago. This data is time sensitive because it is filed as soon as it's created.

Big data analytics
Big data analytics gives companies the opportunity to find hidden patterns and relationships when sifting through large amounts of data. Unused data that would have previously been considered useless can now be considered, giving companies better information about their business. This results in companies being able to increase efficiency, enhance their marketing strategies and increase their bottom line in the long term. Big data analytics is better than conventional business intelligence programmes by enabling users to analyse larger files of unstructured data that is not normally used. A NoSQL database, often interpreted as 'not only SQL' provides a mechanism for storage and retrieval of unstructured data. In the past, Google, Facebook, Amazon and Linkedin dealing with the limitations of older database technology for use with modem web applications used the NoSQL database. Today, The Internet of Things and Cloud Computing are using it. This is because traditional data warehouses cannot cope with the huge amount of extra data being processed.

What are the benefits of big data?
The introduction of big data has given companies access to more data than ever before. In the past, unstructured data would be considered of no value, but with big data it can be collected and analysed to benefit companies. Big data gives companies the opportunity to discover data

correlations and patterns that before would have remained hidden. This allows companies to access more accurate information that can result in them making better business decisions.

Big data can provide benefits to a company by ensuring that it has as much data as possible before making important business decisions. The amount of data available through big data also enables marketing strategies to be improved and more accurately targeted. This can help companies to greatly increase its customer base, and push it ahead of the competition, leading to increased revenue by reducing its cost base and attracting more customers. In summary, the benefits of big data include, better focused data, better business decisions, improved marketing activity and increased revenue due to increased customer base and decreased costs.

Big data connecting with digital marketing

Digital marketing is going through the most significant developments it has ever encountered because of the dramatic expansion of accessible consumer data. Big data is a whole new ball game for digital marketers to discover new and valuable insights about consumers' lifestyles and buying activity. It also brings major challenges about how best to access, analyse, optimise and apply insights from big data. The insights derived from big data analytics will result in future decisions being more accurate, delivering the right message to the right person at the right time for the right price. As a result, intuition-driven marketing is on the decrease. Digital marketing and big data are becoming more interwoven. At the same time, digital marketers are dealing with newly empowered consumers. Today's customers and prospects have ready access to brand, price and quality comparisons from an increasing selection of channels. Digital marketers will have to engage with consumers using consistent relevant and focused content across diverse channels in real- time. Creating a positive consumer experience at the point of sale is a given in marketing. The growth in social media platforms allows consumers to express themselves in every conceivable way that generates an immense amount of data. Millions of consumers are speaking both to each other and directly to companies about what they want and how they feel about it. Success in digital marketing means tuning in to what interests consumers and using real-time content so they know that they are being listened to. Consumers are highly mobile with a choice of small screen devices that gives them uninterrupted access to continuous real-time communication. The growing competition among small screens will drive device prices down and usage up. The audience shift to online will not abate. Digital marketers must keep in touch with their audiences no matter where they go or what device they use. Tablets and smartphones enable consumers to focus in on precise local information about brands. Digital marketing can fulfill growing customer expectations in real- time with personally relevant message content. Moving away from the traditional large demographic approaches toward more data-driven, highly targeted campaigns becomes a necessity.

Key steps in the digital marketing big data journey

- Realise that the increasing amounts of consumer data is a core asset in its digital marketing future. If it doesn't, its more astute competitors will overtake it.

- Companies need to gain access to its own big data starting with a very basic analysis of the data it already owns but hasn't analysed can yield meaningful insights about its customers and prospects.

- Companies can then move to more advanced databased digital marketing which is all about customer engagement based upon elementary analysis and the insights gleaned, remembering that digital marketing lends itself to more accurate ROI measurement than any of the traditional approaches. A company's move into big data digital marketing relies on demonstrating ROI.

- Once a company has proven that small campaigns rooted in basic data analysis can be clearly correlated to improved ROI, it will be in a position exploit tools like data management platforms (DMPs) and demand side platforms (DSPs). These relatively inexpensive platforms dramatically increase a company's access to data using multiple channels providing better customer insights to create better-targeted campaigns.
- Companies eventually need to seek out and invest

in its own big data platform when it knows exactly what it wants from this platform and how much it is willing to invest to achieve its goals.

The bottom-line benefit of enhanced digital marketing
Companies would be well advised to take stock of the wealth of online consumer information that is readily available while developing highly targeted advertising campaigns to boost their business. In addition to profiling online users, big data can also be leveraged in a very pragmatic and operational way. There is no doubt it can make a major contribution to

Chapter 32: Forum marketing

What is it?

Forum marketing involves the use of public or private forums for companies or individuals to share views and knowledge to answer questions that visitors to a particular forum have. The objective can be to have a presence on as many forums as possible to generate traffic to the company's or individual's landing page and to create an online reputation by building trust with other members to the point that they may want to do business with the company or individual. Forum marketing can be appealing because it's free; time investment is all that is needed. The marketing scene has undergone a tremendous amount of change in the way companies and individuals perform day-to-day business transactions. The world is getting smaller due to the technology revolution, particularly the Internet. Technology has given companies a competitive edge in reaching out to customers and prospects. It has created a global village with quick and easy transactions being made irrespective of geographic location or time of day or night. These trends help companies and individuals manage business and marketing in particular.

One digital marketing strategy that is growing in importance is forum marketing. It gives an excellent return on investment because it can create an immediate impact with its first impression among influential and critical forum visitors. Creating a forum marketing strategy can be time consuming, but once successful the efforts are all worth it. A company needs to make sure it picks a good and reputable name and avatar (an icon representing it) for it to become acceptable so other users will notice it. Creating an impressive profile in terms of the company's expertise and experience helps in establishing an effective forum marketing strategy.

In essence, forum marketing is about a company or individual promoting its online business by the means of an online community i.e. a forum. It is a very simple concept. A company posts on forums and uses them to generate traffic, create leads, turn prospects into customers and increase sales via its signature link.

The importance of the signature link

All the good forums allow their users to have a forums signature at the bottom of each of their posts. The way that forums signatures operate depends on the forum. Some have a no-follow feature on links rendering them useless from a search engine ranking point of view. Other forums only show forums signatures to logged in members resulting in smaller audiences. There are four types of forum signatures[69]

- The **descriptive links** is a classic forum signature. It can have a number of links that can easily be easily identified and understood. If the links are on topic with the forum, this type will work well for a company. The problem is when links are not related and as forum visitors people can tell that they are not related, they have no reason to visit the links.

- The personal links forum signature is different to the descriptive links forum signature as it focuses more on the company or individual and not the links. If the website is good, a signature like this can give it more authority in a forum on the same topic.
- The mystery links signature is when a company is linking in a forum to a site that is not related to the current forum, which can at times bring positive results. A mystery link can appear on any site, it may take the browser to an online store, personal home page or similar.
- The graphic banner links are the most unpopular forum signature is the graphical banner due to its typical large size. A graphical banner should not be too high as this means that people have to scroll further to read the conversation.

When designing a forum signature it should be remembered that a badly spelt signature can reflect negatively on a company or individual. It shouldn't have anything too big. Readers can get frustrated if there are too many links, and they might feel that are dealing with a spammer; it also does not seem as professional as one simple link and a description.

The key to successful forum marketing is the forum signature.
A good forum signature will help forum visitors know who the company is and what it does. If written well, it will also motivate visitors to make contact which after all is

the object of forum marketing, it's important to avoid the following.

- Filling a signature line with multiple and irrelevant links will confuse forum visitors and could result in being banned from the forum, not to be recommended to reach the goal of building a business.
- Don't mix up personal and professional forum profiles. Links to a business blog needs to look professional.
- Be clear about the brand that is being sold, with no vagueness, in order to build trust.
- Avoid flashing graphics, they don't build trust in the business world and should not be used in a forum signature.

What should be included in a forum-marketing signature?

- Use a full professional name.

- A simple but concise few sentences will help fellow forum visitors know what the company or individual does and who they are.

- Link the main key word in the company profile to the site. It is more compelling than a link from a blog.

- An email address may be included, and select social network links. Direct links are fine for most sites, but email address should not have direct links.

- Use a professional photo, not too formal, but not to casual. Don't be too casual or readers won't trust the company.

- With a good forum signature the company will be well on the way to successful forum marketing.

Find the right marketing forums

Participating in online forums can be an effective way to get a business in front of the right audience. It can be one of the best forms of online marketing. One potential problem is that it's incredibly easy to get banned from using forums. The temptation with forums is that since they contain some of the most rich and targeted environments to market brands, companies may want to promote their brands actively from the word go and run the risk of being banned from forums

The first rule of online marketing is to not spam. These carefully built communities must be treated with the highest respect while companies are in their patch.

The question that a company should always ask itself when dealing with forums: "Is this good for the brand in the long run?"

When a company starts to think of its business as a brand, then it will begin to understand why spam hurts its ability to grow its business. Finding business forums is very easy. Type "business forums" into Google; by default, the first half a dozen forums will be the ones with the highest traffic. Check through posts to see if the replies are high quality. Forums that rank high in the search results have millions of posts, but can be full of spams and of low quality posts and should be avoided.

A company can pick a few popular brand types it sells and use those words in its forum search. Google are likely to come up with a number of popular forums related to the company's industry or niche. Before a company spends time setting up profiles in these forums it should make sure that they are active.

Once a company finds a forum that attracts its target audience, it should be prepared to go through a long initiation phase to become a part of the group. A company should leave all its salesperson enthusiasm behind and let the forum community transform the company. It should be prepared to give in to their culture and their way of doing things, and in the long run, this approach will lead naturally to the forum's choice of brands.

The process of joining forums

The process of going about joining forums starts with signing up to become a member. This is straightforward. Fill out a biography in "about me" section. Upload a real photo and do not put up links to the company's ecommerce website. Let the communities know that they are dealing with a real person. Then spend time reading the discussions that are happening on these forums, getting used to the community and take notes on what they like and what they don't like. The main point is to learn what makes the forum visitors tick, these are the company's future customers. Start helping people by responding to their questions. Provide information to raise the new member's profile in the forums but it is important not to push links to the company website at this stage. Once it is felt that real relationships have been developed with members of the communities the company can reveal itself by creating a signature that links back to the company website that can provide a way to solve problems for the community.

In most forums people who want to post have to register first by giving their name and email address, this will allow the company running the forum to follow up and email them in the future with information about its brands. At this stage, people won't consider it as spam because they know who the company is.

A forum allows a company to gain creditability with its websites visitors as it can reply to posts that are looking for help and by doing this its letting everyone know that it is an expert on the topic of the website. They're much more likely to buy from a company that appears to know what it is talking about.

Building relationships with visitors becomes easier with forums. If the company post regularly and actively discuss different topics with its forum visitors then gradually it will get to know them and more importantly they'll get to know the company. People are much more likely to buy a brand when someone they know sells or recommends it.

The downside of having a forum is that creating successful forums is not that easy, it involves a tremendous amount of work to get them started and up and running. Nobody likes to post on an empty forum so a company has to actively promote it and create lots of topics for discussion, if these topics are interesting then you should get a few replies, if they are not then it wont get any responses. A company has to do this self-posting on a continuous basis often for months, before its forums members post a steady flow of topics and replies.

That's only to get people talking. Next the company has to administer it or moderate discussions. This means making sure posts are appropriate and that members are not spamming its forum. This has to be done on a daily basis and if the forum gets busy it's going to be very time consuming.

With a glass half full approach, after the initial time involved starting a forum and the time it takes to get people to join in, the company will start to see the benefits that its forum is bringing. The time needed to maintain it will seem less onerous when the company sees traffic and profits increasing making its forum marketing activity all worth while.

Get and give feedback

Most business forums will include a feedback system. When a company sells it should get feedback. Don't let an opportunity pass without getting this vital information. If a company sells a brand it should ask for feedback and acknowledge same. It helps to establish itself as a reputable business. If someone is looking for brands from a company that they trust, they will approach it in preference to a new member with no reputation.

Chapter 33: Disruption in digital marketing

What is digital disruption?
Digital distribution creates a change in the value proposition of a brand due to the effects of adopting new digital technologies and business models brands. The value proposition is an expression that clearly identifies the benefits a customer will get when they purchase a particular brand. The emergence of the Internet and the worldwide web have changed the world we live in, how companies deal with their customers and prospects and how and why they purchase particular brands. Digital disruption emphasises the phenomenon that happens when consumers convert to
new technologies to enhance their lifestyles. Companies embrace digital disruption to promote their brands to consumers in a more enticing way in real time. Things are happening so fast that the new technology very much part of digital marketing is disrupting people's lives and the way companies do their business, usually more often for the common good. Companies that adapt will most likely increase their ROI, but companies that ignore marketing disruption can very easily lose their relevance to their customers and prospects.

The phenomenal increase in the use of mobile phone devices for work and personal use has given rise to digital disruptions across many companies and their respective industries. Significantly, digital disruption is changing how companies go about their business and particularly marketing.

Who and what has been disrupted?
Disruption can happen because of major changes to software and hardware used by companies in the short term. One thing, for sure is that many industries have changed how they operate including:

- The entertainment business
- Banking and Insurance
- Book shops
- Retail trade
- Computers
- Travel companies
- Newspapers and magazines
- Telecoms

In some of the above industries, companies are changing the way they do business in order to get a greater market share in today's digital environment. It has been clear for some time that companies of every description in disruption- affected industries as outlined the above examples need to re-engineer themselves to avail of potential opportunities in the marketplace They need to understand fully how purchase behaviour can be influenced by technological change, how many customers and prospects are empowered by the new technology and how purchase behaviour can adapt to thrive in the new connected world.

Although the web has only been with us for a few years, we have witnessed big companies come and go. We have seen new technologies disrupt existing ones: Take for example the world of publishing and printing, agricultural mechanisation, the telephone and the railways and not forgetting the Web itself. The pace of change seems to be increasing at a fast rate. Marketers from many business sectors today are feeling the effects of new technologies which are changing the way consumers buy brands so they have to adapt the way they sell brands to these end-users or run the risk of going out of business.

There will undoubtedly be the victors and the vanquished. We have vast number of online companies that are completely dependant on the Internet and the Web. They have to adapt to a fast changing environment in order to improve their lot and stay ahead of their competitors. An interesting question is whether companies like Facebook, Google, Apple and others will be so prominent in the years to come. Who knows? What is clear is that we are living in disrupted times. Companies need to focus on what they are about and what exactly they are offering consumers by using the new marketing channels to connect with their customers and prospects, resulting in greater ROI. They need to amass long-term connections using the new platforms not forgetting that the traditional offline media channels are still very much relevant and form a very important part of an integrated marketing strategy.

How does digital disruption affect businesses?

Technologies create changes in most facets of consumer behaviour through disruption activity. Because of this business models are being disrupted because of the impact of technology on society and companies are finding it more difficult to connect with more informed customers and prospects. The question is whether or not companies will choose to adapt or fall by the wayside. Currently several disruptive technologies are converging in real time with social media and mobile technology trends. The result of this is completely altering how people connect and communicate. Digital transformation is a result of companies seeking to adapt to the onslaught of disruptive technologies affecting customer and employee behaviour. As developments in technology become part of everyday life companies have to update their technology to keep pace with the real world. This activity is resulting in greater investment in technology and business models are effectively engaging digital-savvy customers and prospects at all the touch points in the company's purchasing funnel.

Disruption and the publishing industry

The publishing business is very traditional with its own way of doing things. It could be argued that as a result it eventually became inefficient. When you think about it, when people want to communicate a story they have to write it down on paper that then has to go through a long and tedious process before the book can be purchased and read by the customer. Amazon and Kobo marketing people realised this and came up with a solution to shorten the process, making it cheaper for the end user. This opened up the opportunity for people to self- publish

What tools and skills should every business have to accommodate disruption?

To get involved in digital disruption companies need to put the consumer at the centre of things and give them better value when they use the various digital tools and platforms. This requires everybody in the company to take ownership of digital as a major company philosophy. To do this effectively the company has to create more innovative ideas that customers will appreciate. Put simply, if a company doesn't do this someone else will and will use digital tools to take its customers and its business away. In the consumer environment people have the option of switching brands between competitors often at a lower cost. People can easily check out prices, look at the advertising and special promotions. The purchasing decision can be instant if they are walking through the aisle of a supermarket. The ultimate way to win customers is to put them at the centre of all marketing activity.

Is digital disruption an opportunity or threat?

Digital disruption is often portrayed as an obstacle or threat to established businesses and frequently seen as bringing about unwanted changes to our social lives. Indeed the term 'disruption' can carry with it a threatening connotation. As we know the introduction of the mp3 forever disrupted the music entertainment industry. The whole new ball game of online distribution is threatening the traditional retail outlets involving supermarkets and department stores. Consumers interested in domestic appliances can check out competitive brands online, make a decision and click the checkout button and wait for delivery details to know when the item will be delivered to the home at a convenient time with a minimum of fuss. While sometimes disruption can present challenges it creates opportunities to help companies introduce innovative new brands and enables companies to make more informed decisions about their brand purchasing activities.

Are companies ready for digital disruption?
Virtually every industry is feeling disruptive effects. The music entertainment and creative industries in particular have experienced disruption. The term disruption is nothing new. It was brought to our attention by Harvard Professor Clayton Christiansen in 1995 in the article 'Disruptive Technologies: Catching the Wave", and in more detail in his best-selling business book "The innovators dilemma'.
Disruption is effectively a more violent form of competitive innovation. What Christiansen called 'new market disruption' occurs when a new product meets a new customer need – or even better creates customer desire like Apple did with the iPod and iPhone.
What real disruption does is it forces consumers to ask the most primal questions about market places.

Planning for digital disruption

- Adopting digitally disruptive technologies and processes needs to have a considered approach covering detailed analysis of company's capacity for change.
- In better dialogue with its customers and getting its brands to the market in a faster and more efficient way.
- Digital disruption encourages a company to disrupt its way of doing things with its brands to create a more enjoyable customer experience
- Disruption is about improving the people in a company as well as improving or removing processes.
- Digital disruption can only work successfully in a company that is ready for ongoing change.
- Implementing digital technology is also not about replacing a company's workforce, but enabling them to develop their careers, using different skills and at the same time contribute to the company's profits.
- With customers at the centre of a company's activities the emphasis has moved to the technology savvy and more connected companies.
- The company needs to be one step ahead of its competitors to take advantage of digital disruption
- A company should continuously challenge its own processes.
- Always calculate return on technology decisions.
- Competitors shouldn't influence a company's direction with technology. It should decide what's

right for it.

- When it comes to being disruptive, size doesn't matter. Companies should disrupt themselves, step outside of their world, and question it.
- Companies should diversify and differentiate and eliminate fear.

Disruption is the norm today

The concept of 'digital disruption' was with us over 10 years ago when everyone became digital- minded. Today, we revolutionise our lives with technology innovation. Just as movies and TV were once referred to as colour or black and white, today there is no need to talk about anything being digital anymore because everything around us is digital. Disruption is now the norm so companies should assume digital and progress to innovation. This is where companies will have to compete for brand advantage. Digital innovation should be on the agenda of company board meetings to encourage management to start to manage it.

Apple successfully used disruption to reshape its industry

The first occasion was the introduction of the iPod which revolutionised portable music and started a whole new race for creating digital music players when companies were still creating portable CD players.

The second occasion was iTunes which revolutionised online music in an era when record labels were against putting anything online out of fear it would ruin their industry. The advent of iTunes was responsible for the digital music space succeeding and growing as quickly as it did.

The third occasion was the iPhone. Once again, phones were still rather simple and somewhat limited in their uses. Apple came along and created something visually pleasing that was easy to build on and didn't require Java. The iPhone spawned a whole new industry of powerful touchscreen phones and devices.

The fourth time was the iPad starting the tablets race. Before the iPad other companies tried to release their own tablet like devices, but they were crappy and didn't have the nice capacitive touch screen technology Apple already had in their iPhone. The iPad was a success and after it launched, every other company was making a tablet device as well.

Ten companies who enhanced their business with disruptive strategies

- Amazon: Brought shopping online in a major way.

- Starbucks: Redefined and created a successful coffee culture.

- Netflix: Changed the video rental market.

- Google Adsense: Changed advertising online.

- Facebook: Created the gold standard for social networking.

- Ebay: It's online auctions created thousands of online small businesses.

- LinkedIn: Changed business networking and recruiting.

- Monster.com: Brought job searching and resume posting online in a big way.

- Paypal: Redefined online payments for the masses.

- Virgin: Redefined the travelling experience.

A research perspective

According to a KPMG International Survey carried out in 2014 the majority of companies worry about digital disruption but few are ready to address it. Only 36 per cent of companies in the survey had a digital business strategy in place in one or more business units and only 8 per cent had one that was enterprise wide.

Companies that don't manage disruptive technologies stand to lose competitive ground. Disruptive technologies prominent today like social media, mobile, analytics and cloud computing are having an impact on the make up of brand offerings and markets and are changing how businesses are run. Amazon changed the game in retail shopping and Netflix changed how people view videos.

"While digital disruption may threaten current businesses, it also creates opportunities," says Mihai Rada, Director of KPMG Romania Technology, Media and Telecommunications (TMT)Services said that while digital disruption may threaten businesses it can also create opportunities He went on to say that organisations that don't dive in and embrace disruptive technologies can lose competitive ground may find it ever more difficult to catch up as technology advances.

Chapter 34: Sensory branding

What us it?

Sensory branding is about the use of stimuli such as scent, sight, sound, taste and touch to build a person's long-term emotional connection with a brand. It is based on the belief that consumers are more likely to engage emotionally with a brand when multiple senses are engaged. It creates an emotional association with customers by appealing to their senses in order to influence their feelings and behaviour. The belief is therefore that by appealing to people's senses the brand will be more successful from a commercial point of view. More and more companies are experimenting with new ways of reaching customers and prospects that are outside the more traditional methods of building a brand. Digital marketing is very much part of this new process. By using brand sensory attributes marketers are finding new and more effective ways to engage better with customers and prospects in their choice of brands. To do this effectively requires a lot of considered strategic thinking on the part of the company's marketing personnel. Sensory branding can be summed up as a way of using subconscious triggers that influence consumers in their choice of brands.

Types of sensory branding

Sensory branding is about exploiting all the five human senses.

Sight:
Visual communication is the most effective marketing tool that can precede all the other sensory communications. Companies using logos, images, fonts, colours schemes and themes to promote a brand are good examples.

Hearing:
Audio communications is the second most favourite sense used by companies because it is easy and convenient to use for various target audiences.

Smell:
This sense can be more responsive. Smell can be effective in reminding people of pleasant past experiences.

Taste:
The food industry in particular capitalises on the use of taste to build and promote a brand. Taste can be a powerful sense to use to sway a customer and create a habit.

Touch:
The feel or tactility of a product from a smartphone or tablet to the smooth touch of a fabric washed with a specific detergent is a major drive for many brand sales. Many people don't shop for some items online because they miss the tactility of a brand.

Sensory branding can help create more business

While companies obviously know how their brands look do they always know how the brand smells, tastes, feels and sounds? Simon Harrop in his book Brand Sense (source) explains why progressive companies are adopting a sensory approach to give their customers a new emotional feeling for their brands thus improving their bottom line and ROI. For many years marketers have regarded digital and discounting as the only way to sell to customers in difficult times. Many now know that it's important to consider an integrated sensory approach. In the past a company relied on pictures and words for its brand communication strategies. Today marketers realise that sense, smell, taste, touch and sound are processed differently in the consumer's brain. Taste and smell connect to that part of the brain that controls memories and emotions, whereas words and pictures are processed in the brain's cortex which controls a person's rational thought. As a result of this brands can tap into triggers that can prompt consumers o buy on impulse Brand benefits become apparent to consumers when sensory branding is combined with purchasing psychology. Harrop argues that the marketing of brands is at a crossroads. The new ball game is about creating emotionally compelling experiences for the consumer. Many of today's brands do not make it because some brands do not live up to what they are promising the customer. In reality it's only the more progressive companies with marketing expertise that create innovative brands that delight customers across all the senses. Today we live in a world of successful brands that work at an emotional level with customers and on the other hand there are brands that do not live up to the advertising hype and fail to convince customers to part with their hard earned cash.

The importance of sensory branding.

Sensory branding creates emotional and experiential associations with a brand We have seen that sensory branding is when a brand is able to appeal to all five human senses of sight, touch, sound, smell and taste, which enables people to "experience" a brand, ultimately leading to an emotional association and attachment to it. Originally, brands focused solely on visual appeal. The Coca Cola red and iconic glass bottle are instantly recognisable. Later famous people like Marilyn Monroe and Elvis Presley were photographed with the distinguished bottle, which brought happiness to teenagers by way of the brand's presence and sensory experience. Other brands like Shell, McDonald's and Michelin are examples of brands that are instantly recognisable. As TV advertisements became more popular, marketers began incorporating sounds and music in their imagery. Today, sensory branding extends beyond sound, such as Starbucks, which touches people across all five senses and leaves customers with a pleasant memory which enhances their overall brand experience.

Sensory branding influences brand perception

Branding is all about how a brand is positioned by the company and perceived in the mind of the consumer. This can be achieved by strategic thinking including positioning of the brand in the marketplace, creating its name and identity all of which tie together to create one consistent brand image. Sensor branding allows further reinforcement of the brand "perception". Good examples are: Singapore Airlines, Harley Davidson, Apple, Mercedes-Benz and Disney. These brands became icons by embracing sensory marketing techniques. In the case of Singapore Airlines that is often described as the definitive example of sensory branding in action has interesting cabin décor, which blends in with the flight attendants uniforms, their perfume and the scent on their hand towels all make up a very acceptable brand amongst discerning fliers.

Creating a sensory brand experience

For companies to create a successful brand it must continuously re-evaluate its customer's usage experiences from an emotional and rational level. It is now accepted that a brand will emerge and stand out when all the customers' senses are engaged. It is based on the obvious assumption that the most effective way to market a successful brand is to improve the customer experience on an ongoing basis. It is a fact that when customers are happy with a brand they will tell others resulting in word of mouth advertising, which is always desirable. The company will achieve brand loyalty that will help its ROI. An interesting question is what makes some brands memorable and others a failure. It is now believed that a brand makes an emotional impact with the customer when it entices and intrigues all of the customers' senses

Good examples are Apple, Guinness. Proctor & Gamble. Levis, Coca Cola and Pepsi etc. These brands are managed by professional marketing people who understand the importance of constantly changing their brand offerings so that they connect emotionally and rationally with its customers on an going basis

Process for developing a sensory brand profile.
Simon Harrop and Partners [70] have a very helpful and simple process, which includes a number of tools and frameworks for developing a sensory brand profile, summarized below.

Step 1.   Measure and understand the brand. Audit the current brand impact in all its facets

Step 2   Define the brand. What does it to stand for? How should it be different from the competition?

Step 3.   Create a sensory brand. Along with sensory experts start to capture and express these brand values as a five dimensional set of sensory expressions

Step 4.   Translate into a plan of action Map these expressions at all relevant 'touch-points' across the total consumer experience

Step 5.   Implement a programme. Get the best advice on how to apply these sensory brand assets to ensure the brand promise is totally consistent with the customer experience

Step 6.   Refresh when necessary. Periodically revisit and research the brand and sensory attributes to ensure they are still relevant and differentiated from the competition.

Sensory branding, what has the future in store?

We are emotional creatures and we create strong associations using our senses. What is becoming more and more popular is the way companies use the power of sensory impulses to advertise their brands. Companies realize that there is so much advertising and promotional clutter about that the average consumer is bombarded with many messages from the time they get up in the morning till they go to bed at night. Because of this the impact of sensory associations is becoming more and more crucial for companies. The bottom line is that the more senses are stimulated the better the customer brand experience will be. An important aspect of this is that because the influencing factors are often so subtle they can be more effective because consumers may not be aware that they are being influenced by a marketing message which they might normally resent as in the case of traditional advertising and more hard sell approaches

A good way to summarize the increasing importance of sense-based marketing would be to quote Aradhna Krishna, the author of Customer Sense: How the 5 Senses Influence Buying Behavior: [71]"In the past, communications with customers were essentially monologues—companies just talked at consumers. Then they evolved into dialogues, with customers providing feedback. Now they're becoming multidimensional conversations, with products finding their own voices and consumers responding viscerally and subconsciously to them."
So what is going to happen in the future? There is no doubt that sense-based marketing will be used more in the future as companies are finding to differentiate its brand based on visual appearance only. They have to investigate other means of getting its brands to rise above the clutter that's invading the marketplace. It is possible in the future that consumers will be so stimulated on multiple senses by brands that we will reach a state in which their brains will filter out most of it like they do today. Over the next decade we will witness giant shifts in the way consumers perceive brands and who knows what

new techniques will be available for marketers at that stage.

In future, if companies wish to engage consumers at an emotional level to help build loyalty and differentiate themselves from their competitors they will need to embrace the multisensory opportunities that are available to them

In the future, companies will need to take a more holistic view of the senses, consider the symbolism that they bring to human experience, and build brand experiences, which communicate and deliver consistently against the core values of a brand.

Over the next decade or so we will witness changes in the way we perceive brands, and in the ways in which they are presented to customers and prospects. your brand from a two-dimensional existence to five-dimensional life. To succeed with a sensory branding strategy, it is essential that companies do not jump in at the deep end by tweaking and adjusting the sound, smell and tactility of its brand without approaching the issue in a considered way. Companies need to carefully select the channels and the tools it plans

to use and the senses it intends to tap into. It's essential to be perfectly clear about the brand's core message at the start. The trick is not to change every sensory experience at once, but to optimise the brand in stages, sense by sense. Brand's sensory priorities will depend on the category of its brands. From experience it is clear that concentrating on sound, then smell, is more prudent, not only because sound is easy to ideal with, but also because sound is often under used. A company should review its website as well, does it include sound? and if not why not? It should use all opportunities to exploit sensory experience to match the brand's values. Companies should not be deterred by the costs associated with building sensory touch points. The investment in a sensory branding approach will pay off in the end.

Chapter 35: Multicultural marketing and targeting audiences

What is multicultural marketing?

Multicultural marketing (also known as ethnic marketing or cross-cultural marketing) is the practice of marketing to one or more audiences of a particular ethnicity, usually outside of a country's majority culture, which is often referred to as the main market. Multicultural marketing is interested in exploiting the ethnic group's cultural facets including its religious beliefs, its traditions, what it considers important and its language. Advertising is often produced in a particular group's native language and with other features that are specific to the targeted group.

The cost of not creating a considered multicultural marketing strategy can include major losses for businesses either through the misinterpretation of marketing communications and imagery, customer alienation or defection, short- term damage to a brand or worst of all the withdrawal of the brand from the market. Given that there is ethnic diversity worldwide it is imperative for marketers to fully understand the different cultures, how they deal with language and purchasing concepts and how to integrate variations into their traditional and digital marketing strategies and activities. An important point is that multicultural marketing is not different to other marketing concepts because marketers will still have to research, plan, develop and mount campaigns based on the feedback from their various audiences. What may be appealing to one culture may not be appealing to an other. In order to be sensitive to the various ethnic groups marketers should apply web survey technology to pre-test everything from overall messaging to creative layout in order to appeal to a variety of audiences.

Choosing the correct language

Language is just one part of the overall communication activities. When adaptations are required to facilitate cultural issues the marketer will start with things that can easily be achieved by surveying and pre-testing assumptions to better define and use the right mix of cultural options. These options could include something as simple as using multicultural faces in a campaign's photography in order to increase the rapport between the company and its audience or adjusting graphic presentation forms to increase the effectiveness of the company website. To get the upper hand in campaigns marketers must be alert to potential cultural differences to achieve a competitive edge and understand the cultural differences and lifestyle characteristics of the different ethnic groups in their market.

Language or dialect can be a barrier if the particular ethnic group does not understand what a particular brand is all about. Marketers need to conduct local background research for each market they plan to target and for every language they intend to use. Countries will have word meanings that are different from another. For example, there are many variations in the French language spoken in France, Belgium and Canada. Things are further exacerbated when working with the languages of the Middle East, Africa, and Asia and beyond. Never underestimate the importance of good local translation. Marketers should ensure that translation experts who understand how to write marketing copy do their translations; it is no longer enough to use native speakers or journalists. Today marketer need experienced multicultural trained copywriters to write campaigns. To be on the safe side campaigns should be pre tested in focus groups to make sure that they are culturally acceptable. Before spending time, money, and resources a company should make sure that it is in sync with its customers. It is better to leverage surveys and measure the effectiveness of their efforts prior to launching a major campaign. It may save money in the long term and save a brand from a multicultural mishap.

Considering the use of humour

An option for marketers is to consider using humour in its advertising campaigns. Using humour requires great care and sensitivity and is a particular challenge in multicultural marketing, because what might be considered very funny in one culture could be deeply offensive in another. It is relatively easy to use online surveys to pre-test offers and concepts in order to avoid any unpleasant surprises.

Thee effects of acculturation on marketing

The effects of acculturation, which is the process of adopting the cultural traits or social patterns of another group, are significant on marketing. Marketers should:

1.   Know what to say and find a focal point for their communications that resonates with the demographic they are dealing with.

2.   Know the audience, research is a critical part of multicultural marketing. Examine everything about the target group including income, education, media it is interested in and spending habits to make it easier to communicate with them.

3.   In terms of media interest, different cultures are loyal to different media programming. To successfully connect with a community, the marketer needs a campaign that reflects the demographic's nuances, and needs to know where they'll see and hear its communication.

4.   Create messages that are culturally relevant and sensitive. Respect the people who make up the target audience. Craft a campaign that reflects their values and beliefs

5.   The 2008 Barack Obama presidential campaign did a fantastic job of targeting multicultural communities through relevant and sensitive communication. Obama's people figured out how to connect in meaningful ways with people from various backgrounds.

6.   Some things are universal, though one particular culture might seem completely different from

another, everyone wants the same thing: value and quality they can afford. This should be kept in mind all the time.

Consumers' media behaviours may indeed be changing, but what about their response to advertising across these various media? Could imbalances in media consumption and advertising spend relate to advertising effectiveness? How do advertising media stack up against word-of-mouth, consumer reviews, and email marketing?

A total market approach
A total-market approach although well intended can be ambiguous when addressing multicultural groups. Combining different cultures into one message could be interpreted as a removal of personalisation, resulting in a failed attempt at reaching key target audiences.
The risk behind a total-market approach is its lack of focus. By combining a number of cultural segments into one message it lacks impact and falls between too many stools so that the different demographics cannot identify with the message and can feel that the message is not meant specifically for them. The communication leaves no one out which oddly enough can mean that no one feels part of the communication process. Marketers need to understand that while multicultural segments may remain the minority in certain markets, they can be a majority in other markets from a population and consumer-driven revenue perspective. Marketers need to recognise that new mainstream consumers are divided deeply by such

things as subculture, language and country of origin. Marketers need to accumulate a sophisticated level of data and analytics to connect with these consumers with messages presented in context that will catch their attention and appeal to them.

Multicultural consumers

Marketers should set up a team with knowledge of the customs and values of the various demographic groups they are trying to reach. It is important to understand that consumers of diverse cultural backgrounds respond better to messages that are interesting and culturally relevant. Consumers from some backgrounds are more loyal than those of other backgrounds and once a brand becomes a part of their lives, there is a very good chance they will remain loyal to a brand. Use the primary language of the target group. Remember a large percentage of the target audience is happier communicating in their primary language, even if they have skills in other languages. Use a spokesperson with good communication skills that is sensitive to the issues that are important to the audience.

Key strategies for targeting multicultural audiences using social media

For companies that are seeking ways to engage and connect with multicultural consumers and buyers, using social media is a proven successful strategy and tool. Using social media as a tool also requires a specific strategic process in order to implement the right tactics for engaging the targeted audience. Marketers seeking to reach ethnic minorities through social media must reinforce and connect with the culture of their target group with relevant content.

Identify Social Media Marketing Goals and Objectives
The use of social media networks can help with various tasks and goals. For a company those objectives can mean more avenues to reach consumers as well as offering a platform for specific targeted audiences. It is important to establish those business goals and objectives before promotion and advertising especially when targeting a multicultural audience, in order to achieve a more effective campaign.

A successful social media strategy requires a clear definition of objectives, a breakdown of the audience and a strategy to connect with them. Marketers need to assess the cultural materials that are directing the target audiences to social media. They need to establish why they are doing it- is it to talk about music or movies they have seen? and is it to keep in touch with family and friends overseas? What language are they using? By understanding all of this marketers will have a better chance of connecting with the target audience and joining the discussions. Building and creating conversations requires ongoing research and a comprehensive strategic plan.

Understand the cultural landscape
After deciding to target multicultural audiences and then defining marketing goals and objectives, it is important to

develop an understanding of the targeted cultures beyond the obvious areas like music, language and food. Using proper research to establish the online habits of the target audience and an understanding of the social media sites that are most popular is vital in understanding the full cultural landscape that the marketer is dealing with. It is vital for companies to realise that some consumers may move between different cultures from time to time, which may bring an additional need for greater research, and strategic marketing planning.

Mobile is important when dealing with multicultural audiences

Is it a fact that the ethnic minorities are leading the market in adopting the latest mobile devices. It has resulted in mobiles becoming a key component in successful multicultural campaigns. This is often referred to as mobile cultural advertising. Not all ethnic smartphone users will respond to the same advertisement. Nuances like generational differences, country of birth, and level of adopting cultural traits from another culture are also fundamental factors. It is consumer insights like these in all markets and the know-how to act on them that can be the difference between successful and unsuccessful campaigns. The great thing is that it's possible to reach these tech-literate populations wherever they go. Multicultural marketing is key to gaining brand success by identifying the right brand segments anywhere in the world.

Conclusion

To be successful it is important to know that multicultural awareness doesn't mean a marketer has to belong intimately to a particular culture or ethnic grouping. The marketer just needs to research and understand the relevant culture as they would any of the other issues that need consideration prior to making a strategic marketing decision. Enlisting the views of people from the relevant culture or ethnic grouping in the early stages of developing a marketing campaign can be a smart thing to do. This action, together with researching campaign proposals amongst focus groups from the relevant ethic community will go a long way to ensuring a successful marketing approach. It should always be borne in mind that ethnicity is just one of many factors that define consumers as humans and in some cases is not always the most relevant.

Many of the most well- known and successful and global companies like Pepsi, Coca Cola, Proctor & Gamble, Ford Motors, Disney and others have for many years successfully communicated with ethnic consumers worldwide.

Chapter 36: The business of podcasting

What is a Podcast?

What exactly is business podcasting as opposed to personal podcasting? why do people to listen to them? Podcasting in all its forms is simply broadcasting a voice recording for an audience to hear. It's like a radio show, but without all the expense. The word 'podcast' is simply made up of two words – iPod (as in Apple) and broadcast. A podcast is all about a company or individual reaching a specific target audience by recording a message using a microphone and recorder that will be of interest and hopefully will stimulate a series of discussions with the potential customer or community. From a business perspective podcasting is ideal for a company using traditional or digital marketing to entice more customers by giving them information that they will find of interest. Individuals interested in personal podcasting can discuss political, religious, or even entertainment topics with a wider audience.

As we have seen, a podcast is a recording, with good production values, of a voice message which can be done by a company and addressed to existing or potential customers who it would be hoped will become part of a loyal following. Businesses can also utilise podcasting when their audience has specific topics that they need information about. For instance a content marketer could do a podcast about how to write content that converts an audience to paying clients. Then, at the end of the podcast contact information can be given so that potentially interested customers can make contact about the brand being promoted.

A podcast can also be defined as a media file that is distributed over the Internet through making it available as a download on portable media players and personal computers. A podcast is different from direct streaming of content from a website because it is possible to download and store the content of a podcast for future use.

Distributing a podcast

A company can communicate a podcast or web video not only on its own website but can reach many more people by posting its podcast on the company's blog which can be uploaded to sites like You Tube, Hulu and Blip.TV. It should be remembered that podcasts are downloadable files.

When using podcasts:

- Quality content is vital. The marketer will want the brand to be represented well so podcasting can move the business forward.
- Successful podcasters say that frequency and consistency is advisable. Commit to a consistent schedule so the audience will know when to expect the programme.
- Record a few practice shows and post them as test or private on the company website to become

comfortable with the process.

- Repeatedly state the programmes's subject, who the company is and what is going to be provided and the context of each episode. Remember to include a call to action at the start or end of each episode, including the website and phone number.
- Podcasts can be used for communicating company activity, but delivering them requires planning and a regular time commitment.

Why Do People Make Podcasts?

Podcasting is an easy and powerful way to communicate ideas and messages. Companies can potentially reach anyone with a broadband connection who is searching for podcasts and subscribes to shows. People who start podcasts usually want to deliver their posts on a regular basis. There is very little equipment needed and start up costs are low and so this allows anyone to transmit their ideas far beyond the reach of a radio transmitter. Podcasters often start posts with the intention of building a loyal follower base by encouraging interaction with comments and feedback on their posts. People use web blog groups and forums to communicate with other listeners. Businesses are beginning to realise that podcasting is an inexpensive way to advertise to special interest groups. Nowadays, more companies post podcasts to have a dialogue with their customers and prospects as well as their own staff.

Benefits of podcasts

As a marketing tool audiences are highly targetable.

Podcasts can be created on any topic and are very useful as a niche-marketing tool. By focussing on a particular niche a company can understand the needs of the customer and adapt their brands in a way that appeals to them.

- It's also a very good way for companies to differentiate themselves from their competitors. Podcasting is a relatively new medium for companies to promote their brands.
- It represents an extremely efficient and effective way to communicate with not only customers but also with employees and investors. Podcasts are easy and convenient to download as they can be downloaded from the iTunes store or other markets places that are similar for example on Amazon.
- The great thing about podcasts is that they are convenient. They can be listen to at any time and any place, when people are on the go and even when they are in cars. People consume content in different ways. That's why it is important to get your content and brand out using multiple channels
- Some people prefer listening to content as opposed to reading it especially in the form of podcasts.
- Podcasts help to boost PR activities through placing the company in a position of authority.
- People start to see the company as being the expert in the field and, as a result, whenever journalists are looking for a comment about a particular story they are far more likely to approach the company.
- Podcasts are excellent tools at increasing podcasting content can give followers very helpful

information. By expanding their brand experience through relevant content the company can be perceived as helpful and more reputable. As a result there is an increase in customer loyalty.

- Many companies use podcasts to increase sales. This needs to be approached with sensitivity and taste. Followers may be reluctant to download a blatant promotional audio clip.
- If a podcast catches on it can be a medium to sell advertising and sponsorship. I certain cases it may charge people to download its posts but only if they are in high demand.
- Offering regular content helps build brand awareness and keeps people engaged with the company and its brand.
- A company can improve its brand awareness by integrating its podcasts into written blog posts to extend its content reach.
- The podcast can be shared through RSS feeds, emails and a blog, others can embed the link on their site resulting in the podcast being easily shared.
- Podcasting is an ideal way to promote a brand's unique selling proposition to customers and prospects.
- The sound of a human voice can communicate much more meaning through tone and inflection than the printed word ever can.
- Interviews with leaders in a particular niche will establish a company as a respected leader in its niche.

The characteristics of a good podcast and what to avoid:
The podcast should be high quality and provide information of value. It can include items of an educational, information and entertainment nature. By providing information that contains value companies can expand their customer base and keep listeners tuned in and coming back for more. As mentioned earlier, companies should try to avoid just broadcasting blatant advertisements, Although they can be useful in creating awareness, but this should be kept to a minimum, as customers may not be interested and this can possibly lead to subscribers being lost.

Advertising on Podcasts
A company doesn't have to develop a podcast of its own to be able to use them as a marketing tool. Advertising on podcasts, termed podvertising, is becoming more popular as podcast developers look to develop additional revenue streams and monetarise their listeners. Traditional broadcasting pushes its content to viewers, whereas podcasting is described as a pull medium, where users decide what they want to listen to when it suits them. This is welcomed by advertisers as listeners are voluntarily interacting more with the podcasts, thereby making them more receptive to relevant advertising messages. Podcasts audio advertisements tend to last in the region of between 10 and 30 seconds and can appear at the start, in the middle or at the end of the podcast. Advertisers will know that most podcast users are in the age range 25-35 which will have an impact on the type of advertising it attracts.

How does marketing with podcasts work?

We should think of podcasting as one of the digital marketing devices for a company to use. A company usually use its website, newsletters and emails to communicate brand messages to its target audience. However, there can be problems using these marketing channels. People don't always get emails due to overly aggressive spam filters. They may not come back and visit the company website, or read its newsletter. The point is that people have to make a real effort to read a brand's content. With podcasts people can stream the audio and listen to it while they are doing other things. More and more people are multitasking these days to use their time more effectively. Many people tend to prefer the added value of podcasts content, which can be precise and specific if done properly. The important point here is that podcasts have to be done properly with care and attention to detail. Just recording a podcast without any real thought or planning can be a disaster. The best podcasts include multiple episodes or installments and a summary of previous episodes can go down well with followers. Providing value added content is what a company should concentrate on. Podcasting is basically a communication tool, and the podcast is only as good as the content that is provided to the audience.. Once confined to audio only for play on iPods, many podcasts now have audio, video and interactive multimedia – played on mobile phones, tablets and laptops. Podcasts can fill many PR and marketing purposes. They can encourage customers to use a company's brands. Leveraging podcasting technology can give a company a marketing edge that will allow it to increase its online visibility and improve customer loyalty and eventually increase its ROI.

Guidelines for implementing a podcast successfully

- Review discussions on social media and blogs to discover what interests the audience. Develop profiles of typical listeners to create better podcast content.
- Share interesting information and enthusiasm for the topic in question. Do not risk alienating the audience by giving a sales pitch or reading from a script.
- Stay up to date with what the audience is discussing within the chosen topic area. Listening to the social conversations will help stimulate questions and future topics
- Check out the competition to differentiate the podcasts from comparable ones. Think of ways to improve on their format and provide a unique point of view.
- Length and frequency of podcasts are dependent on the time available so there is a need to be realistic about what can be achieved.
- Choose a format that's right for the company. This could be a discussion of current industry news and advice incorporating interviews with prominent industry leaders.
- Plan content to keep it dynamic and focused but not so tightly planned that the podcast sounds odd.

Writing a draft, as you would if you were giving a speech will guard against sounding like the script is being read.
- Include links to other resources that help listeners research the topic further.
- Be sure to provide real value in every episode/installment published. That way subscribers will continue to tune in and recommend the podcast to their own networks.

.

Podcasting and the future

Podcasting is probably the beginning of a new media content era that is empowering individuals with the ability to globally distribute their ideas and create a following of like-minded people. It will continue to impact traditional industries such as journalism, education and entertainment allowing people to freely create and distribute information in the years ahead.

Chapter 37: Defining the target market

Analysing and defining clearly the target market is critical

To build a solid foundation for a business, core potential customers or prospects must be identified to create an effective marketing plan to optimise the success of a brand. As economies can be fragile and fickle at times having a well-defined target market is more important than ever. No company can afford to target everybody in the marketplace. Interestingly, smaller companies can successfully compete with larger operations by targeting niche markets.

For a company to have a policy of targeting anyone interested in the brand is too general. On the other hand, targeting a specific market does not mean that the company has to exclude people that do not fit the criteria from purchasing the brand. Target marketing is about a company concentrating its marketing effort and brand message on a specific market that is more likely to buy than other markets. It is the sensible and more efficient way to appeal to prospects, resulting in a better ROI. When a company spends time analyzing and defining its target audience, it will be much easier to determine where and how to market company brands.

Issues to consider when deciding on the target market

- Analyse the company's current customer base

- Analyse the consumer problem that the brand is solving
- Determine the influencing factors relating to the target market
- Look internally at the company's set up to deal with customers
- Clarify what the brand offering is, including its competitors
- Analyse the company brand for possible improvements to retain target market
- How a company can improve the image of its brand
- What aspects of a brand help generate a strong sales potential?
- Choose specific demographics/ psychographics for target market
- Evaluate the decisions taken

Analysis of a company's current customer base

Who are the company's current customers, and why do they buy from it? Look for common characteristics and what appeals to them. Which of these customers use the brand more often? Can others with similar characteristics who are not customers be considered to sell more of the brand? A two-prong approach may be required to assess how the company's brand is viewed firstly by

- The trade (supermarket and retail buyers) who have the power to delist a brand at any time
- Their customers. This will require discussions with the trade buyers to establish how the brand stacks up against its competitors apart from price.

Secondly, it may be a good idea to carry out quantitative

research to do some number crunching to get a profile of users and non-users of the brand as well as qualitative research to gather key psychographics about users including personality type, preferences and expectations and influences and customer views on the company brand and those of competitors. The value of a customer to a company goes beyond the individual and extends to others who influence and are influenced by them: family, friends and co-workers can influence a customer's buying decisions. As part of this data- gathering exercise, the company should identify the retailers or individuals that form the chain of influence for each customer.

Prior to carrying out research a company can gauge whether it is adequately meeting its customers' needs by looking at a number of characteristics of typical contented customers.

- Contented customers will keep coming back to buy a company's brands and will be interested to see if there are other brands available from that company that they can try.
- Happy customers usually have few complaints. If they do have a problem, for example if a brand is out of stock they will enquire in a calm way and as long as they get a satisfactory explanation they will get on with things. A company needs to monitor customers who have regular complaints and deal with them in an efficient manner to get them back on side.
- One of the best marketing aids is word of mouth. If a company's existing customers are positive about a company's brand they will tell others about it. If this

is the case the company is in a good place.

- Happy customers will be pleased to ask the owner of the brand questions they may have on other issues.
- Happy customers can feel part of a company, which the company can nurture to create a long-term relationship with them to their mutual advantage.
- Happy customers will be more likely to complete company surveys and give feedback on it brand.
- Happy customers are more likely to trust a company that offers other brands accepting that it will be done in both their interests.
- Happy customers know that the company will solve any brand problems that they may have.
- In the end, happy customers will help a business grow.

Analysis of the consumer problem the brand is solving
In defining the target market for the brand proposition the company needs to reflect on the consumer opportunity that it is considering. Once the company has a good idea what this is, it can start to figure out who amongst the population is most likely to have a use for the brand. If it reflects its existing target assumptions well in good. If it doesn't it may have to tweak or revise its key target profile. It should start to list all the different types of customers that the brand will appeal to. When this is done the company can complete a profile of these customers, then group them by location, by market sector, and so on.

What are the influencing factors relating to target markets

- Determining a target market needs analysis to identify who is likely to want the company's brand enough to pay money for it. The target market, however, is also a target for competitors. This fact gives both suppliers and customers an advantage, and a competitive analysis of the target market needs to take this into account. Marketing guru Michael Porter came up with five factors, called the "five forces model," [72]which companies can use to help analyse the target market's make up.

- Entry by Competitors
  If the selection of the target market is right, the company will be able to see results very quickly because the brand will sell well. As soon as the market starts to buy the brand, however, the company risks a competitor entering the same marketplace to try to obtain some of the revenue. This is the risk of entry by competitors; a company creates or succeeds in a particular market because of its hard work, only to have someone else come along and take some of the business away from it.

- Rivalry between Competitors
  The intensity of the rivalry between competitors

can determine the future viability of the target market. If there are not many competitors and their brands are neither identical nor substitutes for one another, rivalry is likely to be less intense and the industry will be more disciplined. All the companies supplying the same target market will be able to conduct business and make a profit. If rivalry is more competitive, it can reduce profitability for everybody where some may fail.

- Buyer Bargaining Power
  The existence of competition in a target market creates buyer-bargaining power. Buyers have the most power when the market consists of mostly small competitors, the buyers purchase in large quantities, and the same or similar brands are available from all the suppliers at similar prices. These situations give buyers the power to force prices down and in some cases, to put supply companies out of   business.

- Supplier Bargaining Power
  The suppliers of raw materials from which a company makes its brands may also have power over a company, especially if it needs materials that are only available from a few sources. The supply companies know who the target market is and who the company's competitors are, and are in a position to squeeze the best prices by refusing to supply some companies. If a company is no longer able to supply its target market because it cannot

get parts or raw materials, or is unable to do it at the same price point as its competitors, that company could go out of business.

- Substitute Products
  If a target market has access to a substitute brand it may compromise the viability of a company. If the choice is much cheaper there could be less demand for the company's brand resulting in reduced profits.

Look internally at the company setup to deal with customers

One way of deciding on the right markets to pursue is to think about the company and its business. Does it have areas of expertise in particular markets? Does it have unique knowledge of a specific geographical area? Is it better at getting on with certain types of people? All these factors could help the company establish a particularly attractive offering.

Clarify what the brand offering is, including its competitors

Write out a list of each feature of the brand. Next to each feature, list the benefits it provides. Once the benefits are listed, make a list of people who have a need that these benefits fulfil. Who are the competitors targeting? Who are their current customers? Don't necessarily go after the same market. Consider a niche market that others are overlooking.

Analyse the company brand for possible improvement to retain the target market

It is a fact that well- managed brands last longer than badly managed brands. Continuous improvement can be an obvious way for a company to deliver on its brand. A marketer may use a number of things including colour, sound, images and memories to support values such as excitement, loyalty, pleasure, or prestige. Brands can't be decreed into existence just by putting a name on something. There has to be a well-defined target market as well as positioning. Doing what everybody else is doing is not the answer. Managing brand improvement never ends. Successful brand managers don't take the easy way out and realise that branding takes a lot of thought and continuous effort.

Developing a personality for a brand is important

The most successful brands, and those with the strongest growth potential, tend to have a clear, distinctive brand positioning based on emotional affinity as well as rational brand benefits. Technical innovation remains a powerful source for brand success, but improving the warmth of a brand's personality may also reap rewards. Finding measures, which relate to future market share is a goal of good brand management but is also a tough one since so many other factors can influence the future beyond the strength of a brand. If a brand is seen as uniquely possessing the attributes which make it distinctive it is much more likely to have stronger brand equity. But is it better to have a distinctive rational or emotional positioning? Variants of this debate have been around for years, and there is a strong argument for brands to adopt an emotional positioning in the face of own-label brands routinely copying the functional innovations of the major brands. Analysis shows that the strongest brands are strong on both rational product performance issues and on emotional appeal. This has substantial implications for marketing activity. Real product differentiation is still of huge significance, but it should be expressed with an emotional appeal. Advertising that communicates on both a rational and emotional level is more likely to generate a sales effect than advertising dependent on a rational or emotional strategy alone. Brands that have the potential for success will have a balanced representation in consumers' minds about what they are, what they do and how they are differentiated from the competition.

Choose specific demographics/psychographics for target market

The marketer should figure out not only who has a need for its brand but also who is most likely to buy it. It needs to consider the brand's demographics including age, location, gender, income, education, marital or family status, occupation and ethnic background. Psychographics are about the more personal make up of a person, including, personality, attitudes, values, interests/hobbies, lifestyles and behaviour. The marketer needs to determine how its brand will fit into its target's lifestyle. How and when will they use the brand? What features are most appealing to them? What media do they use for information?

Evaluate the decisions taken
Once a company has decided on a target market, it should consider:

- Are there enough people that fit the company's criteria?
- Will the target really benefit from the company's brand? Will they see a need for it?
- Does the company understand what drives its target to make decisions?
- Can they afford the brand?
- Can the company reach them with its message? Are they easily accessible?
- As a company can have more than one niche market, consider if the marketing message should be different for each niche market.
- Try searching online to research what others have done on the selected target. Search for magazine articles and blogs that talk about the target market.
- Ask current customers for feedback.

Conclusion
We have seen that defining a target market is the hard part. Once a company knows exactly who it is targeting, it makes the task of figuring out which media it can use to reach them much easier and what marketing messages will resonate with them resulting in greater sales for the brand and a better ROI.

Chapter 38: Getting found online

As we know the Internet has completely transformed the way people learn about and shop for brands. As recently as ten years ago, companies reached their consumers through TV and print advertising, as well as other traditional marketing methods. Many people start shopping by using search engines to surf the Web as well as using blogs and social media channels. To be competitive, company websites have to be easily found online by the consumers who may be doing a search for the type of brands that the company markets. Is your website getting found by consumers looking for your type of brand? This is one of the most talked- about topics amongst companies and individuals when considering their websites. While they concentrate on designing and fine-tuning content they are often at a loss as to how they can get prospects to visit their site. Their biggest challenge is to locate and increase traffic. Obviously, if a website isn't getting any traffic it will not generate any sales. Also, without the benefit of traffic a company cannot test if the key components of its website are maximising the sales process. The ever-increasing dominance of the Internet as a marketing channel has made many things including search engine optimisation a priority for businesses and individuals regardless of what they are selling or where their potential customers are located.

Good, effective website communication is key
Good communication starts with the website. This includes all types of websites regardless of whether it is an e-commerce website, a blog, a brand portfolio website, an information website for a service company, a local authority website or any other type of website, it is always essential to communicate effectively with visitors. Because of the significance of communication with visitors, it is an essential that the website designer and website owner are singing off the same hymn sheet. Unfortunately in some companies communication is often overlooked and plays second fiddle to the visual attractiveness of a website. Ideally, the design and other elements that make up the site's overall look should communicate a clear, unified message to visitors.

Start by evaluating your website's current set up
If your website isn't attracting visitors you need to find out why. Assess your site as objectively as possible. Things to consider:

- Avoid getting traffic from pages with too much repeat content, which Google may see as doorway pages. This approach can eventually have a negative effect on the website. On the other hand cleaning up duplicate content can improve visitor numbers and increase sales and ROI.

- Avoid poor quality on site content. Make sure your site does not have a lot of content that is not of much value. A good test would be to delete the nebulous content pages and see how that impacts the value of the site from a visitor's point of view.

- Are the majority of the site links mediocre?

- Check out the competition and the space they control. How do they go about getting found online?

- Check your current site architecture including your linking structure. Don't have pages with too many clicks from the home page.

- Make sure the titles are not too generic or don't accurately capture the content of the given page.

- Make sure every major topic of interest to the people looking for a brand like yours is covered.

- Check how long it take your website to load a complete page. The longer your site takes to load, the more visitors you will lose.

- When your website opens what grabs your attention on the page? Is it your logo? Your photo? A banner ad? Having the wrong element of your site as the focal point can distract people from the item you want them to take action on.

- Visual appeal is important. Recent studies have shown that the visual appeal of your site makes a measurable impact on its effectiveness. Remember people make a decision about whether or not they like your site within the first few seconds.

- Clear easy to understand content with good grammar is essential to appeal to visitors.

- How does your site compare to your competitors? What do they have that you haven't got?

- Ask the retailers what they think of your site.

- Include surveys on your site to encourage feedback from visitors that may give you pointers to help improve your overall website communication.

Monitor your competitors' activity online

- Set up a Google Alert[73] for your competitors and for any keywords that might be relevant to them. Incorporate the company name, but you could also include alerts for brand names, names of management team, etc and you will be notified as soon as they are mentioned in the media or online.
- Monitor your competition's posts on social media to gain insight into what they are concentrating on or if they are launching a new brand.
- Hubspot[74] has a competitive reporting tool that tells you how your competitors score when it comes to traffic ranking.
- Sign up for competitors' emails and keep abreast of what they are up to.
- Monitor competitors' websites to keep up to date

with their news and brand offerings.
- Use Google's keyword planner tool [75]and find out how you rank in comparison to your competitors and if necessary build a strategy to increase your keyword rankings.

Create a website with clear communication
First of all you need to decide on the correct amount of content to use. Too much information will more likely get in the way of good communication by cluttering the overall effect of the website and confuse visitors. The brand's core message should not be lost in a mass of unwanted information.

When a company is planning a website it needs to keep in mind that each visitor is unique and it is not possible to group them together as a smaller identity. A website needs to be created with a specific target in mind and within that target group there will be some diversity. What makes visitors different? A website can attract visitors from all over the world; people will come from different backgrounds and will have different characteristics, interests and reasons to visit a site; not all visitors ill have similar knowledge or experience of a brand. All of these features will have an effect on the communication between the visitor and the website. When a company is considering a website it should know exactly what needs to be communicated. While this will vary from one site to another the most basic message that needs to be communicated by all websites is its reason for existence. As visitors discover the website they should very quickly understand what the site is all about and what its core offering is. They should be able to discern if the brand offering is of interest to them through good communication.

If the opposite happens and a person visits a website that isn't clear about what it is communicating the result can lead to a visitor's frustration and lack of enthusiasm which will reduce the sites potential sales opportunities.

Ecommerce websites need to clearly communicate to visitors the type of brands they can purchase and the benefits to be gained as a result of such purchases.

Pointers for effective communication

Once you realise the importance of communication in creating a good website there are a number of ideas that can be of practical assistance in developing a site that communicates more effectively.

- Prioritise your message and be precise about what needs to be communicated clearly.
- Make sure your message is very difficult to miss
- Decide what visitors should know about the company and its brands
- Make your message simple and ensure excess copy is eliminated.
- Identify clearly the brand benefits that you want the visitor to learn about.
- The site should be an effective tool to brand the company
- Decide who is the most critical target audience to influence and to stimulate brand purchase.
- Use large text and eye-catching images to communicate the brand message clearly.
- Use headers to break up necessary detailed text.

- Help visitors to find out what they want to know by having good site structure and navigation aids.

Communication goals for creating a website

When a company is creating a website there are a number of objectives it should have to help with the site's overall communications.

- Make the core message appropriate and clear throughout the website
- The core message should be understood by visitors before the exit the website.
- All pages in website should be consistent and clearly understood.
- Make life easier for visitors to find what interests them.
- Text and visuals must be relevant to influence the target audience.
- Create interesting graphics to maximise the impact of the website message
- Make it easy for visitors to discover the brand's forte.
- Provide a resource for visitors to engage with the company and brand issues.

Results of Good Communication

Websites that achieve effective communication with visitors benefit in several ways.

- A website cannot function successfully if it doesn't have clear and persuasive communication.
- Effective communication will improve the company's branding objectives and it own

corporate image in the eyes of the visitors.

- Good communication will help make the site more user friendly and keep visitors on the site longer by viewing more pages.
- Bad communication will frustrate visitors and make them less likely to purchase a brand.
- Good communication is essential to create trust and encourage greater engagement with visitors.

Other suggestions to get found online

- Use search engines to get free traffic.
- Offer free content to other websites to publicise your website.
- Use viral marketing to get free word of mouth publicity.
- Arrange free links on other websites with similar target markets.
- Use email marketing to attract repeat visitors.
- Make your content a 'must read' for your target market.
- Use Google Adwords to promote the site.
- Use social media channels.
- Check out SEO.
- Offer to do a 'guest' blog on a reputable site.
- Create referral traffic.
- Post content to LinkedIn.
- Include video in content strategy.
- Do interviews and post them on the site.
- Consider a rich media approach.
- Consider press releases.

- Consider using 'slide share' and Scribd.
- Add social buttons to site.
- Consider a podcast.
- Use YouTube.
- Suggest to visitors that they share the site with their friends.
- Comment on other websites.

One last but important point

Make sure your site is mobile friendly. More and more searches are taking place on mobile devices of one sort or another and people are using the mobile Internet as their first and more often their only means of going online. It is therefore important for you to use software so that your site automatically detects a mobile browser and can send visitors to a mobile section of your site, which should have a mobile- friendly condensed version of your message for them to engage with.

Chapter 39: Crowdsourcing issues in digital marketing

What is crowdsourcing?

There are a number of explanations and definitions for crowdsourcing.

- It's all about a company getting assistance to implement marketing activity by soliciting contributions from a large group of people and especially from the online community rather than from traditional employees or suppliers.

- Crowdsourcing is gathering collective intelligence from the public and using that information to complete business-related tasks. The company or a third-party service provider normally completes these tasks, but through crowdsourcing the public assists in the completion of them. Crowdsourcing appeals to companies because it expands their talent pool and is often free.

- Crowdsourcing is a linguistic mashup of "crowd" and "sourcing." It means tapping a "crowd" of people to do "sourcing" of work or to collectively contribute to any kind of project.

Examples of crowdsourcing in action
For a number of years students at the University of Austin have been crowdsourcing solutions through the Dell Social Innovation Challenge programme. [76] This project encourages students to think about and come up with practical ideas that can have world changing possibilities. Ideas are voted by members and visitors through the programme website and the students whose ideas are selected win money prizes in return for their efforts. One such winning project was centred on the idea of using old tyres to make rubber shoes for people in need.
Unilever through its 'Open Innovation' programme [77] uses crowdsourcing to encourage people to come up with new designs or technology that can help it grow its business and solve the challenges that it has set itself. Unilever is constantly looking for new ways to work with potential partners through 'Open Innovation.' It will often have specific challenges on where it welcomes collaboration from people outside the company relating to new product formulas, new technologies, new packaging or a fresh design solution to a product that it has in mind. Unilever basically wants to work with partners to solve essential challenges and to make the world and its business better. The term crowdsourcing was first coined in 2006 by Wired magazine author Jeff Howe in an article titled "The Rise of Crowdsourcing." [78] Howe argued that crowdsourcing influences the best-qualified and most creative participants to join in on a project. Despite the rather

informal name, crowdsourcing is a very real and important business tactic. The task of crowdsourcing is to avail of the collective talents of the general public to assist in the development and completion of business-oriented tasks that a company could do in house or outsource to an external resource. Interestingly, the free labour aspect is a very small part of the appeal of crowdsourcing. What is more significant is that it allows marketers to expand the size of their talent pool while also gaining deeper insight into what customers need or desire.

Until social media changed the way companies market their brands consumers were rarely asked to take an active role in the marketing process. In recent times more companies are involved in crowd marketing programmes. A marketer considering crowdsourcing needs to know everything about the 'crowd' and how it can be used most effectively.

Very simply, the 'crowd' is anybody who wishes to provide a service to a company by working on any project being undertaken by that company. Small to medium sized businesses tend to take advantage of it because they lack in-house resources. Crowd sourcing can be the fastest and cheapest way to fulfill a need. Handled efficiently it's a marketing tool to help solve business problems by taking a deep dive into the heart of what are often complex marketing issues.

Who can use crowdsourcing?
Start-ups and established companies big and small, corporate groups, government bodies, non-profit organisations, individuals; in other words almost anyone

who needs resource engagement and ideas.

When to use crowdsourcing

- When you need knowledge and information.
- When you need to improve decision-making.
- When you need funding support.
- When you need to create great ideas.
- When you need opinions.
- When you need support for a cause.
- When you need an objective view of a business.

Ways to implement crowdsourcing

While crowd sourcing can be very worthwhile it can be difficult to implement particularly in smaller companies. It takes both time and money to do well and smaller companies with fewer customers than the bigger companies may find it difficult to get enough meaningful responses. The process should be:

- First of all talk to your existing customers. They will be familiar with your brands and may have very relevant things to say in response to your questions.
- Implement a cohesive crowdsourcing strategy by using all existing communication channels including PR, social media, **website and emails etc.**
- If you've talked to your existing customers through all the appropriate communication channels and you still can't find what you're looking for, as a last resort you should consider looking at dedicated crowdsourcing platforms including Amazon

Mechanical Turk to source small repetitive tasks, and UsabilityHub to test design and layouts among others.

- Utilising your current employee workforce to get feedback on PPC advertisements and landing pages before pushing them live is another important aspect of crowd marketing campaigns. It's smart to get input from other people as to what could be added to a landing page to help them convert at a higher rate for example.

Advantages of crowdsourcing
- Costs less money and time than investing in an expensive R&D department or hiring consultants.
- Very little overhead costs involved.
- The tasks can be outsourced using online crowdsourcing sites to organise the project and recruit interested members.
- Using Facebook or Twitter for crowdsourcing can be free and effective.
- Crowdsourcing engages customers and can build their loyalty to a brand.
- The company can retain the best people for their next project.
- Companies get a large number of applicants to choose from.

Disadvantages of crowdsourcing
- Participants can dispute the ownership of the information gathered.
- You may have no say over the quality of all the

participants, you can get good and bad responses.
- Less talented participants can piggyback on the more talented ones.
- Often difficult to deal efficiently with a great number of people over a short period.
- Disgruntled participants can post bad reviews of the project.

What is crowdsourcing best suited for?
- To perform simple tasks like getting feedback on a website design or a new brand logo before going public with it.
- Holding a competition on a crowdsourcing site to target ideas for a website or logo design.
- You can build a list of photos of competing brands or advertising campaigns from various markets.
- Creating an online shopping website where crowdsourcing can be used to tag and catalogue inventories.
- It can be used as a translation resource like Facebook and Wikipedia do.

Suggestions for using crowdsourcing
Once a company has defined the issue in question and agreed the amount of money it is prepared to spend for it these suggestions may be useful.
- Be very precise. Make it very clear what you expect from the people who are participating. Avoid ambiguous and open-ended questions.
- Be reasonable with what you pay people. If the task is complex and accuracy is essential pay

accordingly.

- Have some system to verify the results of the feedback. Remember when you outsource to a large number of people from different backgrounds the results can vary greatly.
- Evaluate your options carefully before you decide what needs to be done.
- Consider using dedicated crowdsourcing services for issues like usability testing etc.

The better-known crowdsourcing sites

There are a number of sites that involve the response of a crowd to help individuals and companies to deal with a host of tasks from designing a logo to some of the more involved management issues. The following are some of the better-known sites.

Freelancer.com[79]

The site claims that it is the world's largest outsourcing marketplace. It says just post any online project you want done, and one of its 15.8 million freelancers will do it at a fraction of the cost. You post a project you want done, compare and select bidders and you pay when you are satisfied with the final result.

Elance[80]

The site says that Elance is where businesses go to find, hire, collaborate with and pay leading freelancers from more than 180 countries. With a community of over 3 million freelancers and 1 million businesses, it's easy to hire a top freelancer. Find a developer, freelance designers or other talented freelancers with the most in-demand skills. This includes talented application developers, software engineers, testers, network administrators, web designers, graphic designers, copywriters, market researchers, SEO experts, data analysts, social media marketers, translators, customer service agents and moderators.

Upwork[81]

The site says it's a platform for connecting businesses with talented professionals. It accelerates hiring, making it easier for freelancers to update their availability and for companies to find, interview and select freelancers who are ready to work right away. A new messaging experience includes chat and video, where a company plugs into its favourite services, and organises conversations into chat rooms. Companies can communicate with their teams through native Android and iPhone apps. Shared team workspaces will make it easier for multiple freelancers and clients to engage with each other. Businesses can create and engage large freelance teams quickly and safely.

Crowdsite[82]

Launched in 2009 in the Netherlands the site says it is one of the biggest crowdsourcing design marketplace in Europe. More than 50,000 users worldwide work with Crowdsite. The website helps small businesses, start-ups and other organisations with logo, web, template and other graphic design projects.

CrowdFlower[83]
It was founded in 2007 to manage Internet crowdsourcing. It is one of the biggest providers of crowdsourcing solutions for enterprise with over 450 million tasks completed and 2 million contributors.

Some earlier instances of crowdsourcing

- It is said that the earliest record of crowdsourcing is the collection of words for the Oxford Dictionary in 1888 when 800 people were contracted to supply words to be considered for inclusion in the final dictionary which took over 70 years to complete.

- In 1936, Toyota was looking for a new logo and used crowdsourcing to come up with suggestions. Some 26,000 responded and the chosen design didn't change until 1989.

- In 2001 Wikipedia built an encyclopedia using crowdsourcing.

- The Galaxy Zoo Interactive project used crowdsourcing resulting in users participating in a large-scale project of galactic research, which classified millions of galaxies found in the Sloan Digital Sky survey.

- The americanairmuseum.com site states that crowdsources organised information about the men and women of the US Army Air Forces who served from the UK in the Second World War and the British civilians they came into contact with. It collects photographs and information. It was launched in October 2014.

- In 2013, the Chicago History Museum launched a project requesting people to give them ideas for an exhibition it was planning. The American Alliance of Museums claims this was the first crowdsourcing project allowing the public to take part in an exhibition assignment to an American museum.

Summing up

R&D has always been about innovation but in this context the conventional R&D model can be replaced by crowdsourcing, a whole new approach that looks outside the company for new brand ideas. Crowdsourcing is about getting ideas and information by asking a large group of people, usually online, to cultivate ideas as opposed to using traditional methods. Companies are using crowds for more and more tasks from increasing sales to designing advertising campaigns.

The big difference today is that due to major developments in robot technology companies can enlist greater numbers of non technical people to do more complex and creative tasks at a significant lower cost. Crowdsourcing can therefore improve productivity and creativity while minimising labour and research expenses. As we have seen crowdsourcing is not new. However feedback from an active and passionate community of customers can reduce the amount of time spent collecting data through formal focus groups, while also creating enthusiasm for upcoming brands. By involving customers in brand development processes, managers can reduce both staffing costs and the risks associated with uncertain marketplace demand. Taking advantage of the crowd is an efficient, cost- effective approach to a number of different marketing strategies and problems. More and more marketers will have to be convinced to start using the crowd as part of their digital marketing strategies.

Chapter 40: The future of the Internet

It's crystal ball time.

We have seen how the Internet and the World Wide Web have developed since their inception. It's time to review the predictions that are being made about the future of the Internet. At the time of writing this book, two powerful and influential business people, Sir Richard Branson and Elon Musk,[84] announced they were backing competing networks to introduce Internet access to those people who hadn't got it. This covered all third world countries and non-urban areas in developed. Greg Wyler[85], ex Google, stated that his organisation, One Web, was planning to create a micro-satellite network. He secured an investment from Branson and Qualcomm, a California-based global semiconductor company that specialise in wireless telecommunications products and services. Elon Musk stated that his Seattle headquarters were going to concentrate on developing advanced micro-satellites to introduce the Internet to those who didn't have it.

Wyler's goal was to build a network of 648 small satellites, weighing approximately 285 lbs each. The plan was to put the satellites in orbit approximately 750 miles above the earth. It was estimated that each satellite would cost $350,000. Wyler also indicated that Virgin's Space division would also launch satellites. Musk, an experienced space business operator, was starting from scratch in the area of worldwide Internet services. Musk stated that he planned to launch 700 satellites, 250 lbs each, also orbiting the Earth at 750 miles above. Musk[63] said that the long haul potential is to be the essential method for long-remove Internet movement and to serve individuals in scantily populated areas.

It was reported that Musk's business venture would be much more expensive, possibly around $10 billion. It was estimated that it would take around five years to become operational. Some media have suggested that both parties working together rather than separately would be more effective in creating a comprehensive network in a better time frame. However, it works out today there are in excess of over a billion people using the Internet, which is set to spread widely throughout the world. It will provide connectivity almost anywhere in the world. With the advance of wireless technology it is estimated that the number of people with access to the Internet will increase to over four billion in a few years' time. In the future, local groups will operate in virtual space and will exploit well-used communication systems like mailing lists and websites. As a result of this, towns, villages and cities will become more organised and empowered.

The future of Internet wireless communications is mainly about faster wireless facilities. With wireless frequencies there are practically no start-up or maintenance costs. It gives people the opportunity to become mobile. In the future, wireless will create increasingly faster services. The Internet will become more and more part and parcel of phones, television, home appliances and many other devices. People will be able to take advantage of wireless from anywhere on the Internet. People may ask will the Web exist as it is today or will we have a more modern version? In the future, almost everything will be connected to the Internet and emerging virtual technologies will be an everyday experience. It could well be that some time in the future people will be able to do things that seem like science fiction to us now. A possibility will be that companies will be able to hold meetings with people around the world using holographic technology.

The Pew Research Centre Research Report [86]

The Pew Research Centre asked some 3000 Internet experts and scholars questions about how they see it developing in the future. To paraphrase some of the key points from the research report:

- The Internet will become like electricity, always there but less visible.
- The Internet of Things will expand and will make computers behave like humans.
- In the next ten years, many people will want Internet technology to enhance their working and personal lifestyles.
- The Internet will transform human activities like working and learning.

- People will learn a great deal more about themselves and other people from the Internet.
- Routine daily tasks will be taken over by robots, changing the nature of work and home life.
- People will communicate with each other using holograms and take virtual tours of the planet around them.
- The problem of privacy could get worse. The emerging digital world will accumulate more personal data about people.
- A danger that governments may react to the growth of the Internet by changing it into a mass of different networks.
- The majority of people favour a more open Internet based on net neutrality principles but have a fear that powerful corporations may mess things up.

Jonathan Strickland's viewpoint[87]
A senior writer with 'howstuffworks' on technology matters has written extensively about the future of the Internet. To paraphrase his predictions:
- Data transmission speeds will increase around the world.
- At some point, people will download high-definition movies in seconds.
- Play cloud-based video games will have no lag or buffering.
- Portable devices like smartphones, laptops and tablets will continue to grow in popularity.

- The Internet will be faster and more pervasive.

Strickland lets us know that a fight has been brewing over Internet fairness. It can be a controversial theme and a dispute has been simmering for as far back as a quarter century. Internet fairness is an umbrella term for many concepts. It relates to the view that Internet administration suppliers ought to incorporate access to all applications independent of the source without favouring or blocking particular brands or sites. One of the principles is that everyone ought to be in a position to get to everything on the Internet equally. There are Internet Service Providers (ISPs) that don't put stock in this reasoning on the grounds that it may give them less control over their own particular administrations. If an ISP had the capacity to manage content suppliers it would have the capacity to give special treatment to its partners. The destinations individuals can visit depend entirely on the ISP they have. In a few business sectors, they may not even have a choice of ISP; one organisation may dominate the neighbourhood market. This flies in the face of Internet fairness.

Could the Internet of the future affect the way humans think?

On the Internet we have almost unlimited access to information on a vast range of topics. The question is, does the availability of information affect the need to do our own thinking? The fact is that to a large extent we depend on an inanimate object, the Internet, to satisfy our need for information. It doesn't follow, however, that the process makes us less intelligent. What will not change in the future is that information will not equate with intelligence. A person may be able to look up a fact on the Internet but it doesn't follow that the person actually understands what the fact means or its context. It is generally accepted that the Internet is a tool to assist us with learning but it doesn't replace learning itself. It is hoped that the Internet will help people to understand other cultures, to learn from each other, possibly driving people closer, resulting in a more understanding and peaceful world. Sharing of information over the Internet will be so effortlessly interwoven into daily life that it will become invisible, flowing like electricity.

Predictions found online, where else?
Finally, in true Internet fashion I used Google to find out some predictions for the Internet of the future. Here's what I found:

- The growing dominance of the Internet will improve the lives of a lot of people connected to it, resulting in better relationships among societies.
- The Internet of Things, making computers behave like humans, will make people more conscious of their surroundings and how other people behave.
- The Internet will result in an improved version of virtual reality to duplicate the world around us in computers.
- Wearable devices will monitor and give us quicker feedback on our lifestyles and health.

- People will be more politically aware, resulting in a combination of peaceful experiences and public insurrections like the Arab Spring.
- The Internet will become "the Internets" as access, systems and principles are renegotiated.
- The Internet will continue to promote and expand free education among more people in more remote areas worldwide.
- The Internet will create greater divisions between the haves and have nots, which may result in resentment and physical force being used to cause damage to peoples' properties.
- People who advocate violence will have more opportunities using the Internet to make life unbearable for some.
- Governments will come under pressure to bring in legislation to deal with offensive behaviour.
- People will continue to favour greater convenience as a trade off for less privacy.
- There will be significant changes created by communication networks, which will tend to be more disruptive.
- We will see more sensors attached to produces that we use daily that will tell us when they need to be replaced.
- Remote-controlled apps will allow people to monitor household appliances and activate things like running a bath or preheating an oven.
- Sensors and GPS will take over the control of traffic flows in cities.

- The Web will run out of IP addresses, new conventions will be required.
- Software will continue to move from the hard drive onto the network.
- Mobile devices will turn into fully-fledged computers.
- Advances in nanotechnology will mean that sensors can be embedded in anything.
- The Internet of Things will expand in a major way in the years ahead.
- The arrival of mostly US companies like Netflix into European markets will continue to put pressure on traditional media companies.
- Everything we encounter in our daily lives will be connected in some way.
- Voice and touch interfaces will continue to grow.
- Brain- to -network connection is still a long way off.
- Banks will offer more sophisticated services online, with very little personal interface.
- The European Commission will bring in new proposals to tackle illegal content on the Internet and a tightening up ecommerce rules to give consumers better protection when shopping online.
- We could end up living in a world where everything is online and where many things may stop working and nobody will know how get them working again.
- Or, the Internet just won't exist.

Appendices: Social media platform options

The following is a list of the more popular social media platforms used by companies as part of their marketing activities.

Facebook for Business
Running a marketing campaign on Facebook can be a successful and efficient way to increase sales for a business online. A company can decide on the target consumers that it wants to reach, the budget it wants to spend and at the same time it can track the consumers' reaction to its advertising campaigns. Using this platform, a company can try and get Facebook users to make a purchase, ask for more information or make an appointment. The company can check daily if the target market is responding to its advertising campaign and if not it can change the message to make it more appealing. Worldwide there are 1.39 billion monthly active Facebook users. In Europe over 223 million people are on Facebook, 53% of users are female, 47% are male; 16 million local business pages were created as of May 2013.

A Facebook page will give the company an online presence and a way for it to engage and connect with people of a certain age group in specific geographic locations at home and abroad. More on www.facebook.com/business

LinkedIn Business Solutions
A company can accurately target members on LinkedIn with display advertising
that will help it to engage with the world's largest professional audiences. It can drive brand awareness and keep the company on prospects' minds when they go online to ensure its brands stay top of mind. It can target just the right people to increase brand awareness with those who matter most.
LinkedIn has a niche network of 280 million people, who tend to be older and well educated. A company can get its content in front of its target audience with display advertisements and targeted text advertisements. A company can also track the impact of its display advertisements through built-in campaign and website analytics. https://business.linkedin.com/marketing-solutions/company

Pinterest Marketing
Pinterest lets businesses create pages to promote their brands online. These pages can be a virtual storefront. Brand studies show that Pinterest is effective at driving sales and its business pages can include interesting content, including information about company brands. A company can create a 'board' that will communicate its

core values and highlight the company's employee's biographies. It can monitor when it's getting the most likes, comments and referral traffic by regularly analysing both its Pinterest profile and its site traffic stats. It can check out visitor responses on different days of the week and times of day to maximize traffic and audience engagement. The company can allow its best customers to join in on certain 'boards' and make suggestions about how to use the company brands. Pinterest is prominent in social media circles and has become a proven source of traffic for blogs and websites.

A company can use this platform to achieve better customer engagement and help create an appealing brand. It has around 70 million followers, mainly females and mostly in the US, although it is growing considerably in Europe. More details are available on www.pinterest.com

YouTube Marketing

YouTube can help a company to market its business and is a particularly useful marketing platform for small to medium-sized businesses. YouTube is basically about traffic and conversions and works for every type of business, turning traffic into leads and hopefully sales. First and foremost, a company about to use YouTube should establish clear, realistic and achievable goals and then put a plan together to achieve those goals. How does a company successfully market its business on the world's largest video platform and major search engine? YouTube is evolving from a video-based to a channels-based site based on subscriptions. If a company sets up its own channel it's branding will work across all screens, it can turn non-subscribers into loyal fans, and it can show off more of its video content.

Gone are the days when YouTube was exclusively a place for one-hit, user-generated viral videos. The company needs to keep in mind that YouTube is a social network and therefore it is essential that it interacts and engages with its community. Just as a company may thank its readers for comments on its blog, it should apply the same strategy to its viewers on YouTube. Unlike a blog, however, with video, viewers can see and hear what the company has to say, and that establishes a much deeper connection. More on www.youtube.com

Instagram Marketing

Instagram is an interesting way for companies to connect with customers and prospects. There are over 130 million active users on Instagram every month and every day 1 billion+ photos are 'liked'. Using the app correctly, a company could have an instant viral marketing success. Using Instagram a company can tell a visual story about its brand, instantly engage with its followers wherever they are, and even get very real user-generated content through photo contests on the app.

It's easy to set up a business account on Instagram to include an attractive branded photo, a short informative biography and a link to the company website. The account should be connected to both Facebook and Instagram, owned by Facebook. These two very powerful social media sites can help boost the company's marketing efforts.

Making an Instagram tab on the Facebook page will enable the company to instantly share its Instagram photos with its Facebook Fans. A company can keep its Instagram content strategy focused on the brand's unique way of seeing the world. More on https://instagram.com

Google+ Business Solutions

A company can use Google+ to promote its corporate and brand imagery online. To start the process it can customise its page by including the company's name and brands. It can give visitors a comprehensive company profile in the 'about' section and include its website for consumers to find the company across Google, which has published a set of guidelines setting out how a company can use the Google name, logos, icons and language in its marketing activity. The company can put its business on Google Search and Maps. It will give customers and prospects the right information at the right time, whether that is giving driving directions to its place of business in Maps, hours of operation in Search or a phone number they can click to call the company on mobile devices. With AdWords the company can move into advertisements, try new search terms, pause its campaign or restart whenever it likes. It can advertise locally or globally. It can show advertisements to customers and prospects in cities, regions or countries or within a set distance from its company's place of business. It can track and measure advertising and establish how many people notice the advertisements and what percentage click, visit or call. The company can customise its email. Google can synchronise the whole thing with phones and tablets for accessing on the go with 24/7/356 support. Google My Business has many interesting features that companies can use to help build a loyal fan base. More on https://plus.google.com

Twitter and Business

The biggest characteristic of Twitter as a social network lies in its 140-character tweet limit. The updates that are posted are short and clear. While Twitter does offer visual content options, text-based posts are used more often and include links to external websites.

If a company is trying to reach a broad audience that's receptive to marketing messages, Twitter is an option. A recent survey suggested that about 39% of people indicated that they'd rather hear from companies on Twitter than on any other social platform. Twitter currently claims around 650 million users worldwide, and their updates amount to 58 million new tweets per day. Twitter users are more likely to be active on their mobile device than on their PC or Mac, so companies should think of it as a real "on the go" network. An important thing to take into account is that the average lifespan of a tweet is extremely short, so a company needs to be able to post quite frequently – without, of course, spamming its audience – to increase its visibility.

One of the most valuable things that Twitter offers to business owners is the ability to search for keywords that are related to them and track people's conversations. This gives it insights into the way its audience interacts with similar businesses and allows it to improve the content of its tweets. More on https:// twitter.com

Glossary
Definition of terms used in book

Data
Facts and statistics collected together for reference or analysis.

Demographics
Studies of a population based on factors such as age, race, sex, economic status, level of education, income level and employment, among others.

Digital Asset
Any digital material owned by an enterprise or individual including text, graphics, audio, video and animations.

Digitalisation
Digitization is the process of converting information into a digital format and the integration of digital technologies into everyday life by the digitization of everything that can be digitized.

DRM
Short for digital rights management, a system for protecting the copyrights of data circulated via the Internet or other digital media by enabling secure distribution.

Ecommerce
Commercial transactions conducted electronically on the Internet.

EDI
Can be formally defined as the transfer of structured data, by agreed message standards, from one computer system to another without human intervention.

Encryption
The translation of data into a secret code. Encryption is probably the most effective way to achieve data security.

Forum
A public place or opportunity for discussing a subject of interest.

FTP
Short for File Transfer Protocol, the protocol for exchanging files over the Internet.

Going Viral

The spreading of information and opinions about anything from person to person, especially on the Internet or in emails.

Hashtag
A word or phrase preceded by a hash sign (#), used on social media sites such as Twitter to identify messages on a specific topic.

Hyperlink
A link from a hypertext document to another location, activated by clicking on a highlighted word or image.

HTTP
HyperText Transfer Protocol (HTTP) is the underlying protocol used by the World Wide Web to define how messages are formatted and transmitted.

IaaS
Infrastructure as a Service (IaaS) is a form of cloud computing that provides virtualized computing resources over the Internet.

Infographics
A visual representation of information or data, e.g. as a chart or diagram.

IOS
An operating system used for mobile devices manufactured by Apple Inc.

ISP

Short for Internet Service Provider, it refers to a company that provides Internet services, including personal and business access to the Internet.

JIT

'Just In Time' An inventory strategy companies employ to increase efficiency and decrease waste by receiving goods only as they are.

Keyword

A word that serves as a key, as to the meaning of another word, a sentence, passage, or the like.

Landing page

A web page which serves as the entry point for a website or a particular section of a website.

Link

Links from a hypertext file to another location or file; typically activated by clicking on a highlighted word or icon.

Metadata

A set of data that describes and gives information about other data.

Microblog

A social media site to which a user makes short, frequent posts.

Offline

Not controlled by or directly connected to a computer or the Internet.

Online

Controlled by or connected to a computer.

Platform

A platform is an underlying computer system on which application programs can run.

ORM

Object-relational mapping (ORM) is a programming technique in which a metadata descriptor is used to connect object code to a relational database.

Page title tags

Title tags are technically called title elements and define the title of a document. Title tags are often used on search engine results pages (SERPs) to display preview snippets for a given page, and are important both for SEO and social sharing.

Personas

In user centered design and marketing, personas are fictional characters created to help the team have a shared understanding of the real target market makeup.

Podcast

A digital audio file made available on the Internet for downloading to a computer or portable media player, typically available as a series, new instalments of which can be received by subscribers automatically.

PPC
Pay per click also called cost per click, is an internet advertising model used to ... It is defined simply as "the amount spent to get an advertisement clicked.

Protocols
A set of rules governing the exchange or transmission of data between devices.

Pull marketing
Is an approach designed to draw customers to a brand through SEO and other non-intrusive methods.

Push marketing
A push promotional strategy involves taking the product directly to the customer via whatever means, ensuring the customer is aware of your brand at the point of purchase.

Purchasing funnel
Explains the theoretical path a customer follows while deciding whether to make a purchase

Psychographics
The study and classification of people according to their attitudes, aspirations, and other psychological criteria, especially in market research.

Real-time

The actual time during which a process or event occurs.

ROI
Return On Investment, a performance measure used to evaluate the efficiency of an investment.

RSS Feed
A user that can read RSS-distributed content can use the content on a different site. Syndicated content can include data such as news feeds

SaaS
Software as a Service (SaaS) is a software delivery method that provides access to software and its functions remotely as a Web-based service.

SEO
Search engine optimization is the practice of manipulating aspects of a Web site to improve its ranking in search engines.

SERP's
Short for search engine results page, SERP is the Web page that a search engine returns with the results of its search.

SMS
Short Message Service is a service for sending short messages of up to 160 characters (224 characters if using a 5-bit mode) to mobile devices.

SMTP
A protocol for sending e-mail messages between servers. Most email systems that use the Internet use SMTP to send messages from one server to another.

Spam
Irrelevant or unsolicited messages sent over the Internet, typically to large numbers of users, for the purposes of advertising and spreading malware, etc.

SSL
Secure Sockets Layer is a protocol for transmitting private documents via the Internet.

SWOT
A study undertaken by an organization to identify its internal strengths and weaknesses, as well as its external opportunities and threats.

Tagging
Lists other pages on the Web where you can find additional information.

TCP/IP
Transmission Control Protocol/Internet Protocol (TCP/IP) is the suite of communications protocols used to connect hosts on the Internet.

Telemarketing
The marketing of goods or services by means of telephone calls to potential customers.

Touchpoint

Touchpoint is any time a potential customer or customer comes in contact with your brand–before, during, or after they purchase.

Tweet

A post made on the Twitter online message service.

URL

An Internet address usually consisting of the access protocol (http), the domain name (hmhbooks.com), and optionally.

Webcam

A video camera connected to a computer, allowing its images to be seen by Internet users.

Web code

An artificial language used to write instructions that can be translated into machine language and then executed by a computer.

Word of mouth

Spoken communication as a means of transmitting information.

Epilogue

On the evening that I finished the last chapter of this book, coincidentally I had the pleasure of watching on TV the highly respected digital pioneer Baroness Martha Lane Fox deliver the 2015 Richard Dimbleby Lecture at the College of Science Museum in London. She is currently Chancellor of the Open University, where I completed my MBA some years ago. The BBC website, promoting her talk, said the Baroness would "challenge us all, leaders, legislators and users, to understand the Internet more deeply and to be curious and critical in our digital lives in order to tackle the most complex issues facing our society." She certainly did that.

During her fascinating lecture, Martha Lane Fox suggested that a new public Institute be set up to help people understand "the complex moral and ethical issues that the Internet presents." She stated that the Institute should focus on educating the population about the Internet. She reminded her audience that there are about 10 million adults and 70% of small businesses that are not online. She claimed that some businesses are missing out on growth and that estimates shows that helping every small business understand digital would contribute £18 billion to the (British) economy. The following are some other very relevant quotes from her talk in the context of this book.

> "We need a new national institution that would lead an ambitious charge to make us the most digital nation on the planet."

> "It doesn't matter if you're 80 or 8, if you're online once a year or once a minute. Understanding where the Internet came from and what it can do will help you make more sense of the world."

> "And now it's very easy to be on the Internet without really knowing it."

> "This (the Internet) is the fastest technological revolution in history. In the UK, radio took 38 years to reach 50 million users, television took 13 years and the web took just 4. It's perhaps no wonder that we sometimes struggle to work out what it all means."

> "Almost everything you touch uses the Internet in one way or another, banking systems, governments, shops and even some cars.

> "76% of Britons use the Internet every day. Our nation of shopkeepers is now home to the most enthusiastic online shoppers on the planet. In 2014, e-commerce accounted for about 15% of total UK retail sales."

"At all levels of society, we need to get educated and informed about the Internet, so we can all be involved and we can all reap the benefits."

"In this 800th year anniversary of Magna Carta, the document widely upheld as one of the first examples of the rule of law, why don't we establish frameworks to help navigate the online world?"

Sources

[1] Published on Sir Bob Geldof, Keynote Speech at the One Young Summit 2014, Opening ceremony You Tube, October 16, 2014. [Accessed November 2014]

[2] Bill Gates sends a memo, entitled "The Internet Tidal Wave," to all executive staff within Microsoft. May 26th, 1995: www.lettersofnote.com/2011/07/internet-tidal-wave.html [Accessed November 2014]

[3] Now for an Intelligent Internet by Bill Gates. Microsoft: ww.microsoft.com/presspass/ofnote/11-00intelligenti.mspx [Accessed November 2014]

[4] Don Tapscott Quotes: www.brainyquote.com/quotes/authors/d/don_tapscott.htm I [Accessed November 2014]

[5] Ray Tomlinson and the History of Email – Inventors: www.inventors.about.com/od/estartinventions/a/email.htm [Accessed November 2014]

[6] Sir Tim Berners-Lee – World Wide Web Foundation: webfoundation.org/about/sir-tim-berners-lee/7 [Accessed November 2014]

[7] Global Internet User Survey 2012 Key Findings - Internet Society: https://www.internetsociety.org/sites/.../GUIS-2012-Infographic [Accessed November 2014]

[8] The Internet of Things: Dr. John Barrett at TEDxCIT: TEDxTalkstedxtalks.ted.com/video/The-Internet-of-Things-Dr-John [Accessed November 2014]

[9] www.pewinternet.org/2014/05/14/internet-of-things/ [Accessed November 2014]

[10] Tim Berners-Lee: A Magna Carta for the web | Talk Subtitles and ... :

https://www.ted.com/.../tim_berners_lee...magna_carta.../transcript [Accessed November 2014]

[11] Pierre Omidyar | Omidyar Network:om/people/pierre-omidyar [Accessed November 2014)

[12] Eric Schmidt - Google+ https: Biography.com//plus.google.com/+EricSchmidt [Accessed November 2014]

[13] Jeff Bezos – Biography: www.biography.com/people/jeff-bezos-9542209 [Accessed November 2014]

[14] Global Internet Report | Internet Society: www.internetsociety.org/doc/global-internet-report [Accessed November 2014]

[15] 'The Thinker interview with Philip Kotler, the Father of Marketing' by Neelima Mahajan, July 29, 2014: Accessed November 2014]

[16] Wharton Magazine talks to Wes Hutchinson, Professor of Marketing, University of Pennsylvania, October 2012.

[17] Branding in the digital age article by David Edelman, December 2010.

[18] Marketing - Google Books Result: https://24books.google.ie/books?isbn=1486001777Peter Drucker

[Accessed November 2014]

[19] Rethinking Marketing - HBR: https://hbr.org/2010/01/rethinking-marketing [Accessed November 2014]

[20] HubSpot | What is Inbound Marketing?: www.hubspot.com/inbound-marketing [Accessed November 2014]

[21] What is Content Marketing? - Content Marketing Institute: contentmarketinginstitute.com/what-is-content-marketing/ [Accessed November 2014]

[22] Ibid.

[23] Ibid.

[24] Five key elements to create a global content marketing plan | Media: www.theguardian.com/global-content-marketing-plan-pam-didner [Accessed November 2014]

[25] Seth's Blog: Analytics without action: sethgodin.typepad.com/seths_blog/.../analytics-without-action.html [Accessed November 2014]

[26] Crowdbooster: Social Media Analytics crowdbooster.com/ [Accessed November 2014]

[27] Raven Tools: raventools.com [Accessed November 2014]

[28] Business Intelligence Journal - TDWI: tdwi.org/research/list/tdwi-business-intelligence-journal.asp [Accessed November 2014]

[29] The New Conversation: Taking Social Media from Talk to Action: https://hbr.org/product/the-new-conversation.../10815-PDF-ENG [Accessed November 2014]

[30] 2013 Email Marketing Benchmark Report - MarketingSherpa: https://32www.markereports/EXCERPT- BMR-2013-Email Marketing.pdftingsherpa.com/.../reports/benchmark [Accessed

November 2014]

[31] Marketing Cloud: Digital Marketing Software Features – Salesforce: www.salesforce.com/marketing-cloud/features/ [Accessed November 2014]

[32] Why online video is the future of content marketing | Guardian Small: www.theguardian.com/.../video-content-marketing-media-online [Accessed November 2014]

[33] Simplymeasured.com/.../2012 [Accessed November 2014]

[34] TubeMogul | Video Advertising Software: www.tubemogul.com/[Accessed November 2014]

[35] Google Analytics Official Website – Web Analytics & Reporting: www.google.ie/analytics/ [Accessed November 2014]

[36] An introduction to PPC advertising with Google Adwords - Wordtracker: www.wordtracker.com/academy/pay-per-click/.../ppc-introduction [Accessed November 2014]

[37] SEMrush - service for competitors research, shows organic and Ads: ..www.semrush.com/ [Accessed November 2014]

[38] What is reputation management? - Definition from WhatIs.com: whatis.techtarget.com/definition/reputation-management [Accessed November 2014]

[39] Google Docs - create and edit documents online, for free: www.google.com/docs [Accessed November 2014]

[40] Types of Cloud Service Models - Appcore: www.appcore.com/3-types-cloud-service-models/n [Accessed November 2014]

[41] Marketing-made-simple.com: www.marketing-made-simple.com/ [Accessed November 2014]

[42] The consumer decision journey | McKinsey & Company:

www.mckinsey.com/insights/.../the_consumer_decision_journey [Accessed November 2014]

[43] Lars Perner - Consumer Behavior and Marketing Thought: www.larsperner.com/ [Accessed November 2014]

[44] Grant McCracken: Why We Need Chief Culture Officers - PSFK: www.psfk.com/2012/09/culture-jobs-brands.html [Accessed November 2014]

[45] American Demographics - Marketing – Advertising: Ageadage.com/section/american-demographics/195

[46] Marketers From Mars - Subscribers, Fans, and Followers – ExactTarget: pages.exacttarget.com/SFF20-US?...MktrsFromMars... [Accessed November 2014]

[47] Apple - Legal - Software: https://www.apple.com/legal/sla/ [Accessed March 2015]

[48] Permission Marketing by Seth Godin: www.sethgodin.com/permission/ [Accessed February 2014]

[49] Ibid.

[50] Jeffrey F. Rayport - Faculty - Harvard Business Schoolwww.hbs.edu/faculty/Pages/profile.aspx?facId=6536

[51] Gawker MGawker Media - Aboutadvertising.gawker.com/about/edia - About

[52] Ad Workshop Raises More Questions | Adweek www.adweek.com/.../advertising.../native-ad-workshop-leaves-ftc-perp

[53] Solving the Search vs. Display Advertising Quandary - HBS Working: hbswk.hbs.edu/item/7230.html [Accessed January 2015]

[54] What is SSL? - GlobalSign: https://www.globalsign.com/en/ssl-Information-center/what-is-ssl/ [Accessed February 2015]

[55] Online Communities: Researching sociability and usability ... - OzCHI: www.ozchi.org/proceedings/2004/pdfs/keynote-preece.pdf [Accessed February 2015]

[56] The Real Value of On-Line Communities -   HBR: https://hbr.org/1996/05/the-real-value-of-on-line-communities [Accessed February 2015]

[57] Internet Society - The Internet is For Everyone - InternetSociety.org Adwww.internetsociety.org/

[58] CURIOUS - The Desire to Know & Why Your Future- Ian Leslie: ian-leslie.com/books/uk/curious/ [Accessed February 2015]

[59] Digital Vertigo | Andrew Keen | Macmillan: us.macmillan.com/digitalvertigo/andrewkeen [Accessed February 2015]

[60] An enlightening look at the internet by none other than Max du Preez: pessimistincarnate.blogspot.com/.../enlightening-look-at-internet-by-none.html [Accessed February 2015]

[61] Report: Bot traffic is up to 61.5% of all website traffic | Incapsula.com: https://www.incapsula.com/.../bot-traffic-report-2013.htm [Accessed February 2015]

[62] Schneier on Security: Data and Goliath: Bruce Schneier on the ...: https://www.schneier.com/news/.../2015/.../data_and_goliath_bru.html [Accessed February 2015]

[63] foreignpolicy.com/2012/10/08/big-data-a-short-history. {Accessed February 2015}

[64] Article | Harper's Magazine - Part 2
        207harpers.org/departments/article/page/207/.{ Accessed February 2015}

[65] Visually exploring gigabyte data sets in real time - ACM Digital Librarydl.acm.org/citation.cfm?id=310977&preflayout=tabs. {Accessed February 2015}

[66] Hamming's Reviews - MacTutor History of Mathematicswww-history.mcs.st-and.ac.uk/Extras/HammingReviews.html {Accessed February 2015}

[67]Eric Schmidt: Every 2 Days We Create As Much Information As We   techcrunch.com/2010/08/04/schmidt-data/   {Accessed February 2015}

[68] whatis.techtarget.com/definition/3Vs {Accessed February 2015}

[69] www.syncrat.com/posts/5105/writing-a-good-forum-signature { Accessed February 2015}

[70] www.simonharrop.com/why-sensory-branding-means-business/ {Accessed February 2015}

[71]www.aradhnakrishna.com/ { Accessed February 2015}

[72] www.quickmba.com/strategy/porter.shtml {Accessed February 2015}

[73]https://www.google.ie/alerts { Accessed February 2015}

[74] www.hubspot.com/ { Accessed February 2015}

[75]https://adwords.google.com/KeywordPlanner { Accessed February 2015}

[76] www.dellchallenge.org/ { Accessed February 2015}

[77] www.unilever.com/about/innovation/ { Accessed February 2015}

[78] www.crowdsourcing.org/.../jeff-howe...the-rise-of-crowdsourcing/4749 { Accessed February 2015}

[79] Adwww.freelancer.com/ {accessed February 2015}

[80] www.elance.com (Accessed February 2015}

[81] www.upwork.com ({ Accessed February 2015}

[82] https://www.crowdsite.com { Accessed February 2015}

[83] www.crowdflower.com { Accessed February 2015}

[84] arstechnica.com/.../satellite-internet-meet-the-hip-new-investment-for-richard -branson-elon-musk/ { Accessed February 2015}

[85] ww.wsj.com/.../greg-wylers-oneweb-satellite-internet-company-secures- funding-1421278832 { Accessed February 2015}

[86] www.pewresearch.org/ { Accessed February 2015}

[87] science.howstuffworks.com/jonathan-strickland-author.htm

www.ingramcontent.com/pod-product-compliance
Lightning Source LLC
Chambersburg PA
CBHW051849170526
45168CB00001B/42